For 14 years (1987-2001) Todd Crowell worked as Senior Writer for *Asiaweek*, the leading English-language news magazine published in Hong Kong by Time Warner. He has contributed regularly to the *Christian Science Monitor* and *Asian Wall Street Journal* among other publications and has worked as an editor and freelance writer in Hong Kong, Thailand and now Japan, where he serves as Japan correspondent for Asia Sentinel.

The Dictionary
of the
Asian Language

TODD CROWELL

The Dictionary of the Asian Language
ISBN 978-988-16139-8-1

Published by Blacksmith Books
Unit 26, 19/F, Block B, Wah Lok Industrial Centre,
37-41 Shan Mei Street, Fo Tan, Hong Kong
Tel: (+852) 2877 7899
www.blacksmithbooks.com
www.facebook.com/blacksmithbooks

Illustrations by Ming

Also by Todd Crowell:
Tales from Victoria Park
Explore Macau: A walking guide and history
Farewell, My Colony: Last Years in the Life of British Hong Kong
Tokyo: City on the Edge

CONTENTS

INTRODUCTION

The Dictionary of the Asian Language was one of the more popular features of *Asiaweek* newsmagazine when I worked there in the 1990s. It took about five years to run its course from A (***Aaiiiyah!*** CANTONESE, what a Hong Kong real estate speculator bellows when he finds that his Mercedes has been stolen and put on a fast boat to China while he was at an all-night mahjong session) to Z (**Zhang Yimou**, the most prominent of China's "fifth generation" film makers, known for testing the limits drawn by the communist party.) I confess that when the editor-in-chief, the late Michael O'Neill, introduced the idea, I thought it was loony. In time I got hooked, as did many readers. One of my regrets is that the Dictionary moved inexorably forward from A to Z. If you happened to be in the Ms, for example, and came across a fascinating word beginning with C, you were out of luck.

In a way this book is a way of making up for that by including words I wish I had known back then. Yet as soon as it is published, newer words will crop up making me say, "I wish I had learned that one sooner". Hopefully, there will be additions.

Of course, a lot has happened in Asia in the decade since the Dictionary ran its course. *Asiaweek* itself stopped publication in 2001 after a 25-year run. New words, expressions and vogue words crop up all the time. Publication allows me to begin afresh. This book is entirely new, not simply a compilation of the old work. I have written this work from scratch, with only a handful of holdovers from the old Dictionary.

Don't be put off by the word "Dictionary". This book is not meant to be a comprehensive catalogue of any Asian language, much less all of them. Such a project would take an army of scholars working for decades and producing volumes. This book is meant to be a collection of vogue words and items that illuminate little corners of Asian life, culture, arts, politics and business. Think of each entry as a bite-sized story in itself.

The definition of "Asia" is not as cut-and-dried as one might think. For the purposes of this book, "Asia" is defined mainly as Northeast Asia (Japan, China and Korea) and Southeast Asia (Indonesia, the Philippines, Thailand, etc.) I make an occasional side glance at South Asia (the Indian subcontinent) but not Central Asia or what some prefer to call "West Asia," aka the Middle East. Whether Australia and New Zealand are really a part of Asia is a matter of dispute, but I cannot resist including some items.

The book is not an encyclopedia. I don't feel constrained to include everything. Such well-known figures from history as Mao Zedong or contemporary Asia such as Aung San Suu Kyi are not to be found, but lesser known but influential people are included such as Beate Gordon, the American who wrote the equal rights provision in Japan's American-drafted constitution. The book is meant to be idiosyncratic, and eclectic. The main rule is that there are no rules, except one: No item shall be boring.

Todd Crowell

A

aaiiiyah! CANTONESE What a Hong Kong real estate speculator bellows when he finds out that his new Mercedes 420 has been put on a fast boat to China while he was at an all-night mahjong session.

abacus An ancient instrument for doing sums, first invented in Babylon or China depending on sources and still in common use throughout much of Asia. It comes in two basic forms: a seven-bead abacus and a five-bead version once used in Japan and called a *soroban*. Experienced practitioners can outperform electronic calculators.

Abenomics A widespread popular buzzword to describe the economic policies instituted by Japan's Prime Minister Shinzo Abe shortly after his party won a landslide victory. The use of the "-nomics" suffix probably goes back to US President Ronald Reagan. His economic policies, based mainly on large tax cuts, were called "Reaganomics" but they were considerably different from Abe's pump-priming initiatives.

Abu Sayyaf A Philippine Muslim terror organization founded on Basilan Island in the 1990s as an offshoot of the Moro insurgency that has raged for decades. The group, numbering in the hundreds, operates mainly in the Sulu islands that extend from Zamboanga in the Philippines to Sabah in Malaysia. It is uncertain whether the group is motivated by jihad or simply likes to kidnap people for ransom. Several hundred US troops rotate in and out of the region to train and equip the Philippine Armed Forces fighting the Abu Sayyaf.

Aceh Indonesian province at the extreme western end of Sumatra. Given its proximity to trade routes in the Indian Ocean, it became the first part

of the country to embrace Islam and is still noted for its piety. About 98 per cent of the population is Muslim. It was the last region of the archipelago to be pacified by the Dutch, if that is the right word. Rebel groups under the common banner of *Gerekan Aceh Merdeka,* or Free Aceh, conducted a long insurgency against the central government in Jakarta over religion and the sharing of natural resources. The Indian

Ocean Earthquake in late 2004 precipitated a tsunami that devastated the capital, Banda Aceh, and hinterland, killing an estimated 170,000 in Indonesia plus thousands more in Thailand and Sri Lanka. However the disaster seemed to sober both sides which concluded a peace treaty the following August, mediated by the former president of Finland, Martti Ahtisaari. As part of the deal, Aceh is the only province in Indonesia that imposes Shariah law, albeit a relatively mild version of it.

Acer Taiwanese maker of desktop computers and laptops which became the first Asian company outside of Japan to score big internationally using its own brand name. Acer was founded in 1976 by Stan Shih, his wife and five others. Shih had started out selling eggs on the street with his mother.

Ade Pen name of Jose de Santos Ferreira (1919-1993), a 20th-century poet who was probably Macau's most famous writer (not counting Luis Vaz de Camoes, Portugal's most famous poet who may or may not have lived in Macau). He wrote plays and poems in the Macanese *patua* full of nostalgia for a dying people and their fading culture. He is still a much loved figure in the **Macanese** community. *Patua*, a pastiche of Portuguese, Chinese and Malay, is not much used today though there are local groups dedicated to keeping it alive.

Agent Orange A chemical herbicide sprayed by the millions of gallons over a large area of South Vietnam for the better part of a decade from 1961. It has had long-lasting consequences both for former American soldiers and especially for the Vietnamese in terms of stunted lives and deformed babies, as it contained toxic dioxin. The chemical was mainly spread by the USAF in "Operation Ranch Hand" with the stated purpose of depriving the Viet Cong enemy of forest cover. An unstated purpose was to destroy crops and force farmers into the cities where they could be better controlled.

ah chaan CANTONESE A patronizing term that Hong Kong people often applied to new immigrants from mainland China (formally *dai* *luk sun yee man*) derived from a bumpkin-like character in a popular television series. Illustrative of the way Hong Kongers looked down on their mainland "compatriots" in the years immediately preceding and after the 1997 handover. With the growing prosperity in mainland China and Beijing's decision to permit individuals to visit the territory, friction has increased, especially as tourists flaunt their wealth and buy up real estate, helping to inflate property prices. They still consider mainlanders country bumpkins, only rich country bumpkins. (See **sandwich class**)

AKB48 Spacy name for a large group of teenage performers, founded in 2005, that has become the most popular girls' revue in Japan. The group is made up of 88 girls, of 14 to 20 years of age, who are then subdivided into four "teams" for performances, making it the largest and one of the highest-earning pop music groups in the world. Unlike other pop groups, AKB48 has its own theater in the Akihabara district of Tokyo, usually noted for its many electronics stores, hence the initials AKB. There is a constant churn of members as girls "graduate", i.e. age out, and replacements are recruited in endless auditions. The management makes a big deal out of the girls' supposed purity – they are not allowed to have boyfriends under the terms of their contract – despite the often risqué performances on stage. The management has been criticized for the unrealistic and often hypocritical demands that it makes on its performers. Members have been known to make tearful apologies on YouTube for having a boyfriend.

Ahmadiyya A Muslim sect, founded in 1889 by Mirza Ghulan Ahmed, that is considered heretical by both Shia and Sunni Muslims. Mainstream Muslim clerics accuse it of violating a central tenet of Islam, that Muhammad was the final prophet. Adherents are scattered throughout Muslim Asia, where they often face persecution. Indonesia is said to be the home of about 200,000 Ahmadi. Under pressure from conservative Muslims, the Indonesian government banned the sect from proselytizing in 2008 but stopped short of formally banning the group. Frequently the subject of violent mobs. Followers believe that Jesus Christ is buried somewhere near Srinagar, Kashmir.

ah quah [ah kwah] HOKKIEN Straits Chinese word for transvestites. For many years they entertained tourists along Singapore's Bugis Street, gorgeously outfitted in colorful gowns and hairstyles. Cases of drug and theft assaults on single male tourists (many of whom mistook *ah quah* for the real thing) caused the government to crack down. Some of them moved to Orchard Street. (See **lady boys**)

aiguo renshi MANDARIN for patriot (literally "love country person"). Basically an honorific bestowed by Beijing on rich overseas Chinese who make large investments in the country, often in their ancestral provinces (even if they were actually born and raised in Hong Kong or Indonesia). In Taiwan a similar honor, *chung chen* (faithful-true), is bestowed on overseas Chinese who support the old Nationalist cause and hang a picture of Chiang Kai-shek over the television.

aisatsu JAPANESE The word *aisatsu* is often translated as "greetings" but it is more accurately described as a "courtesy call." It refers to a kind of meeting where no real business is conducted but where relationships are cultivated. The presidents of two corporations under merger may have an *aisatsu* to put their final seal on a deal that has actually been worked out well in advance. A variation is *aisatsu mawari* or "walking around meeting", usually during the New Year break, to pay respects to customers and business clients.

Ai Weiwei (1957-) Chinese avant-garde artist, sculptor, designer and now political dissident. Ai was in sufficient official favor to play a major role in China's most important modern prestige project, the design of the National Stadium, the chief venue of the 2008 Olympic Games in Beijing, commonly called the **Bird's Nest**. He was also the son of an important modern Chinese poet, Ai Qing. He ran afoul of the authorities when he very publicly denounced the government for the consequences stemming from the 2008 Sichuan earthquake. Some 5,000 schoolchildren were killed in the quake as a result of crumbling, shoddy school buildings. He was arrested, allegedly for tax evasion, in 2011 but conditionally released two months later.

Airlangga, King (991-1049) Balinese king who consolidated his rule in his birthplace and then extended it into east and central Java, supplanting the dying Srivijaya empire. Airlangga means "he who crossed the water" and describes how he crossed the Bali Strait to conquer the eastern part of Java, creating the Kingdom of Kahuripan. He abdicated and went with his guru into the woods to seek truth. During his reign the north-coast city of Surabaya became an important center of trade, as it has remained for the past millennium. He is revered as a hero in Indonesian history textbooks.

aircraft carriers Several Asian navies have aircraft carriers, although they don't advertise it. Japan calls its two *Hyuga*-class carriers "helicopter destroyers" though the 13,500-ton flat-tops hardly look like conventional destroyers. Japanese avoid calling them aircraft carriers as the term suggests an offensive capability constitutionally denied the Maritime Self-Defense Force (see **Article 9**). Their main mission is anti-submarine warfare. The flagship of South Korea's navy is an 18,000-ton helicopter carrier called the **Dokdo**. Seoul is planning to build four more. China, of course, has long aspired to acquiring aircraft carriers and in 2011 put to sea a training carrier that it bought from Ukraine. The purchase was made through a travel agency connected with the People's Liberation Army, ostensibly as a floating casino for Macau, but was towed (it lacked propulsion) to Dalian for refitting. In 1997 Thailand acquired a carrier, HTMS *Chakri Naruebet* ("Chakri Dynasty"), from Spain. It made Thailand the only Southeast Asian nation to have an aircraft carrier, albeit a small one. It spends most of its time in port. (See **Blue Water Navy**)

akachochin JAPANESE for red lanterns of the kind seen in entertainment districts. Often hung from *yakitori* (skewered chicken) stalls, where **salarymen** booze after work and complain about their bosses.

Aksai Chin A remote corner of northeast Kashmir disputed by India and China and occupied by the Chinese since 1962. It has colored relations between the two countries for some 50 years, although in the 1990s the two countries signed agreements to recognize the "actual line of control" as the de facto border. The region is unbelievably remote and virtually uninhabited. It has no permanent settlements and few if any natural resources of any consequence. It is important to China as it contains an all-weather highway linking Tibet to the Xinjiang Autonomous Region. It is administered as part of Xinjiang but is also officially recognized by New Delhi as part of Jammu and Kashmir. The 1962 war led to the severing of direct air links between India and China that were not revived until 2002, during a period of improving bilateral relations.

Akubra AUSTRALIAN ABORIGINAL for a distinctive Australian brand of bush hat with a wide brim that makes good use of the fur of Australia's burgeoning rabbit population. The name is derived from the Aboriginal word for a head covering and has been trademarked since 1912. The hats are made by the Akubra Company, which is still a family-owned concern. The current owners are the great-great-grandchildren of Benjamin Dunkerley, who made the first Akubra hats in 1870.

Akutagawa Prize Japan's most prestigious literary award named after Ryunosuke Akutagawa (1892-1927), the country's celebrated short story writer, who killed himself at the height of his popularity. It has been awarded twice yearly since 1935. Awards go mainly to short story writers rather than novelists. The winners receive one million yen and buckets of publicity. Several famous Japanese writers, such as Nobel laureate Kenzaburo Oe and Kobo Abe, have won the prize, but other distinguished writers, such as Yukio Mishima and **Haruki Murakami**, have not. Mishima has an award in his name and Murakami has gone on to be an international best-selling novelist. Among the winners of the Akutagawa Prize is Shintaro Ishihara, the longtime conservative politician and governor of Tokyo. He won in 1955 for *Seasons of the Sun.*

Allah ARABIC The word Allah for God is usually associated with Islam. However, many Southeast Asian Christians use "Allah" for "God" in their own languages. The Bible (*Alkitab*) translated into the Indonesian language is one example. Christians in Indonesia and Malaysia say that the word is simply interchangeable with God, but some Muslims feel that Christians are misappropriating their sacred word. They find particularly offensive the phrase *anak Allah*, or "Son of God", since the God of Islam has no son. The word *tuhan*, a neutral term for God, is used in Malaysia for official oaths. The first translation of any portion of the Bible outside of a European language was into Malay in 1612 (one year after the King James version was completed). It used the word Allah for God.

All Blacks The name for the New Zealand national Rugby Union team, taken, of course, from the team uniform. For more than 100 years the national rugby players have been wearing a black jersey and matching black shorts with the silver New Zealand fern emblem on the chest. By most measurements the All Blacks are the most successful rugby team in world sporting history. But though often ranked number one in the world, the All Blacks have a strangely poor record in Rugby World Cup competition, winning the inaugural event hosted jointly with Australia in 1987 before finally triumphing again in 2011. Before each international competition the All Blacks perform a traditional Maori *haka* challenge dance to psych out their opponents. New Zealanders are obsessively loyal to their national team and any prominent defeat, such as in the 2007 world cup competition, is cause for a national funk and an avalanche of criticism of the team and the coach. (See **Rugby Sevens**)

amah From PORTUGUESE, an almost universal Asian word for maid. In India the word is *ayah*, also from Portuguese. In Hong Kong the word *amah* usually refers to aging Chinese maids who are now very few compared with tens of thousands of maids, or as they prefer "domestic helpers", from the Philippines, Indonesia and Sri Lanka. Maids are not restricted to the rich. In Hong Kong and Singapore even middle-class families often have at least one maid, allowing the wife to hold an outside job. Japan has the riches to pay for domestic help, but for cultural reasons and a prejudice against allowing tens of thousands of Southeast Asians into the country, relatively few Japanese employ maids. For the same reasons, they restrict Asian caregivers, despite a growing need to care for an aging population.

amakudari JAPANESE for "descent from heaven", taken from Amaterasu Omikami, in Japanese mythology the sun goddess and the most important Shinto deity. In its modern, political connotation, the practice of senior civil servants finding post-retirement jobs in the private or semi-private sector. In this construction the bureaucrats are the "gods", the civil service "heaven" and the earth the hard landing which they are trying to avoid. It is brought about by the practice of retiring senior civil servants in their mid-50s, when they are still in their prime of life, but with few public corporations in which to find post-retirement jobs. Successive reformist administrations have sought to end or curb *amakudari* without much success.

Amaral, Joao Maria Ferreira do (1803-1849) Portuguese governor of Macau who arrived in the enclave in 1846 and immediately began to assert Portuguese sovereignty over Macau (before then, it was mainly a self-governing trading outpost). In 1849 he was assassinated while riding near the border. For many years a large equestrian statue of Amaral dominated the roundabout leading to the bridge to Taipa Island in front of the Lisboa Hotel. It was taken down and returned to Portugal several years before the handover of Macau to China in 1999.

Amputuan Massacre The term for a particularly gruesome, politically motivated massacre that occurred on November 23, 2009, in Manguindano province on Mindanao in the southern Philippines. Some 58 people, women and journalists, were ambushed, allegedly by members of the locally dominant Amputuan family, while on their way to witness a candidate filing to run against an Amputuan family member for provincial governor in the 2010 elections. It is considered the single deadliest mass killing of journalists in recorded history. Of the 37 reporters trailing the candidate, some 34 were murdered.

amuk MALAY One of the few English words borrowed from Malay, to describe uncontrollable rage often described as "running amok." It refers to an individual (always a man; women do not run amok) who shows no signs of previous anger or disposition to violence, but who acquires some kind of weapon and then tries to kill everyone he encounters, ending, usually, in his own death. In Malaysia, it is described as someone possessed by some kind of evil spirit and who thus is not really responsible for his actions. That may be why one European visitor said "homicide is here a joke and goes without punishment." Amok entered English through the diaries of British explorer Captain James Cook. It is thought to be a form of suicide where it is forbidden by the tenets of Islam.

Anak FILIPINO for "child" and the title for what is unquestionably the most popular and most widely known ballad in the Philippines. Composed by Freddie Aguilar in 1978, it has been translated into 26 languages and has sold 30 million albums. *Anak* is also part of the word *peranakan* for Straits-born Chinese.

Angka Loau CAMBODIAN Literally the "organization on high," what the Khmer Rouge called their regime. Within days of winning power in 1975 Pol Pot set about enforcing a revolution that probably went farther and faster in destroying a society than any other in history. Cities were emptied, schools and hospitals closed, money forbidden, all in an effort to turn the clock back to **Year Zero** and turn Cambodia – or Kampuchea as it was temporarily renamed – into some kind of rural paradise. Many were tortured and killed in the special **S-21** prison, but many more died of starvation and disease due to the gross mishandling of the economy.

angklung An Indonesian musical instrument sort of like a xylophone made from bamboo tubes set in a bamboo frame. The oldest surviving *angklung* is about 400 years old. Though now widespread throughout Southeast Asia, it is closely identified with the Sundanese of West Java and an institute for promoting its preservation and development is in the Sundanese capital **Bandung**.

Anjin-san JAPANESE name for William Adams (1564-1620), the first Englishman to debark and live in Japan after his ship got lost in a storm around 1600. The local *daimyo* valued his shipbuilding skills so much that he overlooked the *bakufu* prohibition against contact with foreigners save for a small Dutch enclave in Nagasaki. James Clavell made his life the center of his novel *Shogun*.

Anpanman JAPANESE Anime cartoon figure for children that has been popular for more than two decades. The figure with round, dough-like head and two red cheeks is as ubiquitous in Japan as Mickey Mouse used to be in America. The face appears on every children's product imaginable from toys to snack foods and is, of course, the star of numerous cartoon series. The term *anpan* is an amalgamation of the word for bread, *pan*, which is one of Japan's oldest borrowed words from Portuguese, and *an*, which means red bean paste.

ao dai VIETNAMESE [ao zai] A distinctive costume for women in Vietnam, often called the country's national dress. It is comprised of a tight-fitting silk tunic worn over pantaloons. Though dating back to the 18th century, the modern look coalesced in the 1920s under the influence of French fashion, and found its final refinement in the 1950s. It has generally been more commonly worn in the free-wheeling south rather than in the stern north, but it is rapidly gaining stature as perhaps the best-known Vietnamese cultural artifact. Commonly, it is worn at weddings, during the **Tet** celebrations and other formal occasions. A pure white version serves as a high-school uniform. The *ao dai* is also worn by flight attendants, hotel and restaurant staff and others that interface with tourists.

Aotea-roa MAORI For "land of the long white cloud", or New Zealand. It probably looked like a cloud on the horizon when the first transoceanic canoes were making their landfall about a thousand years ago. The

Maoris, Polynesians related to Samoans and Hawaiians, spread across the two main islands.

Apo Active volcano in southeastern Mindanao that is the highest point, at 2,954 meters, in the Philippines. Open to climbers, it is a protected area as the principal home of the nearly extinct Philippine Eagle (sometimes called the "monkey-eating eagle" from its presumed favorite meal). It is one of the largest and most majestic of the eagles and the Philippines' national bird.

Aquinaldo, Emilio (1869-1964) The leader of the Philippine resistance, first against Spain and later against the US, in a war that the Filipinos call the Philippine-American War and Americans the Philippine Insurgency. He formally declared the Philippines independent on June 16, 1898, which today is celebrated as Independence Day. He welcomed the Japanese in 1942, buying into their propaganda of liberating Asians from colonial rule. As such he was briefly imprisoned after the war but later released. He lived to be a feisty 94.

Aquino, Corazon (1933-2010) Eleventh president of the Philippines, elevated in the People Power revolt of 1986 that ousted longtime strongman Ferdinand Marcos. Known universally as "Cory," she was the widow of longtime opposition leader Benigno S. Aquino Jr., who was murdered on returning to the country from the US in 1983. She was the daughter of a rich ethnic Chinese landowner (family name Cojuangco) whose family still has extensive land holdings. She served one six-year term, as stipulated by the post-1986 constitution, characterized by several aborted coups. Her son, Benigno S. Aquino III, was elected president in 2010.

Area Licensing Scheme One of several ways in which Singapore manages to avoid the kind of traffic gridlock that seems endemic to other Asian capitals. Introduced in 1975, the ALS (everybody calls it by its initials) charges drivers for entering a designated central business district, also known as the "restricted zone" during the day. This was the world's first urban traffic congestion pricing scheme to be successfully implemented. Singapore has other means for restraining the growth in private automobile ownership and use. In 1990 it introduced the Vehicle Quota System, in which the potential car owner must first purchase a permit to buy a car, then pay for the car itself. It is a kind of social engineering that one could label "only in Singapore". These measures have however been successful in limiting the growth of automobile ownership to about a third of Singaporean households.

arigato JAPANESE for "thank you". In full: *domo arigato gozaimasus*, which has the same meaning but is considered more polite. The word *arigato* alone is a bit abrupt. The greater the obligation and thanks, the greater the bow that goes with it.

Arirang Festival Unquestionably the world's largest choreographed extravaganza, featuring a cast not just of thousands but tens of thousands.

Named after a traditional Korean love song, the Arirang Festival was first held in 2002 to commemorate the 90th anniversary of the birth of North Korea's founder Kim Il-sung (he had actually been dead for several years), but it goes on for two months. The most impressive feature is the massed card flippers composed of about 30,000 schoolchildren seated in one bank of the huge May Day Stadium in Pyongyang, whose synchronized card flipping produces a mosaic of images. Somehow it seems fitting that the mass gymnastics should be held in Stalinist North Korea since nowhere else is the individual so effectively submerged in the mass. Some foreigners have witnessed the Arirang Festival, but it is a question whether North Korea really exploits the tourist value of this unique performance. Most outsiders who have seen it have only one word to describe the experience: awesome.

Asia pivot A foreign policy term identified with the administration of US President Barack Obama, which purportedly means refocusing America's attention on Asia, broadly defined to include the arc of countries running from India to Japan, and away from the overwhelming focus on the Middle East and Afghanistan. In more practical terms it has meant paying closer attention to organizations such as ASEAN and the East Asia Summit. Secretary of State Hillary Clinton made her first trip abroad to Asia and has made about a dozen more, visiting some countries, such as Cambodia, that don't often get such senior-level attention. It has also meant deploying additional military assets to the region, such as a contingent of Marines to be stationed in northern Australia.

"assassins" When in 2005 several veterans of Japan's Liberal Democratic Party (LDP) voted down former Prime Minister **Junichiro Koizumi's** pet plan to privatize the Japanese postal service, including its extensive banking system, the premier decided to call a snap election on the issue. Using his powers as party president Koizumi read the rebels out of the party and handpicked candidates to oppose them in the election as legitimate LDP representatives. The press immediately dubbed these stand-in candidates meant to punish the rebels as "assassins." Before the press got tired of this story angle the election was held, and it turned out to be a Koizumi triumph. Some rebels running as independents got back in; some others did not. Many of the freshmen **Diet** members were women, dubbed "Koizumi's daughters". Most were swept away in the 2009 general election. (See **Ozawa, Ichiro**)

"astronaut" An expression for Hong Kong men who sent their families abroad to establish foreign residency and obtain passports while they stayed behind to make money. It was current in the years before 1997 as people sought "insurance" against things turning out badly after the handover of Hong Kong to China. It often involved separations of three years or more until the family member established foreign residency and obtained the precious document. Relatively few were interested in actually emigrating. The term is a pun on the CANTONESE *tai hung yan*, which means astronaut in the globe-orbiting sense but also can mean a man without his wife (*tai tai*). The Chinese term for a real astronaut is *taikongnaut*.

Aum Shinrikyo "Shining Light", a Japanese cult that in 1995 perpetrated the world's first and, so far, only act of urban terrorism using a weapon of mass destruction delivered in a *bento* (lunch) box. The cult spread sarin nerve gas at several locations on Tokyo's extensive subway system. Twelve people died and many more were injured, some for life. The cult leader Chizuo Matsumoto (alias Shoko Asahara) and 11 other followers were convicted of murder, although the guru himself was convicted only after a trial that lasted nine years! Japanese justice grinds slowly. One of his lieutenants, Fumihiro Joyu, became something of a pop hero to many teenagers who thought he was cute (see **kawaii**). Interestingly, Japan never banned the cult outright. Japan's most famous contemporary writer, **Haruki Murakami**, wrote about the cult in a book called *Under Ground: The Tokyo Gas Attacks and the Japanese Psyche* published in 1997. The cult members, he wrote, "found a purity of purpose they could not find in ordinary society."

Australian Labor Party Although Australia mainly uses British spelling, the name of the Australian Labor Party is spelled in the American style. The New Zealand Labour Party uses the British spelling.

Ayutthaya The capital of Siam from 1350, when it was founded by King U-thong, to 1767, when it was sacked by the invading Burmese army. For four centuries it was the seat of 33 Siamese kings from several dynasties, some of whom, such as King Narusuan, were among the country's greatest monarchs. It was named after Ayothaya, the capital of King Rama, the hero of the great Hindu epic *The Ramayama*. King Narusuan changed the name to Ayutthaya, meaning "undefeatable city", during his short reign. Protected on three sides by rivers and a canal on the fourth, making it practically impregnable, until the Burmese arrived. Now a thriving tourist city about an hour north of Bangkok.

B

baburu keizai Bubble economy. A term for the frenzy of rising real estate prices and inflated stock prices in late-1980s Japan. Many of the newly rich splurged on Western art, which they used as collateral to raise more loans to buy more property or stocks. Ordinary people found that the humble family abode had made them millionaires, at least on paper, only to feel like paupers in the post-bubble recession or if they were forced to sell out to avoid exorbitant inheritance taxes. Those not eager to sell were "encouraged" by a gangster element known as *jiageya* who created disturbances, loud noise and damaged property to intimidate the property owner. During the Bubble era, this was the greatest source of income for the *yakuza*, eclipsing the sex trade and drugs. It all ended predictably in a big bust, which was followed by a more sober period of anemic growth that has lasted for some 20 years and is often referred to as Japan's **lost decades**.

Bac Bo VIETNAMESE for northern Vietnam, or what the French called Tonkin (they called the middle Annam and the south Cochin China). *Bac Viet* is what Hanoi called North Vietnam until the two halves of the country were united following the communist victory in 1975. *Bac* has the same meaning as *Bei* in MANDARIN – as in Beijing, the northern capital.

Badaling Site of the best preserved and most frequently visited section of the Great Wall of China, located conveniently only about 80 km northwest of Beijing. Visited by millions of people every year and the spot where visiting dignitaries, such as Presidents Richard Nixon and Barack Obama, are brought to have their pictures taken.

Baekdu (Paekdu) Mountain A volcanic mountain located on the border of China and North Korea that is sacred to Koreans, even though most of it is in China, where it is known as Mt. Changbai. For generations the mountain has been considered the ancestral home of the Korean people (and of the Manchu, though they have all but disappeared as a separate ethnic group). For the Han Chinese it is merely a scenic spot. The beautiful crater lake, called the Heavenly Lake (*Tianchi* in MANDARIN), was formed after the mountain erupted in the 10th century. Some believe it is the home of a plesiosaur creature similar to the Loch Ness Monster of Scotland. According to communist mythology, North Korea's late dictator Kim Jong-il was born on the slopes of Mt. Baekdu, although in reality he was born in Siberia.

Baguio Scenic Philippine mountain retreat in northern Luzon, one of several mountain retreats that Europeans and Americans built in Asia to escape the blazing summer heat of their lowland capitals. The town was laid out in 1904 during the early American occupation period by Daniel Burnham as the "summer capital" where the governor general went to cool off. Now it is a retreat for presidents of the republic. The Philippine military academy is located there. (See **Karuizawa** in Japan and Dalat in Vietnam)

baijiu A distilled clear liquor often called China's national drink in the way that vodka is the national drink of Russia – though *baijiu* outsells vodka by a wide margin, if that is possible – whisky in Scotland, *slivovitz* in Poland or *soju* in Korea. Similar to Japanese *shochu*, except it is distilled from grains rather than potatoes and has a heavier alcohol content. It is often served in small cups like *sake* cups. It is not generally popular with women, and foreigners find it very much an acquired taste. As one American resident reported: "It began with a nose-filling, cloying floral aroma like that of a fabric softener, then washed through the mouth like smoky kerosene, leaving in its trail the stinging acrid taste of vomit after a vodka binge" (*Beijing Welcomes You*, Tom Scocca).

bajak laut INDONESIAN for pirate (literally "plow of the sea"), sometimes shortened to just *bajak*. It can mean the kinds of marine marauders that lurk along the Strait of Malacca or, in a more modern sense, a copyright pirate. Pirated software or other protected intellectual property is known as *bajak*.

Bali An Indonesian island, separated by only a 4 km channel from east Java, that is the only surviving outpost of the Hindu culture that once flourished in Southeast Asia. Java's Hindus took refuge on the island following the advance of Islam in the 16th century. The Dutch took possession in 1906 after a last battle with natives which ended in one of the world's largest mass suicides when 3,600 died at Denpasar, something the masses of Australian and other tourists are not likely to take note of as they admire the many temples and exotic dances of the native Balinese. Site of a major Islamist terrorist attack in October, 2002. (See ***puputan***)

Bali Ha'i Mythical South Pacific island of mystery, not to be confused with the very real Indonesian island of mystery, **Bali**. The American author James A. Michener wrote in his autobiography that he came across the word "Bali Ha'i" written on a sign on the Solomon Islands during World War II, liked the sound of it and scribbled a note for future use. It later appeared in his Pulitzer Prize-winning novel *Tales from the South Pacific*, which was made into a fabulously successful Rodgers and Hammerstein musical *South Pacific*. It features a haunting ballad of the same name:

> *Bali Ha'i will call you*
> *Any night, any day . . .*

Balikbayan FILIPINO A word meaning roughly return to your homeland that was coined in the 1970s by the tourism ministry to encourage overseas nationals to return home for a visit. The *Balikbayan* were given specially reduced airline fares and permitted to bring in their cars duty free. These inducements have been considerably scaled back, and tens of thousands of Filipinos still work abroad often as one of the three Ms: maids, musicians and mariners. Perhaps the most famous *balikbayan* was

Benigno S. Aquino Jr., who was assassinated in 1983 on the tarmac at Manila airport returning from long exile in the U.S.

baling hou MANDARIN for the post-1980s generation of Chinese young people born between 1980 and 1990, after the death of Mao Zedong and the advent of the **One Child Policy** (see **Little Emperors**). It is similar to the Western Generation Y as a reference point for any discussion of values and national character. These young people, numbering about 240 million of China's population, have been born into probably the most prosperous era of Chinese history. They have a great affinity for the new media represented by the country's most famous young blogger, Han Han.

Banaue rice terraces Rice-growing terraces carved out of mountains in northern Ifugao province in the Philippines. They are said to be more than 2,000 years old, and were built by ancient indigenous peoples. The terraces constitute one of the most important cultural and tourist attractions in the country. Probably more people in the province earn their living from people wanting to see the terraces than actually farm them. They are fed from rainwater flowing down from higher elevations and require some attention, as some of the terraces are beginning to crumble.

Bando, Tamasaburo V (1950-) Famous Japanese *kabuki* actor. Since his breakout role in 1970, Bando has been the leading *onnagato* or male actor performing female roles. Even though he was not a member of one of the ancient *kabuki* families he later adopted the name as the fifth in a long line. (In *kabuki* all roles are played by men.) In a long theatrical career Bando has shown remarkable versatility. Besides *kabuki*, he has had roles or participated as artistic director in *Noh*, ballet and even Shakespeare. In 2008 he played the lead in the *Peony Pavilion*, one of the more famous Chinese Kunqu Opera roles. In 2011 he was awarded the Kyoto Prize for his accomplishments in the performing arts.

Bandung Indonesia's third-largest city and the capital of Sundanese-speaking West Java, founded by the Dutch in 1810 as a refuge for Dutch plantation owners and their families. The Dutch considered moving the capital from Batavia (now Jakarta), and the Indonesian parliament actually did meet there from 1955 to 1966. During the colonial period Braga Street was lined with shops and boutiques featuring the latest French fashions. Indeed, it was nicknamed "Parijs van Java" (Paris of Java) during colonial times. Bandung is noted for its cool climate and its stately Art Deco architecture, which may be a reason why it is often chosen as a site for international and regional conferences. It is best known for the 1955 Bandung Conference, convened by President Sukarno that set up the **Non-Aligned Movement** among 29 newly independent and developing nations – non-alignment being defined as standing aloof from the Cold War conflict between the USSR, the US and their allies and clients. In recent year Bandung has lost out to Bali as a venue for international conferences.

Bangsamoro MALAY for nation (*bangsa*) and SPANISH for Moro, which was the name the Spaniards gave in colonial times to the Muslims living in the southern Philippines, hence Bangsamoro is the Nation of the Moros. Moro was once a derogatory term taken from Moors, the Muslim inhabitants of Spain driven out of the peninsula. The term now encompasses parts of the Sulu Archipelago, Mindanao and parts of Palawan given a degree of autonomy though not independence as part of a peace agreement reached in 2012 with the largest insurgent group, the Moro Islamic Liberation Front.

Banteng A wild jungle ox common throughout Southeast Asia (except Sumatra) thought to be similar to the domesticated ox. The Banteng's distinctive feature is its white fore and back legs, which make it look like the creature is wearing socks.

banyan An Asian tree long associated with mythical qualities. The Buddha is said to have found enlightenment sitting and meditating under its branches (although the actual tree was a pipal, or fig tree.

The current tree in the town of Bodhgaya in Bihar state is said to be a direct descendant from the one the Buddha sheltered under. The nearby Mahabodhi Temple is a common destination for Buddhist pilgrims. The name banyan comes from the PORTUGUESE *banian* for trader, which in turn has roots in GUJARATI and SANSKRIT. The Banyan's branches sprout roots, which droop to the ground and become new trunks.

banzai! JAPANESE from CHINESE for "may you live ten thousand years." Once a common cry of triumph, it has fallen out of use of late due to its association with Japanese aggression during World War II, when troops shouted it before an attack. Modern Japanese are more likely to shout ***ganbare!*** in such situations.

bau hua qifeng MANDARIN for "let a hundred flowers bloom." With these words Mao Zedong launched a campaign ostensibly aimed at enriching social culture and allowing free expression from dissidents, but in reality designed to lure "snakes from their lairs." Mao announced the campaign in 1956, by inviting intellectuals to say what they thought of the party. Many naïvely did just that and were fired from their jobs, jailed or sent to the countryside to labor and eat cabbage.

Bao Ninh (1952-) Pen name for Vietnam's most celebrated contemporary writer. A former soldier in the North Vietnamese Army during the Vietnam War, he is famous for his widely acclaimed 1990 novel *The Sorrow of War*, which is sometimes compared with *All Quiet on the Western Front* for its depiction of life in the ranks. He lives quietly in Hanoi.

Baotou A city in China's province of Inner Mongolia that is the center of China's rare earth metals production, both in mining and in processing. Baotou Iron and Steel, founded as part of Mao Zedong's efforts to move vital industries away from the vulnerable coastline, has now been resurrected as Baotou Steel and Rear Earth and is world's largest processor of these light metals that are increasingly important to the production of electronics, car components and other leading-edge technologies. China has a virtual lock on the production and export of these vital metals, a fact that the world woke up to in 2010 when Beijing supposedly threatened to block exports to Japan in a dispute over the **Senkaku** islands. The region is rich in other minerals and industry.

baramee THAI for charisma, derived from the same root as the word *barom*, which means great, literally the highest form of excellence. In Buddhist terms, *baramee* means the highest virtue performed by a Bodhisattva in order to get rid of desires and reach enlightenment. But in Thai is also denotes a quality in a person that makes other people love and respect him. Aside from being divine, Thai people believe that King Bhumibol is also a Bodhisattva with charisma, who is not only loved but practices the virtues necessary to becoming enlightened. It gained some political meaning in 2006 when then Thai Prime Minister **Thaksin Shinawatra** cryptically remarked that a "charismatic person" was working to undermine his constitutional rule. It was believed to be an oblique reference to Privy Council president and former premier Gen. Prem Tinsulanonda. A few months later Thaksin was overthrown in a coup.

barangay FILIPINO The basic administrative district in the Philippines. Originally, the name for a vessel that brought over Malay settlers. The travelers on each ***barangay*** would form their own community once they had landed. The clan-based districts carried over into the Spanish era and beyond.

"barefoot doctors" Rural health workers trained in the millions during the Cultural Revolution who provided rudimentary health care to China's vast peasantry. Barefoot doctors were neither barefoot nor doctors. But they carried out simple tasks such as immunizations and gave advice on hygiene. In 1980 there were still about 1.5 million of them. Under Mao, Chinese health services were provided either through work brigades at major state-owned enterprises (SOE) in the cities or by the "barefoot doctors" in the country-side. This system broke down following the economic reforms initiated in 1979 which saw the gradual demise of SOEs, vast movement of people to the cities and the demise of the rural practitioners. The system has not been fully replaced by the kinds of universal health care systems common in other Asian countries. Although

nominally a communist country, in China health care is not free. Parents even pay to have their children immunized.

barong FILIPINO Full name *barong tagalong*, a *barong* is a formal dress for men. It consists of a pure white tunic with a high collar that is worn untucked. It said to have been popularized by former president Ramon Magsaysay, who wore a *barong* on most official occasions. It is also the word for the leader of the good people against the evil ones in traditional Balinese dance.

Your barong looks very light and nearly transparent.

Yes, you should try it.

basa kedaton INDONESIAN This is the courtly language of Indonesia, now seldom used as royalty has withered away after 60 years of republican government outside of Jogjakarta and Surakarta palace circles. Few retain more than a couple words, such as "romo" for father (*bapak* in modern Indonesian).

Bataan Philippine province on Luzon commanding the entrance to Manila Bay. It is famous as Gen. Douglas MacArthur's last stand in World War II. Following the Japanese invasion in late 1941, American and Philippine forces withdrew, as planned, to the Bataan peninsula to hold out until reinforcements arrived. They never came until MacArthur's "I have returned" landings in 1944. Long before that, some 65,000 Filipinos and 15,000 Americans surrendered. They were marched to a railhead that would take them to prison camps. About 10,000 died along the way in the infamous Bataan Death March. The word is often mispronounced. It is *ba-ta-an*, not BaTAN.

batik INDONESIAN A method of dying using wax, and also the name for the finished fabric. Colorful batik shirts are almost a national dress. The techniques have been used by Javanese for a millennium. Originally organic dyes, such as indigo, were used, but in the 19th century the Europeans introduced synthetic dyes. Colors and design vary according to the region, but the main batik-producing centers are in the cities of Jogjakarta, Solo and Pekalongon. In Malaysia the best batik comes from Kelantan.

Bayinnaung, King Famous Burmese warrior king, who reigned for 30 years in the 16th century. During his reign he assembled the largest empire in the history of Southeast Asia, encompassing much of present-day Myanmar, Thailand and Laos. He is also credited with first conquering the Shan states, even though they are not fully integrated into Myanmar even today. The king's forces captured the Siamese capital of Ayutthaya in 1563, taking members of the Siamese royal family to his capital at Pegu as hostages, including a prince named Naresuan, who would later free Siam of Burma. Today King Bayinnaung is considered one of the country's greatest historical figures, and his name is remembered in monuments and statues round the country. One such statue is near the still undefined northern border of Thailand and Myanmar, where the two armies exchanged artillery fire as recently as 2001. The Thais wanted to build an opposing statue to their hero king, Naresuan, across the border with sword pointing toward Myanmar, although the foreign ministry prevailed in muting the aggressiveness. So the ancient fuel continues on down to this day. (See **Naresuan, King**)

becak INDONESIAN The Indonesian incarnation of the common pedicab or cycled rickshaw. Pedicabs are found everywhere in Asia from Bangladesh to Taiwan, under various names. Basically a tricycle, the customer sits up front while the driver peddles from behind (or sometimes reversed). Indonesian authorities going back to the Dutch era have waged war on pedicabs as emblems of poverty and snarler of traffic. In 1988 the Jakarta city council banned *becaks* in the city, confiscated them and dumped them in Jakarta Bay. But they are still seen everywhere in the country, including parts of Jakarta. Man-powered rickshaws were first developed in Japan, where they ironically are no longer found. Of late there is a small resurgence of pedaled cabs known as **velotaxis** as being free of carbon emissions.

Beidaihe A beach resort on the Bay of Bohai on the Yellow Sea where China's communist leaders used to gather each summer to hold a retreat to plot strategy and play cards. Mao Zedong himself had a seaside villa here. President Hu Jintao discontinued the annual retreats in 2004 sensing that a conference in a resort would undermine the appearances of frugality and equality that he wanted to project. Now popular with Russian tourists.

Beijing Consensus A geopolitical term that purports to describe a Chinese model of economic development combining authoritarian political control with market and quasi-capitalist economic policies. It is seen as being an alternative to the **Washington Consensus** of democratic government and free markets. The model appeals especially to certain countries in Africa and elsewhere which want to emulate China's economic miracle without opening the government to change through the ballot box. It has gained credence as China's economy has zoomed to second place, displacing Japan, and as many Western countries seem mired in recession. However, there is no real "consensus" on what really constitutes the Beijing Consensus.

Bejaratana, Princess (1925-2011) The only child of Thailand's King Rama VI, who died in 1925 not long after her birth. If Thailand had then allowed for women to inherit the throne, she would have reigned for 85 years, making her possibly the longest reigning monarch in history. Her childless uncle ascended the throne but abdicated following the 1932 coup that ended the absolute monarchy. He was replaced by one of his many siblings, who became Rama VIII but was succeeded by his brother King Bhumibol (Rama IX) after his mysterious death in 1946 by a single gunshot wound. The princess was kept mainly in seclusion all her life, and few Thais had heard of her until the elaborate funeral procession in 2012, conducted with all the regal pageantry that only the Thais (and maybe the British) can muster.

Bells of Balangiga Three Catholic church bells from the town of Balangiga in Eastern Samar province. They were taken by American troops as war trophies following reprisals for a deadly ambush by Filipino insurgents in the same village. Two of the bells are displayed at Warren Air Force Base in Wyoming and one with the 2nd Infantry division at its headquarters in Seoul, Korea. Successive Philippine administrations have requested their return, but have been rebuffed by veterans groups and Wyoming state officials (though the bells are actually on federal property). The massacre took place in 1901 during what Americans call the Philippine Insurgency or what the Filipinos call the **Philippine-American War**.

bersih MALAY for clean. It is the latest manifestation of discontent with Malaysia's electoral system, which has kept the ruling Barisan Nasional coalition in power since independence in 1957. Full name is the Coalition for Free and Fair elections, and it is made up of 62 organizations and political parties. The reform agenda seems fairly modest, such as lengthening the election period from eight to 21 days. Nonetheless, the government came down hard on its July 9, 2011 rally in Kuala Lumpur

(**Bersih 2.0**) arresting several hundred leaders after Bersih leaders defied restrictions on gatherings of more than five people without a permit. Berseih's leader, Ambiga Sreenevasan, and ethnic Indian, is emerging as Malaysia's most prominent opposition figure. (See *reformasi*)

Bhopal A city in central India that is the capital of Madhya Pradesh and the site of the worst industrial accident in modern history when leakage from the Union Carbide insecticide factory killed some 2,500 people. Compensation is still being disputed.

Bhutto, Benazir (1953-2007) Former prime minister of Pakistan and the first woman to head a government in a Muslim country. She was the grandee daughter of former prime minister Zulfikar Ali Bhutto, who in 1979 was executed on the order of military dictator Zia ul-Haq, allegedly for ordering the assassination of a political opponent. She herself was assassinated by jihadist fanatics in 2007. Her husband, Asif Ali Zardari, was jailed for corruption but in 2008 became president of Pakistan.

billabong AUSTRALIAN Stagnant water or a water course that only flows following a downpour. Made famous by the bush ballad *Waltzing Matilda* (the swagman camped by one). A swagman is an itinerant worker who wanders with all of his possessions in a bag (matilda) slung over his shoulder. The first notes of the folk song immediately conjure up Australia in a way that the official national anthem, *Advance Australia Fair,* does not. The original lyrics were written in 1895 and published as sheet music in 1903, two years after Australia gained independence. The song is full of other Australianisms including: "coolibah tree", a kind of eucalyptus growing next to a billabong; "jumbak", a sheep; "tucker bag", a bag to carry food and "billy", a can for boiling water. (See **Winton**)

Big One Monstrous earthquake that is about to hit Japan according to historical calculations. One might think that the Great East Japan Earthquake and tsunami of March 11, 2011, which registered 9 on the Richter scale and was the largest earthquake in Japan's recorded history, was the Big One. But it happened in the wrong place. When Japanese think of the Big One, they refer either to a massive quake hitting Tokyo, as it did in 1923, or further south in Suruga Bay. This is a place where three giant tectonic plates rub together: The Eurasian plate, the Philippine Sea plate and the Pacific plate. The last Big One occurred there in 1854, and Japanese records (which are pretty complete, going back a thousand years), show that it recurs every 100-150 years. Most of the country's considerable investment in earthquake prediction is directed at predicting this anticipated cataclysm, also known as the **Tokai Earthquake**.

bintabat THAI for receiving alms. In the morning in any Thai town or village, one sees the saffron-clothed Buddhist monks are out and about collecting rice and other food in brass bowls, often erroneously called "begging bowls". But the monks are not begging. They are graciously receiving voluntary offerings from the laity, who themselves receive merit by their actions in giving the monks their daily meal.

Bird's Nest Popular nickname for the National Stadium in Beijing built for the 2008 Olympic Games in China's capital. It is constructed in two parts: a red concrete seating area for 80,000 sports fans, and the lattice-like steel outer frame which is said to resemble a bird's nest, although the architects would prefer that it be seen as a imitating a traditional Chinese ceramic pillow. The design was created by the Swiss architectural firm Herzog & de Meuron with collaboration from one of China's leading contemporary artist-designers **Ai Weiwei**. It is one of several spectacular edifices erected in Beijing and designed by expensive Western architects either for the Olympic Games or concurrent with them. They include the National Center for the Performing Arts, designed by Paul Andreu of France and popularly known as "The Egg" from its shape; the National Aquatics Center, site of swimming competition, and known also from its shape as the "Water Cube". The walls are built entirely of polygonal, cell-like strutwork, each cell framing an inflated plastic membrane, so that it presents a solid surface of different-sized bubbles.

Birds' Nest Soup A peculiarly Chinese cuisine known in MANDARIN as *yan wo*, or swallows' soup. It is one of the world's most expensive delicacies and has been a part of Chinese cuisine for some 400 years.

Black Dragon Forest Fire China is known for earthquakes, floods, famine, epidemics and other natural disasters, but one of the worst disasters was a forest fire which raged over northeast China and parts of Siberia from May to June 1987. It consumed about a third of China's prime conifer timber resources, covering an area about the size of New England. The conflagration was so vast, that fully two People's Liberation Army regional armies plus many civilians were mobilized to bring it under control, although it was not until heavy rain fell in June that the fire sputtered out. It has had profound ecological consequences that are hard to quantify such as desertification and climate change. The term Black Dragon is the Chinese name for what the rest of the world calls the Amur River. The Russian government has been even less forthcoming than the Chinese in detailing the extent of the fire on its side of the river.

Blue House The official residence and office of the President of South Korea, known in Korean as *Cheong Wa Dae*. It is constructed in the traditional Korean fashion and takes its name from the blue roof tiles. In 1968 the Blue House and the compound was attacked by North Korean commandos seeking to assassinate President Park Chung-hee. Park survived but many guards were killed. Later Park was assassinated by one of his own staff members at an outlying building. The term Blue House is used generically for the president, much as White House is used in the U.S.

Blue Water Navy What China supposedly aspires to as part of its naval buildup. For years the Chinese navy was seen as being mainly interested in coastal security. Beijing now sees its acquisition of modern destroyers, submarines and eventually an aircraft carrier or two as a means of projecting power and influence beyond. As part of this strategy the Chinese navy has participated in anti-piracy patrols off the coast of Somalia. China isn't alone in wanting a blue-water navy. South Korea too has been acquiring sophisticated vessels meant to project power offshore. The Japanese have the capability with its modern **Maritime Self Defense Force**, but does not proclaim any global aspirations, although for several years it helped to refuel allied ships in the Indian Ocean, and it too participates in anti-piracy patrols. Japan has acquired its first permanent offshore naval base in Djibouti to support such far-flung operations. (See **First Island Chain**)

Bnei Menashe HEBREW for "Children of Menasseh". Name for a group of people, also known as the "Chin", comprised of several thousand tribesmen living in the two northeastern Indian states of Mizoram and Manipur and in Myanmar's extreme northwest who claim to be descended from the ten lost tribes of Israel exiled more than 2,700 years ago by the Assyrians. In 2005 Israel's chief rabbinate officially recognized the tribesmen as authentic "descendants of Israel", allowing them the right of return to the Jewish state. Several thousand have moved there in recent years. Western academics believe the tribesmen were essentially animist, who converted to Christianity and who are now converting to Judaism. It is a source of some controversy over "massed" conversions.

Boao Forum for Asia A meeting that draws a thousand or more political leaders, businessmen and academics from Asia and Oceania to the town of Boao on the resort island of Hainan. Sometimes billed as the Asian version of the World Economic Forum held in Davos, Switzerland. It held its first meeting in April 2002. It is one of several ways in which China has attempted to copy the more famous and successful international institutions that project influence. Some, like the **Confucius Institute,** patterned after the British Council, have been successful. Others like the Chinese "Nobel" prize have flopped. The Boao Forum has not yet gained the global cachet of Davos.

boat people A general term for desperate people who take to sea on rickety boats to flee to other countries with a coastline. For many years the term referred mainly to refugees from Vietnam fleeing political persecution after the collapse of Saigon in 1975. In later years the exodus consisted mainly of economic refugees seeking a better life. Throughout the 1970s and 1980s some 675,000 set off for destinations all over Asia, especially Hong Kong, where they languished for years in camps. It has been estimated that a third of those who embarked died in storms at sea, of dehydration or in the hands of pirates. The exodus from Vietnam has tapered off with the increasing prosperity from from *doi moi* reforms, but other boat people flee persecution in Myanmar (see **Rohingyas**) or seek refuge in Australia, where the issue of boat people has taken on outsized political significance despite the relatively small numbers.

Bolkiah, Hassanal (1946-) The Sultan of Brunei, and the only absolute monarch in Asia aside from Bhutan. He is also reputed to be the world's richest man. His sultanate is the small but exceedingly rich country on Borneo's east coast. Once the focus of an empire that stretched across Borneo, it became a British Protectorate in 1888. Reluctant to share its huge oil resources, it elected to remain independent while the other two British colonial states on Borneo, Sabah and Sarawak, joined Malaysia. Hotel lobbies in the capital Bandar Seri Begawan (formerly Brunei Town) display portrait pictures of the Sultan and his two wives.

Bollywood A term for Hindi-language films produced in Mumbai (formerly Bombay). The term gained currency in the 1970s as India overtook America as the world's largest film producer. Bollywood encompasses only one part of India's gigantic film output, as there are other film centers producing films in other Indian languages, especially Bengali (known as "tollywood"). The name of Bombay fell out of use replaced by Mumbai, but that has not given rise to a new term "Mollywood."

bomba films The FILIPINO term for "bold films", or films that contain a lot of nudity and sexual themes, though not straight out pornography. They are often produced by serious directors and actors and aspire to some artistic merit. Official tolerance for bomba films waxes and wanes in the Philippines depending on social-political climate and the extent to which the president wishes to curry favor with the powerful Catholic Church or new alternative Christian groups such as **El Shaddai**. Other Asian countries have their own versions of sexually charged films. In

Japan they are known as "pink films," in Hong Kong simply as Category III films.

Boryeong Festival An annual mud-slinging event dreamed up in 1998 and now possibly the most popular festival in South Korea. Boryeong is a coastal town about 200 km south of Seoul, and its nearby mudflats are said to be rich in nutrients and thus famous for cosmetics. The festival was dreamed up specifically to promote Boryeong cosmetics and advertise their soil to be the best mud in the world. The summer festival now attracts huge crowds to a fun week of mud wrestling, tug of wars, mud sliding and other games.

bosozoku JAPANESE for motorcycle gangs, a kind of Japanese version of the Hell's Angels. Comprised mainly of teenagers, they ride their souped-up machines along Japan's highways, often removing the mufflers to cause as much noise and disruption as possible. Though seeing themselves as outcasts, they are prime recruits for gangsters and right-wingers. By some estimates, from 30-40 percent of *bosozoku* end up with the *yakuza*. Participation probably peaked in 1982 when the national police reported 42,510 members. By 2011 this had declined to under 10,000, police say.

"Bridge of No Return" A narrow concrete bridge that crosses the Military Demarcation Line between the two Koreas at Panmunjom. It was used during the Korean War for prisoner exchanges, and it got its nickname as North Korean and Chinese POWs were given a choice – either to stay in South Korea or return via the bridge. If they chose the latter but changed their mind, they were not allowed to return. The last prisoners to cross the Bridge of No Return were the 82 captives from the *U.S.S. Pueblo* in December, 1968. (See **Pueblo Incident**)

Budi Tek (1957-) Chinese-Indonesian businessman, also known by his Chinese name Yu Deyao, who made his fortune in poultry feed and livestock and used it to become one of the world's most influential new art buyers. His focus is on contemporary Chinese art, and in a few years he has amassed a collection of works by such figures as Zhong Xiaogong and Wang Guongyu. He has an art museum in Jakarta and is planning one in Shanghai. The art world took notice of this rising figure when in 2010 he paid $6.7 million for a Zhong painting: "Chapter of a New Century, Birth of People's Republic II", which he planned to display in Shanghai.

bugaku JAPANESE court music and dance. Dating back to the 7th century, it is thought to be the oldest example of Japanese performing art, predating Noh or Kabuki. It is also thought to be the oldest ensemble music in the world. The dancers wear bright red gowns and wooden masks. Masks are important as they convey the characters of the persons they represent. The dance is characterized by slow, precise and regal movements accompanied by *gakaku*, or court music imported from China. These days *bugaku* is mostly performed in important temple grounds. The first Shogun, Minamoto Yoritomo, brought the dance to Kamakura from Kyoto in 1189, and it has been performed annually at the Tsurugoaka Hachimangu temple there.

Bugis [boo-gis] One of the many ethnic groups of the Indonesian island of Sulawesi. A maritime people, the Bugis have always been good shipbuilders, sailors, merchants, warriors and fearsome pirates. The word may be the origin of the English term "boogey man" used to scare children. The term is thought to have been brought back to Europe by sailors who encountered the fierce Buginese pirates. There are other sources for the term. Bugis were among the first Malays to convert to Islam in the 17th century.

bulgogi KOREAN for "fire meat," more commonly Korean barbecue. Marinated slices of beef are cooked over fire on a metal grill. Along with *kimchi*, bulgogi has come to symbolize Korean cuisine, although it is only recently that *bulgogi* has appeared regularly on most Korean tables.

bumiputra MALAY Literally sons of the soil, it refers to ethnic Malays and other indigenous peoples.

bund From HINDI meaning an embankment or seaside landing place. The most famous bunds in Asia are in Shanghai and Yokohama which were centers of European influence. The Shanghai Bund demarcated the international settlement along the Huangpu River. Famous buildings along the bund include the Hongkong and Shanghai Bank and Peace Hotel. For years the other side of the river was virtually empty but has now filled up with modern buildings that provide startling contrast with the 1930s-style edifices on the bund. The Hotel New Grand, where Gen. Douglas MacArthur spent his first days in Japan, is on the Yokohama Bund, now better known as Yamanashita Park. (See **Pudong**)

bundok FILIPINO for mountain. From this Tagalog word comes the English word boondocks, or the "boonies", meaning somewhere in the hinterland. The word boondocks entered the American usage during the Philippine-American War, as mountainous terrain offered the Filipino irregulars a place to hide from American troops.

Bung INDONESIAN for brother. But it is not used simply for a biological sibling but as a kind of soul mate. Sukarno, the country's first president and father of the nation is frequently referred to as **Bung Karno**. Even U.S. president Barack Obama, who lived in Jakarta as a child, is affectionately known as Bung Barry. The word ***bapak*** means a respected father, and, shortened to Pak, is another term of respect for an elder.

Burakumin JAPANESE The term for a class of Japanese people ostracized since feudal times because they engaged in work Buddhists considered unclean or associated with death, such a being undertakers, or leather workers. They were often relegated to isolated hamlets, hence the name which means "village people". Most *burakumin* are concentrated in western Japan; there are fewer in Tokyo or the Northeast. Prejudice has abated; several are members of parliament and at least once served as chief cabinet secretary in the 1990s.

burasagaru JAPANESE for impromptu hallway interviews in which a mob of Japanese reporters buttonhole the prime minister in the corridors of his official office and pepper him with questions. Former prime minister Junichiro Koizumi initiated the practice but was the only premier who seemed to have the verbal agility to bring it off. His successors found it a minefield of potential gaffes, especially Yukio Hatoyama, the first opposition leader, who once said, "I think I had to resign [after less than a year in office] because I held so many [impromptu] interviews". If the premier's approval ratings are falling, as they usually are, the reporters are especially likely to pounce. Prime Minister Yoshihiko Noda discontinued the practice fearful of being trapped into making embarrassing or contradictory statements. The media mob was usually made up of young inexperienced junior reporters, not political veterans. Their editors dispatched them in the belief that it was good "training."

Busan South Korea's second city and largest port, formerly known as Pusan under the **McCune-Reischauer** system of rendering Korean words into Roman characters. The system was created in 1939 and named after the two American scholars who devised it, George M. McCune and Edwin O. Reischauer (the latter the famed East Asian scholar and former US Ambassador to Japan). The system was revised in 2000 to conform more closely to the way the words were really pronounced, which resulted in new spellings for several important cities and provinces: Thus Pusan is now Busan; Kwangju is now Gywangju; Cheju, now Jeju, Inchon is Incheon, Taegu is Daegu and Taejon is now Daejeon. The names of South Korea's capital, Seoul, and North Korea's capital Pyongyang, remain unchanged in the old and new systems. Historical references, such as the Pusan Perimeter of the Korean War, retain the old spelling. (See *hangul*)

bye bye Increasingly what Asians, especially Asian women, say to each other on parting. From ENGLISH for goodbye, but it has transcended English to become an almost universal word, sort of like taxi or variations on the word police. In Japan it is used mostly by office ladies, rather than men. It is trendy in Jakarta and Malaysia too.

C

Caixin Magazine MANDARIN for financial magazine. It was founded in 1998 by Hu Shuli and became a pioneer in reporting business and financial news in China. It is famous for investigative reporting, strong writing and pushing the limits. It seems to have a great deal of latitude in its reporting, in part because, unlike most Chinese publications, it is not directly linked to a government agency. It is supported by advertising and the Stock Exchange Executive Council. It earned a reputation for serious muckraking by exposing the SARS epidemic in China in 2003. It seems to be tolerated because it aims its sights more on economics rather than politics.

Camp 14 Just one concentration camp in the North Korean gulag but one made famous by the chilling 2012 book *Escape from Camp 14* by veteran journalist Blaine Harden. The book focuses on one inmate, Shin Dong-hyuk, who was born in the camp and probably would have lived his entire life there except that he managed to break out and make his way to the West – becoming, the author says, the only person to make a break and live to tell about it.

Canberra Purpose-built capital of Australia, it was created shortly after Australia became independent in 1901 to avoid having to choose between Melbourne or Sydney. The national parliament moved to Canberra in 1927 and now meets in a new parliament building, opened in 1988, which looks sort of like a burial mound topped by a humongous flagpole. Despite being the capital for some 100 years, much of the business of governing the country still takes place in Sydney, where the prime minister has a separate residence called Kirribilli House. Canberra is located in a federal district separate from Victoria or New South Wales called the Australian Capital Territory. With a population of about 350,000, it is Australia's largest city without a coastline. Unlike the District of Columbia in the U.S., the ACT has voting representation in parliament.

caning A form of punishment using a bamboo stick applied across the buttocks on a court order. It is still used in Malaysia, Brunei and Singapore for relatively minor crimes such as vandalism or against illegal immigrants. In 2002 Malaysia passed a stiff anti-immigration statute which allowed or up to six lashes for illegal immigrants. From 2002-2008 some 34,000 illegal immigrants were whipped. Singapore provides caning for some 30 offenses. It was source for international concern when Singapore sentenced an American youth named Michael Fay to be whipped for vandalism in 1993. Singapore reduced but did not eliminate the punishment under protest from Washington. It seemed to strike a chord in crime-weary America, judging by the many letters of approval. Hong Kong formally did away with caning in 1990.

Cao Dai [cow dye] VIETNAMESE for "supreme being." Religious and nationalist sect that took root in southern Vietnam in the 1920s. It was founded by Ngo Van Chieu, a civil servant and comprises an eclectic mix of Confucianism, Buddhism, Daoism, Christianity and Islam. It mimics the Roman Catholic Church for its hierarchical structure – it even has a "pope". Among its "saints" is Joan of Arc. The center of worship is in Tay Ninh. In 1955-56 former South Vietnam president Ngo Dinh Diem disbanded the Cao Dai army and sent its "pope" into exile. It continues to flourish along the Mekong River delta even under the communist regime. The sect is said to have about 2 million faithful and about 1,000 temples in Vietnam.

capsule hotel A modern, low-cost kind of temporary lodging introduced in Japan in the 1980s. They consist of rows of plastic capsules about 6 feet long and 3 x 3 feet wide and high, equipped with a bunk and a small television. At one time it was a symbol of prosperity, as salarymen working too late to catch a train home could spend the night in a capsule hotel (usually far cheaper than a late-night taxi ride). Now it is more a symbol of decline as more and more of the working poor use them as a kind of flophouse.

catty A traditional Asian unit of weight, especially for tea and other foods sold in open markets. The word is taken from MALAY *kati*, which is freely used throughout Indonesia, Malaysia, Singapore, and Hong Kong. Weight varies but a catty is about 600 grams in Southeast Asia, and an even 500 grams in China. Also a word for tea container, pronounced **caddy**, first applied to the porcelain jars imported from China in the 19th century. (See **wet market**)

cha-cha Not a dance from Latin America, it is shorthand for "charter change", meaning amending the Philippines' 1986 Constitution to allow the president to serve more than one term. The six-year term limit was written into the charter following the People Power revolt in the wake of the long rule of Ferdinand Marcos. Filipinos began to get buyers' remorse for this provision toward the end of President Fidel Ramos's term as president (1992-1998), especially as his likely successor was the buffoonish ex-actor Joseph Estrada. The *cha-cha* movement died out, and Estrada duly won election as president. And equally predictably, he made a botch of it and was overthrown and replaced by his vice-president, Gloria Macapagal Arroyo.

chaebol KOREAN A term for large family-owned conglomerates in South Korea. Korean dictators, especially Park Chung-hee, adopted a policy of favoring a handful of families with tax benefits, special loans, cheap energy and other subsidies. They grew into industrial giants, each commanding a huge family of subsidiaries and huge swaths of the economy. They are both a source of pride to many Koreans as engines of the country's rise from poverty but also resentment at the special favors and frequent corruption scandals that emanate from these giant concerns. Today they dominate the country's export economy, outpacing Japan and other rivals in such industries as shipbuilding and computer chips, and most recently, in sales of nuclear power plants to the Middle East. They

are similar to the pre-war Japanese ***zaibatsu***, which were largely broken up under the American occupation, in that they are dominated by one powerful family. There are a couple dozen *chaebol* in South Korea, but the most widely known are probably Hyundai, Samsung and LG.

Chakri Dynasty The ruling royal family of Thailand. The dynasty was founded in 1782 by a general Chao Phya Chakri, who became Rama I. The accession of Chakri to the throne marked not only the beginning of modern Thailand but also of Bangkok, as his first act was to move his capital from Dhonburi across the river to Bangkok. He made the decision on military grounds as Bangkok was better protected by water. Other notable monarchs in the line include King Mongkut, Rama IV (1851-1868), and King **Chulalongkorn,** Rama V (1868-1910). The reigning monarch, King Bhumibol Adulyadej, Rama IX, ascended in 1946 and is one of the world's longest-serving kings.

Champasak The name for an ancient independent Lao state that was abolished by the French in 1945 and amalgamated with the Kingdom of Laos. It is home to Wat Phou, which is considered the birthplace of Khmer civilization. Essentially a village now, it is close to Pakse, the largest town in southern Laos, now connected by airline to Vientiane and Bangkok. Numerous guesthouses and boutique hotels are springing up to accommodate tourists wanting to explore southern Laos.

Chang, Iris (1968-2004) A second-generation Chinese-American who wrote several books of which the most famous was *The Rape of Nanking*, the first full-length, non-fiction account of what happened in China's former capital when the Japanese Imperial Army occupied the city in 1937. The book spent ten weeks on the *New York Times* best-seller list, but Chang had a hard time finding a Japanese publisher. Many Japanese conservatives, not just fringe right-wingers but mainstream figures such as Tokyo Governor Shintaro Ishihara, deny that the event, generally referred to as the **Nanjing Massacre**, ever happened or was greatly exaggerated. Chang was as much an activist as a detached historian and that may have played a role in her 2004 suicide.

Changi Name of Singapore's international airport, opened in 1981 and often considered the world's best, the international benchmark for service excellence. The airport has added luster to a name that was once associated with some of the worst prisoner abuses during World War II. After Singapore's garrison surrendered to the Japanese, the former civilian prison was used to intern British and other civilians as well as ordinary POWs. Among the prisoners was one James Clavell, who turned his experiences into a novel, *King Rat*, and later went on to write other best-selling novels set in Asia. There is a Changi Museum, which has become a tourist attraction, similar to the Bridge on the River Kwai.

chengguan MANDARIN an abbreviation for Chinese City Management Administration and Implementation of Law, a quasi-official urban and township police force charged mainly with enforcing regulations against street hawkers, beggars, unlicensed taxis and residency permit violations. The *chengguan* are frequently the butt as well as the spark for the protests and riots that break out daily in China. They are often caused by the heavy-handed "arrest" or beating of unlicensed hawkers or owners of property that the local authorities wish to condemn for other purposes.

The ranks are drawn from demobilized PLA soldiers or workmen made redundant by the closing of state-owned enterprises and are seen as enforcers for local communist cadres. The phrase "don't be a *chengguan*" is a way of saying "don't be a bully".

Chin Chin Densha "Ding Dong Trolley" (formally the Arakawa line), so called because of its clanging bell. It is all that remains of the extensive network of trolley lines that once criss-crossed Tokyo. At one time close to 40 streetcar lines served the public, but as buses and subways were built, they gradually closed so that by 1972 only the Arakawa line remained. About 67,000 daily commuters still use the line, and it has a kind of cult following complete with souvenirs such as bean-paste cakes in the shape of the trolley car. The width of the rail line is 372mm, the same as that of an English horse carriage circa 1911, when the tracks were first laid down. A one-way trip from Waseda to Minowa-bashi takes about 50 minutes.

Chin Peng (1924-2013) Communist guerilla who led the insurrection known as the "Emergency" against British rule in what was then called Malaya in the 1940s and 1950s. He led about 10,000 guerillas against a larger force of British and other Commonwealth troops. The rebellion petered out in the late 1950s, and Chin fled to China and then to Thailand, where he remained exiled until his death, even after signing a peace treaty in 1989 and pledging loyalty to Malaysia. The British-led operation was considered a textbook case of successful counter-insurgency, and was taken as a model by the Americans, with much less success, in Vietnam. Some of the "emergency" measures, such as the **Internal Security Act**, remain in force to this day.

China Airlines Despite the name, this airline is Taiwan's flag-carrier — except that its aircraft have no flag painted on the tail, just a big pink plum blossom. China's flag carrier is called Air China. China Airlines has many flights throughout Southeast Asia, and since July 2008 has been able to make direct flights to mainland China. (See **Taiwanization**)

China Dream A term that Xi Jinping took as the theme of his administration when he took over the reins of government in late 2012 and early 2013. Officially, it is meant to describe the rejuvenation of the Chinese nation, and it seems to be replacing the **"Peaceful Rise"** locution promoted by his predecessors. The theme is supposedly not meant to be jingoistic or expansionist, although observers note that the term seems to be taken from the title of a very popular 2010 book, *The China Dream,* by People's Liberation Army Colonel Liu Mingfu, which advocated China's dominance both regionally and globally. The controversial book postulates a different and more nationalist role for China beyond the official "peaceful rise" (See *heping jueqi*) rhetoric of the government. It declares that China's ultimate goal is to become the world's dominant power, restoring a modern version of its historic Middle Kingdom role but on a wider canvas. Liu rejects the "peaceful rise" concept and argues that China should build sufficient military power to prevail in any showdown with the West.

China Lobby During the 1950s and 1960s the China Lobby was considered one of the most successful and feared pressure groups in Washington, on par with the Israeli AIPAC and the National Rifle Association today. The lobby acted on behalf of the Nationalist regime of Chiang Kai-shek and against any recognition or reconciliation with the PRC (aka **"Red China"**). At its peak the lobby boasted influential members of Congress, usually from the Republican Party, and important journalists such as Henry R. Luce of *Time*. President Richard Nixon took much of the wind out of the sails of the China Lobby in his 1972 visit to Beijing and the subsequent official recognition of the PRC and the downgrading of the U.S. mission in Taipei. Little is heard of the "China Lobby" anymore, even though both Beijing and Taipei continue to lobby for their respective interests.

China price Literally, the price of goods and services produced in China, a catch word for how the cost of producing these goods in China has become a benchmark for global competitiveness. Foreign businesses that cannot meet the China price find their products edged out of the market and either close up shop or move their factories to countries that are even cheaper than China, such as Vietnam. "The China price has become the three scariest words in U.S. industry," stated *BusinessWeek* in 2004.

China watcher One of an intrepid band of journalists and academics who analyze public appearances and closely parse official statements and newspapers for clues as to who is up and who is down in China's internal political power struggles. For many years the China watching had to be done from safe perches such as Hong Kong, since China was largely closed to foreign media. Since its opening, journalists have been allowed to live and report in China. Yet China watchers still ply their trade because the elite that rules the country still does not appreciate outsiders (or Chinese journalists, for that matter) probing too deeply into what goes on behind the gates of the **Zhongnanhai** compound. Politics and, to an extent economics, are their stock in trade. Persons interested in an

We are watchers of those China watchers. Everything under control.

Gong On

China Watcher

academic study of Chinese culture, art and literature are more properly called **sinologists**.

chindonya JAPANESE [cheen don ya] Term for troupes of urban troubadours, once the favored way to advertise the opening of new stores and sales but now mainly a venue for hobbyists and those interested in preserving traditional customs. Each troupe is comprised of three to seven people with the women dressed in colorful kimonos, carrying paper umbrellas, beating drums and playing Western or Japanese wind instruments. The practice is said to have developed in Osaka near the end of the Edo period, but the golden age of *chindonya* was just after World War II as commerce slowly recovered, and businesses moved out of street stalls and black markets into permanent locations. Advertising for new businesses has been taken over by newspaper supplements, television and the Internet. Aficionados strive to keep the tradition alive against these modern ad mediums. Toyama city hosts an annual national *chindonya* festival.

Chinese Patriotic Catholic Association The name for the state-sponsored church in China to which all "patriotic" Catholics are supposed to belong. China has a long and complicated relationship with the Vatican. Supposedly, reconciliation is blocked by the Vatican's formal relationship with Taiwan, although there hasn't been a Papal Nuncio in Taipei for decades. The main issue is the choosing of bishops, as Beijing insists on naming or at least approving elevation of new bishops. Relations have soured when the Association, a government body, has gone ahead and named bishops without reference to the Pope. These strictures do not apply to Hong Kong, where the local bishop is appointed by the Pope without reference to Beijing. (See **Three Self Movement**)

Chinese Taipei A studiously neutral term that allows Taiwanese people to participate in many international organizations and events, even beauty pageants, without raising the wrath of Beijing. Under this name athletes participate in the Olympics, the World Baseball Classic and other sporting events. It is also how Taiwan is addressed by the World Bank and the International Monetary Fund. The athletes march under the banner of their sporting organization, not the flag of the Republic of China. (See **One China Policy**)

Chiyoda-ku, Tokyo 100 One of the most famous addresses in the world, the SW1 of Japan. Chiyoda Ward (*ku*) encompasses the heart of power in downtown Tokyo, including the Marunouchi financial district, the Imperial Palace, the national **Diet** building (but not **Ginza** which is in Chuo Ward). Every day about a million commuters emerge from the district's numerous subway stations for a day's work. Every evening, they descend to the railroad stations for the commute back home. The permanent population is only around 40,000 and has been steadily falling to the point where some worry it may have to be merged with one of the adjoining wards.

Cho, David Yonggi (1935-) South Korean Protestant evangelist who built the **Yoido Full Gospel Church** into the world's largest single congregation, with from 750,000 to one million members. He began his ministry in 1958 after attending a gospel seminary in Seoul. His church grew exponentially, reaching 450,000 members in 1984 and 700,000 in 1992. The main sanctuary is located on Yoido island in the middle of the Han River in Seoul and seats about 25,000 for each of seven Sunday services (Cho still preaches at two of them). People begin lining up an hour ahead of time to get a seat. He and his fellow megachurch pastors had the clout to kill a law that would have eased the purchase in Korea of Islamic bonds known as *sukuk*. But in 2011 he came under a cloud after two dozen of his pastors accused him of embezzling millions in church funds.

Choeung Ek CAMBODIAN Execution grounds known as the "killing fields" situated 15 km south of Phnom Penh, where the skeletal remains of some 8,985 people were found in 1980, shortly after the Vietnamese army invaded Cambodia and overthrew the Khmer Rouge government. An estimated 17,000 people were executed at the extermination camp at Choeung Ek as part of the Khmer Rouge's attempt to exterminate religious, ethnic and racial minorities. Cracked skulls arranged by sex and age are now displayed as a memorial in a glass pyramid.

chow fan CANTONESE Fried rice in all its forms, shapes and sizes, the staple dish in Hong Kong in much the same way as *ramen* is in Japan. It usually comes with chicken or pork and a large dollop of monosodium glutamate. It is known in Japan as *chahan*.

Chulalongkorn, King (1853-1910) Remembered as one of Thailand's greatest kings of the present dynasty, of which he was the fifth reigning monarch (Rama V). Though forced to cede portions of his kingdom, such as Laos and western Cambodia to France and several Malay states to Britain, he managed to maintain his country's independence during a time when European powers had a firm upper hand in Asia. He also undertook many far-reaching reforms, such as the abolition of slavery, and promoted transportation and educational reforms. Thailand's premier institution of higher learning, Chulalongkorn University, is named after him.

Chusok (Chuseok) KOREAN Harvest festival that is by far Korea's most important national holiday. It takes place over three days usually in September or October, by the lunar calendar. Koreans by the millions descend on their ancestral homes to visit family grave sites, make offerings, commune with relatives and in general celebrate the bountiful harvest.

Class A (war criminal) Unlike at Nuremberg, the post-World War II International Tribunal for the Far East, better known as the Tokyo Trials, distinguished three types of war crimes: crimes against peace, conventional war crimes and crimes against humanity, designated Class A, B and C respectively. Some 300,000 Japanese were charged with Class B and C crimes, mainly involving prisoner abuse. The more controversial class of crimes, a controversy that resonates down to this day, were the 25 military and civilian leaders who were convicted of: "being the leaders, organizers, instigators or accomplices in the formulation or execution of a common plan or conspiracy to wage wars of aggression..." Even today most Japanese nationalists, and even some more disinterested people, claim that the charges were invented by victors with no precedent in international law. Twelve Class A defendants, including former prime minister Hideki Tojo, were hanged. In 1972 the **Yasukuni** shrine inducted 14 Class A defendants into the shrine. The action is a source of continuing friction between Japan and China, which objects to Japanese leaders making official visits to the shrine. (See **Pal, Radhabinod**)

combini JAPANESE for convenience store. The Japanese language has no "v" sound, so the "b" substitutes in a kind of compressed English. Such Japanese-English terms are becoming increasingly common as Japanese find new words for new instruments and concepts – like convenience stores. Others include *"wopuro"* for word processor, *"famicom"* for personal computer, and *"comisen"* for community center. Convenience stores are everywhere in urban Japan and offer more goods and services than similar American stores. Executives bring their golf clubs for delivery to the course for Sunday games, busy mothers pick up their laundry, grandmothers buy their noodles there instead of making them. The venerable American 7-Eleven chain, founded in 1927 in Dallas, Texas, but since 1991 almost totally owned by Ito-Yokato, Japan's largest retail conglomerate, led the march beginning in 1974. The convenience store business is highly competitive. Other major *combini* in Japan are Family Mart, Lawsons and SunKus [pronounced sunks].

Commissioner Lin A figure of rectitude in China. Lin Zexu (1785-1850) was dispatched to Guangzhou in southern China to try to stop shipments of foreign opium into the country. He gave it a good try, but the direct result of his crackdown was the first Anglo-Chinese War (1839-1842), also known as the Opium War. That resulted in the cession of Hong Kong Island to Britain "in perpetuity".

Confucius Institute A major element in projection of China's "**soft power**". These institutes are devoted to teaching Chinese language and customs throughout the world and are generally modeled after the British Council or Alliance Française. The name Confucius Institute is well-chosen as it conveys no direct link to China's communist government. If Beijing had formed such institutes in an earlier age, it might have named them the Mao Zedong Institute, which means they would have been banned just about everywhere.

Cool biz JAPANESE/English term for businessmen and politicians who ostentatiously shuck their neckties during the summer to emphasize their commitment to conservation and the environment. Originally it was meant as a statement to cut down on carbon emissions, but after the Fukushima nuclear disaster of 2011 severely curtailed electric power production, it became a symbol of conservation by cutting down or shutting off air conditioning, especially in Tokyo and other large cities.

Cui Jian [sway-jen] (1966-) Famous Chinese singer and pioneer of rock music, often described as the "father of Chinese rock". His career took off in 1986 with his first hit *Nothing to My Name*. The song became the unofficial anthem of the student protesters in Tiananmen Square in 1989, and has remained China's most popular contemporary ballad. Cui was not arrested after the June 4-5 crackdown, but he was barred from large-scale performances for years until his final rehabilitation after 2000. He might be described, along with other artists such as novelist **Wei Hui** or film director **Zhang Yimou**, as a quasi-dissident, meaning performers in China who have pushed the limits, been harassed and censored, but never imprisoned or exiled. His CDs have sold in the millions.

Cyclone Nargis The worst natural disaster in Myanmar's recorded history made landfall at the Irrawaddy River Delta on May 2, 2008. The official death toll was 138,000, though likely higher. International assistance was delayed by the regime's reluctance to have foreign aid workers freely roaming about the country and by the fact that the **Sichuan Earthquake**, China's greatest recorded natural disaster, struck only 10 days later. A referendum on a new constitution was held almost simultaneously with the cyclone and thus is known informally as the **Nargis Constitution**. Nargis is URDU for daffodil.

D

Dabbawallah Lunch box carriers. They deliver roughly 200,000 hot, home-cooked meals to busy Mumbaikers – as residents of Mumbai are called – at their workplaces and return empty lunch boxes to their homes the same evening. The Dabbawallah Association of Mumbai consists of about 5,000 carriers, all men, who ensure that the right meal reaches the right customer. The mistake rate is said to be just one in about 16 million deliveries.

Dai Sam Ba CANTONESE for the ruins of St. Paul's Church, probably the most recognizable artifact of Macau. It refers to big San Pa(olo) as opposed to San Pa(olo) *chai*, or the little St. Paul, which is the Chinese name for St. Joseph's church and seminary. The church and a nearby seminary were erected by the Jesuits around 1630, with most of the work on the church being done by Japanese Christian artisans. The Jesuits were expelled in 1762 and the seminary turned into an army barracks. On the night of January 29, 1835, a fire broke out in the kitchen of the barracks and destroyed the college and all of the church except for one stone face. The church was never rebuilt; only the stone façade remains.

Dalai Lama Title for the head of the Yellow-hat order of Tibetan Buddhism and also the spiritual and temporal ruler of Tibet. Tibetan Buddhists believe he is a god. When he dies, the search begins for his reincarnated successor. The current Dalai Lama, Tenzin Gyatso, was born in 1940 in Hongai in Qinghai province, and he is the 14th incarnation. He fled Tibet in 1959 and has lived and maintained a kind of government-in-exile in Dharamsala, northern India, ever since. The Dalai Lama won the Nobel Prize for Peace in 1989 for his consistent efforts in trying to negotiate a meaningful autonomy and has generated much support from non-Buddhists worldwide. His predecessor, the 13th Dalai Lama, ruled for nearly 60 years as the head of a sovereign state. That ended in 1950 when China seized Tibet. The current Dalai Lama was only a child then.

dalang JAVANESE for puppet master, the man who manipulates the puppets in Indonesia's shadow theater, the **Wayang Kulit** (so-called because the puppet silhouettes are projected onto a screen). The *dalang* sits behind the screen, manipulates the puppets, speaks the lines and cues the orchestra. To perform these tasks takes considerable training, not to mention sheer physical stamina (the puppets are heavy and performances can run all night). The plays draw on the country's Hindu heritage with tales from the *Ramayama* and other epics from the subcontinent. Sukarno, Indonesia's first president, was often referred to as the *dalang* – the puppet master of the Indonesian people, the one who gave them voice and directed them in their new state, leading them, so to speak, in their new national epic.

Dal Lake Situated near Srinagar in the disputed territory of Jammu and **Kashmir**. With its breathtaking scenery and houseboat hotels, ranging from the basic to the most palatial, it was once a popular destination for tourists and honeymooners. The houseboats are still there, although many have fallen into a state of disrepair as communal troubles and insurgency have kept tourists away in recent years.

Dalit HINDI Currently the politically correct term for India's lowest caste, formerly known as "untouchables" or, as Gandhi called them, "Harijans", the people of God. It refers to those at the bottom of the Hindu caste structure. About 170 million of India's billion people are Dalit, and the vast majority live in poverty, despite the emergence in recent years of several Dalit millionaires. Caste discrimination has been illegal in India for more than 60 years, but informal discrimination is much harder to eradicate.

danwei MANDARIN A Chinese unit of social organization and care under communism. Organizing the people of China into work units was one of the ways in which Mao Zedong dealt with the task of restructuring the economy. All workers were registered with a *danwei*, which provided work, rudimentary healthcare, lodging and other life-time social amenities, sometimes known as the **iron rice bowl**. On the other hand, party leaders wielded enormous power over members, as their approval had to be obtained for everything from work assignments to marriage and child-bearing. With the market reforms begun under Deng Xiaoping, the power of the *danwei* has declined significantly, along with that of the state-owned enterprises. But the regime is challenged to find new means of providing a social safety net.

Daqing [dah-ching] China's largest oilfield, located in the northeastern Heilongjiang province and developed in the 1950s with Russian help (until Moscow withdrew aid in 1959). It once provided some 80 percent of China's petroleum needs, which is more a comment on paucity of automobiles in the years before China's economic reforms and opening to the world. Now, of course, it provides only a fraction of China's fast-growing demand, which much be met by imports from many sources.

datu FILIPINO Basically the local ruler or chieftain in the pre-Spanish Philippines. The head man of the ***baranguy*** boats that brought Malays to the Philippines was the *datu*. They had a hard time under the Spanish, who made them responsible for raising taxes. Philippine history is replete with stories of rebellions led by *datu*. The most famous chieftain in Philippine history was **Lapu-lapu**, the *datu* of Mactan, whose soldiers killed Ferdinand Magellan.

Dayak A term that refers to the indigenous peoples of Borneo, in both East Malaysia and Indonesia's Kalimantan territories. The term once had derogatory connotations similar to "savage" but today it is a neutral collective term for ethnic peoples such as the Iban and Orang Ulu. Dayaks make up about half the population of Malaysia's Sarawak state. Most Dayak villages have been incorporated into the administrative systems of Malaysia and Indonesia.

Dazhai The name of a "model" Chinese farming commune in Shanxi province, made famous by Mao Zedong's 1964 campaign to "Learn from Dazhai in Agriculture." The village of only a few hundred people achieved unbelievably bountiful harvests and constructed large dams, aqueducts and other infrastructure by applying "Mao thought." The village party secretary Chen Yonggui was promoted to the national Politburo and made a vice-minister for agriculture. Later Dazhai was ridiculed as an example of ultra left-wing zeal accompanied by falsified harvest reports that greatly exaggerated its successes. The truth may be somewhere in between as Chen introduced some practical ideas, such as combining small fields into larger ones, that improved harvests. Deng Xiaoping deliberately blackened the Dazhai legend in his campaign to end collectivization. Chen was dismissed from his posts in 1980 and held under house arrest until his death in 1986. (See **Lei Feng**)

Democracy Wall A kind of Hyde Park-type reservation for free speech that existed in Beijing for about one year from 1978 and was considered part of China's short-lived **Beijing Spring**. Anybody could post a large-character poster on a red-brick wall on Xidan Street. For a while,

Deng Xiaoping was happy to tolerate this free speech as much of it was directed at his old enemies, such as the **Gang of Four**. But as he grew more secure in power, he closed down the Democracy Wall. There were always limits to what one could post. Wei Jingsheng was arrested and imprisoned for a large-character poster on Democracy Wall calling for a **Fifth Modernization**, namely democracy itself.

Democrat Party The oldest political party in Thailand, founded in 1946. It is spelled Democrat (not Democratic) in English renderings. It is historically conservative and royalist but of late has been defined mainly by opposition to former premier Thaksin Shinawatra. The last Democrat Party government, headed by Abhisit Vejjajiva, was defeated in the 2010 elections by Thaksin's sister Yingluck Shinawatra. (See **yellow shirts**)

depato JAPANESE from English for department store. Many of the world's oldest department stores are Japanese, such as Daimaru (founded 1717), Mitsubishi (1673) and Matsuzakaya (1611).

deru kui wa utareru JAPANESE for "The nail (or stake) that sticks out gets hammered in," which is probably the best-known Japanese proverb. It underscores the general cultural bias toward conformity.

Diaoyu See **Senkaku**

Dice-K Sportswriter and headline lingo for Daisuke Matsuzaka, ace pitcher for the Seibu Lions, who in 2007 moved over to the Major Leagues to pitch for the Boston Red Sox for a combined payout of about $100 million (combining posting fee with compensation.) Dice-K earned his salary his first year, helping the Red Sox win the World Series but has been something of a disappointment since then. (See **posting system**)

Diet The word normally used by foreigners for Japan's bicameral parliament. It is not Japanese but a common term used for medieval German assemblies. Japanese call their legislature ***kokkai gijido***. The word Diet reflects the German origin of many Japanese legislative traditions. The Diet was created under the Meiji Constitution, patterned after the Prussian constitution, and first convened in 1890. One can see German influences even today in the way the ministers sit on benches facing the circular seats of the backbenchers and how the leaders sit in the back row rather than the front. It operates under the 1947 constitution, written by the Americans (see **Article 9**). The main changes were to replace the former House of Peers, made up of aristocrats and Imperial nominees, with the directly elected House of Councilors and to give women the right to vote. The Diet meets in the severe-looking, granite and white marble art deco style Diet Building, which was completed in 1936.

dim sum bonds A bond denominated in Chinese yuan or **renminbi**, issued in Hong Kong and named after Hong Kong's favorite dining pastime. The bonds are popular with foreign investors who desire exposure to yuan-denominated assets but are restricted by Chinese capital controls from investing in domestic Chinese debt. The first dim sum bond was sold by China Development Bank in 2007 to help raise capital for major infrastructure projects on the mainland. There are also **samurai bonds**, yen-denominated instruments issued in Tokyo by a Japanese firm and **sushi bonds**, Eurobonds issued by a Japanese issuer that does not count against Japanese restrictions on holdings of foreign securities.

dingo Free-roaming wild dog unique to the Australian outback (but not Tasmania). Originally they are believed to have been brought to Australia by the first Aborigines, but are now thought to have come via Asian traders 3,500-5,000 years ago. Even so, they became an essential part of Aboriginal life. Dingos are an example of partial domestication, not really a domestic dog but some form of early dog. The term dingo goes back to colonial times and probably stems from one of the Aboriginal languages. They hunt rabbits and feral cats and sometimes sheep. It is a matter of debate how dangerous they are to humans.

Diwali Hindu festival of lights which precedes the beginning of the New Year. It is held on the day of the new moon between mid-October and mid-November.

DMZ Well-known wildlife sanctuary between North and South Korea. Actually it is an abbreviation for demilitarized zone, a four km-wide buffer zone that stretches 151 miles across the Korean peninsula. Almost no humans venture into this zone, so it has become a kind of informal sanctuary for all kinds of birds and beasts that have vanished from other parts of Korea – among them, the Manchurian crane, the Korean wildcat and the small Korean bears. (See "**Bridge of No Return**")

doi moi VIETNAMESE term given to a series of economic reforms initiated in Communist Vietnam in 1986 with the goal of creating a more open market economy with socialist characteristics. These reforms were obviously inspired by the market-opening reforms begun in Communist China a few years previously. Among other reforms, it opened the country to foreign investment, permitted privately owned companies and abandoned collectivized agriculture. The reforms made things easier for the US to normalize diplomatic relations with the former enemy in 1995. It has led to greater personal freedom, although the party still arrests dissidents and democracy advocates.

dojo JAPANESE Depending on the way the word is pronounced, *dojo* could mean a special training area for martial arts students or any other physical training activity. Or it could mean a kind of common bottom-feeding eel found slithering in the mud of rivers and canals. On taking office in 2011, Japan's Prime Minister Yoshihiko Noda modestly described himself as a *dojo* rather than a goldfish. Noda was quoting the calligrapher and poet Mitsuo Aida (1924-1991), who wrote that "a *dojo* does not have to emulate a goldfish." In the English vernacular, it was sort of like saying he considered himself a work horse, not a show horse. For the average Japanese the *dojo* is a staple of hot-pot dishes. It contains high levels of calcium and vitamins, which supposedly boost stamina.

Dokdo The Dokdo, or "lonely islands", are comprised of two rocky islets in the middle of the Sea of Japan (see **East Sea**) 200 km off the coast of Japan. Ownership is disputed between South Korea and Japan, which calls them the **Takeshima** islands. They are also known as the **Liancourt Rocks**, named after the French vessel *Le Liancourt*, which carried the first Europeans to set eyes on them. The U.S. Board of Geographic Names uses this neutral term. Koreans claim they were first incorporated into the **Shilla Kingdom** by King Jijeung in 512. In 1952 President Syngman Rhee established the Syngman Rhee line in the Sea of Japan including the rocks inside South Korea's purported boundaries. The Japanese claim they were a part of Shimane prefecture, which roils the waters by such things as proclaiming "Takeshima Day" observations. Seoul maintains a small garrison and lighthouse. The issue flares from time to time, sparking protest marches, the burning of Japanese flags and temporary recalling of ambassadors. Also the name for the South Korean Navy's largest warship, an 18,000-ton amphibious assault carrier.

dolphin Several species of dolphin are native to, but no longer common in, Asia. The **Irrawaddy dolphin** is an ocean-going mammal that is found in the estuaries of mayor rivers throughout Southeast Asia. It has a large, rounded, blunt face and an indistinct beak. Though called Irrawaddy, they are found in other river systems. Recent surveys found only 85 such dolphins in the Mekong. Several river-going dolphins are found in Asia, including the **pink dolphin** in the Pearl River estuary (they really are pink). Hong Kong people often go on dolphin-watching boat trips to view the animals. The **Yangzi dolphin**, also known as the *baiji,* once common along the river, is either very endangered or, indeed, already extinct. The Yangzi finless porpoise is likely to meet the same fate. As of 2011, the World Wildlife Fund estimated the population at about 1,000 (even fewer than giant pandas) and declining steadily. All species of river dolphin are endangered due to gill net fishing in these waters or poisoning from nearby coastal factories.

Dongbei The name for China's northeast – often, though erroneously, referred to in the West as Manchuria. The region encompasses the three provinces of Heilongjiang, Jilin and Liaoning. Because of its location close to the Russian and Korean borders it was for many years a crossroads of conflict, especially between Russia and Japan. It was the site of China's heavy industry, building on facilities erected first by the Japanese and later with help from Russia. But since the market reforms initiated by Deng Xiaoping, the region has become something of a backwater, with much of the action moving to the coastal cities further south. Jilin province includes a large number of ethnic Koreans in the Yanbian Autonomous Region. *Dongbei-cai*, or Dongbei food, is becoming recognized as a distinctive regional cuisine, though not quite ranking with the eight "traditional" Chinese cuisines. Its use of cabbage and vinegar reflects Korean influence; that of lamb, Mongolian influence.

Dongguan The quintessential Chinese factory town, if the word "town" can cover a metropolis with a population larger than New York City. It is located in the Pearl River Delta factory belt near to Hong Kong and is home to hundreds of assembly plants, many owned by Taiwanese concerns. Dongguan ranks behind only Shanghai and Shenzhen as China's largest exporter. The faceless, characterless city has no real amenities or attractions, not even an airport, but it does boast the world's largest shopping mall, the **New South China Mall** opened in 2005. Rather, it would be the world's largest mall if it ever attracted any tenants. The mall has space for 2,350 stores but as of 2012, it was still virtually empty.

Dong Son VIETNAMESE for an ancient prehistoric culture centered on the Red River Valley of northern Vietnam which flourished circa 500-300 BC. The culture is known for the high quality of its bronze works, especially the bronze ritual kettle drums. The Dong Son culture is considered a precursor to many subsequent civilizations in Southeast Asia. It was named for a village in northern Vietnam, where many of the bronze artifacts were found, but they are also found throughout the region.

Double Happiness The two Chinese characters for joy, 喜喜, joined together to form one image – 囍 – is a common ornamental design in China, often used in various ways at weddings and New Year celebrations. In MANDARIN the characters form the words *shuang xi*. Also the English name for a common brand of Chinese cigarettes said to be favored by Deng Xiaoping and often found at airport duty free shops.

Dragonboat racing A team paddling sport with ancient pedigree but which has become popular across the globe only in the past two or three decades. It got its boost in Hong Kong where the annual Dragonboat Festival in the summer is a major event, with dozens of contests held along the coast in the territory. The boats are richly decorated, usually with a dragon's head at the front and a tail at the rear. It differs from other rowing sports in that the contestants use paddles, not oars, and the coxswain beats the pace with a drum. It is a recognized sport in the Asian Games.

Driglam Namza DZONGKHA A policy announced by **King Jigme Singye** of Bhutan in 1989 calling on all citizens to wear traditional costume in public. The measure was also aimed at limiting the number of foreigners entering the country and stopped television broadcasts from

India, all in the interests of reviving tradition and culture. **Dzongkha** is the official language of Bhutan. Originally the language spoken in the western part of the country, it is now the language of the government and taught in schools. It is similar to Tibetan and has only had a written form for the past 40 years.

dukun INDONESIAN Shaman, faith healer or soothsayer still followed in one of those versions by many modern Indonesians and respected even in Muslim areas. *Dukuns* are more prevalent on Java, where many ancient, semi-pagan practices continue under a veneer of Islam, but they are also prominent in Madura and Bali.

durian A large fruit with a tough spiky skin that makes it look like the head of a battle ax, grown throughout Southeast Asia. It has a famously repellent odor – it is said to taste like heaven but smell like hell – but also many devotees who are willing to ignore the smell to get to the creamy insides. Sometimes banned in close spaces, such as elevators or mass transit trains.

E

East Sea What Koreans, North and South, would like the rest of the world to call the body of water between Korea and Japan, now known almost universally as the **Sea of Japan**. Understanding that getting the rest of the world to drop "Sea of Japan" in favor of "East Sea" is near impossible, Seoul has taken the middle course, with some success, of advocating that other nations put "also known as the East Sea" in parentheses. Korea asked the International Hydrographic Organization to follow this course, but Washington officially advised that organization to use the name Sea of Japan alone. That is also the position of the U.S. Board of Geographic Names, which guides the government. China and Russia, two other nations that border the waters, use variations of Sea of Japan. (See **Dokdo**)

Edo The original name for Tokyo up until the Meiji Restoration of 1868, when the emperor moved from Kyoto to the shogun's palace and renamed the city "Eastern Capital" – or Tokyo. Human habitation goes back to prehistoric times, and the famous Sensoji Temple traces its history back at least to the 800s. However, officially Edo was founded in 1457 when a minor feudal lord named Ota Dokan established a fortress where the current Imperial palace now lies. It fell into disrepair, but was transformed into a mighty fortress-palace by Ieyasu Tokugawa who arrived in 1600 to found the shogunate and rule Japan from Edo. In Japanese history the time from 1600 to 1868 is known as the Edo Period. Even today longtime residents of Tokyo are known as **Edokko**.

EDSA FILIPINO Acronym for Epifanio de los Santos Avenue, Manila's main highway linking the suburbs to the two main business districts,

Makati and Ortigas. Named after the biographer of Filipino hero Andres Bonifacio and also forever linked as a mass meeting venue to the February 1986 People Power rebellion.

Eid ARABIC Islam's most important festivals. It's important to note that there are two Eids. Eid Ul-Fitr is celebrated at the end of the Ramadan fasting month. The second is Eid Ul-Adha, which is the day after the Haj pilgrimage to Mecca. Both festivals last two or three days, when Muslims dress up, make visits and bestow presents.

eki bento JAPANESE for railway lunch box. A selection of food, attractively arranged in a hygienic, light-wood box and sold at kiosks in almost every railroad station. Prawns, fish, chicken and various kinds of pickles and vegetables dressed in sesame seed water plants are all placed on a bed of underlying rice. The travel cuisine is usually restricted to longer *shinkansen* routes rather than commuter trains, but it can also serve as a light lunch at the office.

El Shaddai HEBREW for God. El Shaddai is a charismatic Christian movement in the Philippines which blends Pentecostal-type religious fervor with some Roman Catholic rituals. It was founded in 1984 by a radio preacher named Mariano (Mike) Verlarde and boasts more than 8 million members. El Shaddai is part and parcel of the broad Christian evangelism movement that has swept through the Philippines in recent years and has a special appeal to poorer Filipinos and their many fellow countrymen working overseas. The church unabashedly preaches the "prosperity gospel", in which the faithful will be rewarded with greater riches in this life. It is technically part of the Catholic Church but is barely tolerated by the Vatican, which is concerned about the steady drop in membership as many former parishioners move to the more evangelical Protestant churches. In 2009 the sect opened its main headquarters in Paranaque, Metro Manila, which is now one of the largest Christian churches in the world, rivaling the Yoido mega-church in Seoul. The new church seats 16,000 people with room for 25,000 standees. President Gloria Macapagal-Arroyo attended the opening, an indication of the sect's vast political clout. (See **Velarde, Mariano**)

Emerald Buddha Large Buddha statue made of jasper or nephrite (not emerald) that sits on the altar of the Temple of the Emerald Buddha in the Grand Palace in Bangkok. It has a colorful history that is shrouded in mystery and legend. Some believe it was originally carved in Afghanistan, others that it was made in heaven by angels. It has passed through the hands of many would-be owners and is thought to have traveled from India to Sri Lanka to Vientiane (where it remained for two centuries). It has been at its present location for 200 years. The King performs religious rites three times a year, when the statue's robes are changed.

empu INDONESIAN for a particular kind of blacksmith and maker of the **keris**, the fabled ceremonial knives of Java. An *empu* must be a spiritual person meditating before he makes a knife to allow *wahyu*, or spiritual force, to enter his creation. It is said that a skilled *empu* can, through meditation, stop any feeling of pain and shape the blade with his hands while it is red-hot.

Emu A large flightless bird of the Australian outback. After the ostrich, it is the world's largest bird, often reaching a height of 1.5 meters. It can run at speeds of 50 km/h. The emu appears on the Australian coat of arms.

endaka JAPANESE A state in which the yen (*en*) is high or overvalued in relation to other world currencies, especially the dollar. One could say that Japan has been in a state of almost perpetual *endaka* at least since the **Plaza Accord** of 1984, in which Tokyo agreed to strengthen the yen dramatically under pressure from Washington, which was then worried about the influx of Japanese automobiles and other imports. Since then the yen has gone through spasms of *endaka*, especially in 1995, 2008 and following the Great East Japan Earthquake of 2011. The finance ministry and Bank of Japan have intervened repeatedly to sell yen and buy dollars, which has served to increase foreign exchange holdings, but has never actually pegged the yen to the dollar (see **Hong Kong dollar peg**). The opposite of *endaka* is *enyasu* (cheap yen) but that hasn't happened very much in recent years.

erhu A kind of Chinese violin with only two strings. Its origin goes back to the Tang Dynasty (618-907), but its development into a modern instrument took place in the last century. It consists of a drum-like little case at the base of the instrument, made of ebony and covered with snakeskin. It has a long and slim neck and is played with a similarly long bow. The posture that the player must assume is similar to that of the cello. The *erhu* can be played solo or in Chinese orchestras where it takes on the role of the violin in Western ensembles.

erkuai A type of rice cake that is particular to Yunnan province in southwest China. The word literally means "ear piece", a reference to one of its common shapes. The cake is made out of rice, and the best quality is washed and then soaked in cold water. After that it is steamed twice. Yunnan is home to numerous minorities, which is why it is famous for many different kinds of dishes, but *erkuai* is prevalent throughout the province. The best quality cake is said to be made in the Guandu district of the provincial capital, Kunming, where it is said to have originated about 400 years ago. The traditional method of making *erkuai* in Guandu was listed as an "intangible cultural relic" in 2005, and the provincial government has taken steps to ensure that the traditional way of making the delicacy does not die out. (See **mooncake**)

Everest The name by which the West calls the world's highest point, on the border of Nepal and China. The British named the mountain in 1865 after Sir George Everest, a former surveyor general of India. The TIBETAN name is Chomolungma, or Goddess Mother of the World. It was first climbed on May 29, 1953, by Nepali Tenzing Norgay and New Zealander Edmund Hillary, and subsequently by many other climbers.

F

fai di, fai di CANTONESE for hurry, hurry. Life is never in the slow lane in Hong Kong, where people always seem to be in a hurry, a hurry to get someplace, a hurry to better themselves or to make their fortunes.

Falungong A quasi-religion that combines traditional Chinese *qigong* deep breathing exercises with some philosophical precepts drawn from Buddhism and Taoism, though most mainline Buddhist organizations disavow the Falungong as legitimate practitioners of their faith. The leader is one Li Hongzhi, a former government grain clerk and *qigong* master who moved to New York and is believed to be in hiding somewhere overseas, probably in the US. The Falungong have ascribed many supernatural attributes to Li including an ability to heal the sick. The sect came to international attention on April 25, 1999, when 10,000 followers surrounded the compounds (see **Zhongnanhai**) where China's leaders live and work, seeking official recognition as a religion. Instead, a panicky leadership branded the Falungong an "evil cult" and banned their practice, and shows no signs of loosening the ban. The Falungong practice their beliefs legally in Hong Kong under the "**one country, two systems**" regime.

"Fat Pang" A generally affectionate local term for Hong Kong's last governor, Chris Patten (1992-1997). "Pang" is the CANTONESE approximation of his last name. "Fat" because he was a little bit plump. Better known to the editorial writers of the communist *People's Daily* newspaper as the "sinner of a thousand antiquities," the "tango dancer" and other choice epithets during the long discord over his pre-1997 democratic reforms.

feng shui Meaning wind and water, it is the Chinese term for the balancing of the energies of any given space and finding the correct location for everything from an ancestral grave to the new premises of a brassiere factory in relation to winds, water and the spirits of the dragon. *Feng shui* remains very much alive in the Chinese world today. In Hong Kong the rich still shower money on practitioners to make sure that their latest property project is properly aligned.

fenqing MANDARIN for "angry youth". A term for a particularly obnoxious group of super-nationalist Chinese netizens. Modern-day **Red Guards**, they infest the Chinese Internet picking fights with anyone who dares to be even slightly critical of China. They go into overdrive whenever there is an incident, such as a show of sympathy for Tibet, that can be seen as besmirching China's honor. The government occasionally blocks their websites if their outbursts against foreigners are seen as going too far and impacting its relations with other countries.

Feroci, Corrado (1892-1962) Few *farangs* have put their personal stamp on Thailand as did the Italian, Corrado Feroci. He would rank with **Jim Thompson** but far higher than **Anna Leonowens**, the purported inspiration for novels and musicals. He came to Thailand in 1923 at the invitation of King Rama VI to help develop Thai arts. A sculptor by trade, he designed some of the most famous landmarks in Bangkok, including the statue to King Rama I, founder of the **Chakri Dynasty**, the **Victory Monument** and the Democracy Monument among others. In 1943 he became a Thai citizen and changed his name to Silpa Bhirasri. He founded the Silpakorn University of Fine Arts, which is a going concern to this day.

Filipino nicknames Filipinos love nicknames. Bizarre, sometimes unflattering nicknames are as quintessential to Philippine culture as **jeepneys**. They are not just prosaic diminutives like Mike or Pete or Cory, but nonsense names like Danding, Peping, Ting Ting, Yang Yang or Bum Bum (repetitive names are popular). All sectors of Philippine society sport nicknames. Famous Filipinos are known by their nicknames such as Bong Bong (the son of Ferdinand Marcos), Ninoy (Benigno Aquino,

Jr. – his son is Noynoy); Erap (former president Joseph Estrada – Erap is *pare* or "buddy" spelled backwards). And many, many more.

First Island Chain Chinese military doctrine conceives of two island "chains" as forming the basis for China's extended defensive perimeter. The precise boundaries are not officially defined, but the first chain generally extends from southern Japan along the Ryukyus, east of Taiwan and the northern Philippines and then loops around the boundary of the South China Sea (see **Spratlys**). They include the South China Sea, the East China Sea and the Yellow Sea. The First Island Chain is seen as the current limit of Chinese naval operations, but Beijing's planners envision operations extending to the "Second Island Chain" – extending from Japan past the Bonin and Marshall islands and as far as Guam.

Flores man One of the world's greatest human fossil discoveries was made in 2004 in a cave on the Indonesian island of Flores. The skeletons of nine people in a cave were discovered by an Australian-Indonesian team of archaeologists seeking clues to the human migration to Australia. The remains are believed to have belonged to a small species of archaic humans who lived more or less at the same time as modern man. They gave it the formal name *homo floresiensis* and the informal name of "hobbits". Some scientists dispute this analysis and say they are deformed modern humans that happened to suffer from certain pathologies that made them small. Some of the remains have been dated back only as early as 12,000 years, which means they possibly survived longer than Neanderthals, who became extinct about 25,000 years ago. That would make them the longest-lasting non-modern humans. Indonesia has been the site of important archaeological findings, including **Java Man**, whose remains were discovered in the 19th century in one of the earliest discoveries of fossilized human bones.

Flying Horse of Wuwei A beautiful bronze statue of a galloping horse unearthed in 1969 in a Han Dynasty tomb in Wuwei, Gansu province, a modest-sized city of some importance during the height of the Silk Road trade. The statue, one of the finest works of the period, is magnificently depicted in full stride, three hooves in mid-air and a fourth just touching the back of a sparrow, nostrils flaring, tail blowing in the wind. The tomb was discovered by a working party digging an air-raid shelter and included a procession of warriors, chariots and other less dramatic horses. Packed away in a storehouse at a local museum, the statue was "rediscovered" in the early 1970s and eventually became an icon for China tourism. The Flying Horse is now displayed in the Gansu Museum in the provincial capital Lanzhou.

Foal Eagle The designation for annual joint South Korean and U.S. maneuvers, usually held at the beginning of March and extending into April. They involve thousands of U.S. forces, both stationed in Korea and from bases abroad, and tens of thousands of South Korean troops. It is probably the largest such exercise in the world. Foal Eagle exercises take place in the rear area and are labeled as purely defensive. North Korea, however, considers them dress rehearsals for an invasion. In recent years Foal Eagle has been especially controversial, taking place against the backdrop of provocations such as the 2010 sinking of a Korean corvette and later missile and nuclear tests in the North. Pyongyang also objects to their continuing into April when they celebrate the birth of Kim Il-sung.

foreign devils The terms that Asians use for white people make a fascinating study. In CANTONESE, the term *gweilo* is most widely used and is often translated as "foreign devil", although its more literal meaning is "ghost person". It has a slight pejorative flavor. Most Chinese will refrain from using the word with their foreign friends until they know them well, then in a kind of teasing manner. In MANDARIN the term **yangquiziy** means foreign devil but it has been supplanted mostly by the more neutral term **waiguoren**, which simply means somebody from a foreign country. It is often shortened in colloquial speech to **laowai**, "old foreigner". The terms usually refer only to Caucasians; other Asians or Africans have their own special terms. In THAI the word for foreigner of European descent, *farang*, is generally considered neutral.

In JAPANESE the word *gaijin* (outside person) is slightly pejorative and is being replaced with more neutral term *gaikokujin*, or foreign land person. In INDONESIAN the term for white people is *bule*, which literally means "piggy", taken from the pinkish complexion of Caucasians compared with Indonesians.

fugu JAPANESE Puffer or blow fish, expensive and sometimes deadly. This delicacy is the biggest thrill on the Japanese menu. Prepared by anyone less than an expert and the dish could be the last one you enjoy. If a chef loses a customer in the most permanent way, the only honorable course of action for him is *seppuku*, or ritual suicide.

Fujiyama Mount Fuji is the eternal symbol of Japan. Its name, meaning everlasting life, is Ainu in origin. The mountain is a dormant volcano lying about 112 km from Tokyo. It stands 3,776 meters tall and is surrounded by five lakes. The last eruption occurred in 1707, blanketing Edo/Tokyo with a thick layer of ash. It is easy to climb, and every summer thousands of people, armed with walking poles known as "Fuji sticks", trek to the top, having their sticks marked at various stages along the way. Many climb overnight so that they can observe a spectacular sunrise from the summit.

fukoku kyohei JAPANESE Meaning "affluent nation, strong military", this was the battle cry of the leaders of the 19th-century Meiji Revolution, which overthrew the shogunate, promoted the emperor, moved the capital of Japan to Edo (renamed Tokyo) and set in train Japan's modernization and opening to the world after three centuries of isolation. In an era of European colonialism, many of the Meiji revolutionaries believed that only a strong military backed by a powerful industrial establishment could preserve the country's independence. (See *Ishin*)

fukubukuro JAPANESE for good fortune bags, a marketing gimmick that combines January clearance sales with the Japanese focus on good luck at the beginning of the New Year. Shoppers buy the bags without knowing what is actually inside. Depending on how much you pay, where you shop and how lucky you are, you can walk away with some amazing bargains – or just a bunch of socks. Deluxe *fukubukuro*, can cost the equivalent of $1,000 and offer chances to win holidays abroad, jewelry or new cars. Shoppers can get some hints about the contents by perusing specialty magazines and television programs.

Fukushima Japan's third-largest prefecture, about 200 km north of Tokyo, larger than Jamaica or Lebanon. The name means "fortunate island" (the first character is a famous character for good fortune). But it had the bad fortune to host the Fukushima Daiichi nuclear power plant, which suffered multiple meltdowns on March 11, 2011. The name, like Three Mile Island, will forever be associated with nuclear disaster. Before the **Great East Japan Earthquake** and tsunami, it was mainly known for picturesque scenery, peaches and rice. The term Fukushima 50 was the popular reference to a small but intrepid band of nuclear power plant workers who braved high levels of radiation to help bring the damaged power plant under control during the height of the crisis. It was always a bit of hype, more popular in the West than in Japan, in that many more nuclear power plant workers, Self-Defense Force soldiers and others labored to bring the plant safely under control – which isn't to denigrate the bravery of those numbering in the thousands who, over a period of months, worked at the plant under difficult conditions, exposing themselves to relatively high levels of radiation. The term *fly-jin* (*jin* meaning person) enjoyed a brief vogue for those expatriates who fled Japan – or at least Tokyo – shortly after the nuclear crisis, only to return sheepishly later. It is a takeoff on *gaijin,* a word for foreigner.

G

gado gado Probably Indonesia's best-known cuisine – to foreigners, at least. What makes it special is the peanut sauce that is spread over the traditional mixed vegetable salad.

gaiatsu JAPANESE for foreign pressure ton (the word is similar to *gaijin*, or foreigner). The term refers mainly to pressure from Washington, usually in the fields of trade or security. It is often secretly welcomed by people in Japan who want to see change but are frustrated by conservatism in their own country. This way they can argue that they are regrettably being forced to change to keep Japan's partner and protector happy.

gamelan INDONESIAN An indigenous orchestra in Java and Bali consisting of various gongs and tuned instruments that are struck with mallets to produce haunting and hypnotic tones. They often accompany the productions of shadow plays.

gan xie guo jia MANDARIN for give thanks to the nation, which became popular after Chinese speed skater Zhou Yang used the term while receiving the gold medal in the awards ceremony at the 2010 Winter Olympics in Vancouver.

ganbare! JAPANESE A difficult-to-translate popular word that roughly means "hang in there" or "hang tough". It is a means of exhorting people, more commonly sporting teams, to do their best to win or succeed. Following the March 11, 2011, **Great East Japan Earthquake**, the phrase *ganbare Tohoku!* became a kind of catchword to encourage the people of the devastated region to recover. (Tohoku is the name given to the northern third of Honshu). The MANDARIN equivalent is *jia you!,* which means something like "step on the gas". It became a Chinese battle cry during the 2008 Olympic Games, with the expression *Zhongguo jia you!* or "go China!" Following the devastating 2008 earthquake many substituted Sichuan for China, as in *Sichuan jia you!*

Gang of Four Members of a powerful and radical political elite in China responsible for implementing the policies of Mao Zedong during the Cultural Revolution in the late 1960s and early 1970s. The group comprised Mao's third wife, **Jiang Qing**, Wang Hongwen, Zhang Chunqiao and Yao Wenyuan. Aside from Jiang Qing, all were relatively low-ranking officials, but they were clever enough to overthrow many moderates such as President Liu Shaoqi, who was murdered, and Deng Xiaoping, who was exiled. Even as the Cultural Revolution waned, the Gang continued to exert influence though their control over media and propaganda outlets. After Mao's death in 1976, the four were arrested and given long prison sentences. Jiang was found hanged in her cell in 1991.

Gangnam Style KOREAN The title of a rap song by a singer who goes by the name Psy, released in mid-2012. In only a few months it became a worldwide pop culture phenomenon. The *Guinness Book of World Records* says that by October of that year it had become the "most liked" video in YouTube history, with more than a billion views. It is a testimony to the extraordinary continuing worldwide appeal of Korean pop culture. Gangnam is a subdivision, or *gu,* of Seoul and has emerged in recent years from poverty to become perhaps the most affluent, dynamic and influential locality in Seoul or even in all of South Korea. (See **K-pop**)

gangren zhigang [gong.ren zha.gang] MANDARIN Literally "Hong Kong people ruling Hong Kong". A reassuring maxim that emerged in the early 1980s to describe what Hong Kong would be like after it was restored to China. The phrase, attributed to Deng Xiaoping, was meant to show that after 155 years of colonial rule by Britain, Hong Kong people would have control over their own destiny. Similar to the "**one country, two systems**" formulation, which meant that after the 1997 handover, there will be one sovereign state but a different set of political and economical arrangements in Hong Kong (also see **Xianggang**).

Gao Xingjian (1940-) Chinese writer, the first to win the Nobel Prize for Literature in 2000. He spent much of the Cultural Revolution doing forced farm labor. He was exiled to Paris, where he became a French citizen. Gao is *persona non grata* in his native country, where his books are banned, but highly popular in Europe as they seem to read better in French than in English.

Garuda A mythical bird associated with Hinduism. The image traveled from India to Southeast Asia, where it can be seen carved into various monuments. The Garuda was chosen as part of the Indonesian national coat of arms, and it is also the name of the country's national airline, Garuda Indonesia, formed in 1950.

"gazetted" A journalistic term that describes how the Singaporean government polices the foreign press by selectively curtailing or expanding the publication's circulation in the island state. The word comes from the fact that the order from the Information Ministry is published in the National Gazette. But used as a verb, it has a sinister connotation, sort of like being garroted or guillotined. Most of the foreign press circulating in Singapore, such as *Asiaweek,* the *Far Eastern Economic Review* and the *Economist,* have been gazetted at one time or another.

Gini coefficient A mathematical representation of a country's income distribution, in which 0 equals total equality and 1 equals maximum inequality. It was developed by the Italian statistician Corrado Gini. In Asia the Gini coefficients, as of 2012, range from approximately 0.3 for Japan, South Korea and Taiwan to 0.48 for Singapore, 0.47 for China and 0.51 for Hong Kong.

Ginza The most glittering and expensive shopping district in Tokyo, located within an easy stroll from the Imperial Palace grounds. The name comes from JAPANESE *gin*, meaning silver and *za*, meaning guild, recalling the days during the Edo Period when the mint was located there. It is packed with boutiques, trendy bars and restaurants and sits on some of the most expensive real estate in the world. All of the fashionable luxury stores, such as Giorgio Armani, Dior, Hermes and so on have outlets on the Ginza catering to the huge demand for brand-name luxury goods in Japan.

godown BRITISH ENGLISH for warehouse. Though technically English, it has a distinctive flavor of Asia, reflecting a time when many of the British colonial era *hongs* operated godowns in Hong Kong, Guangzhou and Shanghai. The word comes from the MALAY word *gudang*. Also the name for a Hong Kong pub popular with British and other expatriates before the 1997 handover.

Godzilla One of the most universal and instantly recognized symbols of Japanese pop culture and star of the longest running series – 50 years – in movie history. The name is a romanization of the Japanese *Gojira,* meaning gorilla. In 1954 Godzilla made his debut in the movie of that name, produced by Toho Productions which retains the rights to the image and name. Godzilla's size and powers were attributed in the films to radioactive fallout, which was topical in Japan because the atomic bombings only nine years previously were still fresh in memory. America's open-air atom bomb tests in the South Pacific, which famously blanketed a Japanese fishing vessel, the *Fukuryu Maru*, when it ventured unawares into the test zone were also fresh. Later versions touched on other topical

issues. *Godzilla and King Ghidozal* alluded to the then-burning topic of **Japan bashing** in America. The 24th and last Godzilla epic, *Godzilla Final Wars,* was released in 2004. That year, the rampaging monster achieved the ultimate film accolade, a star on Hollywood's Walk of Fame.

Golden Triangle Notorious opium-producing district in Southeast Asia, called "golden" because of the profitability of the drug trade. The triangle falls mainly on the Shan plateau of Myanmar, while overlapping parts of Thailand, Laos and Yunnan province in China. It was the world's largest supplier of opium, hence heroin until the early 21st century, when overtaken by Afghanistan. The generally high altitude is said to provide optimum conditions for poppy growing, while the hilly terrain makes it difficult for governments to send in troops to enforce the ban on narcotics production. Various groups have used the profits of the drug trade to finance their operations. They once included remnants of the Nationalist army, expelled from China in 1949, and Burmese communist rebels. The most notorious drug dealer/rebel was Khun Sa, the self-proclaimed leader of the Shan state, who died in 2007.

goldfish The ubiquitous aquarium fish is native to China and common throughout Asia. In its natural state, a goldfish is actually dull brown or gray in color; the gold pigment is the result of mutations. Going back 2,000 years, the Chinese bred goldfish to emphasize the mutant variety, and now they can be found in myriad colors, shapes and sizes. Among the varieties, Veiltail has a flowing three-lobed tail, Celestial is characterized by bulbous eyes, and Lionhead possesses a large knobby head. Released into the wild, goldfish usually revert to their natural lackluster pigmentation.

Golkar *Golongan Karya* Indonesia's dominant political party for the past 45 years. It was created in 1964 and was designed to mobilize mass support for long-time dictator Suharto and his immediate successors. Though it has lost much of its previous dominance, it remains one of the country's main political organizations, especially powerful in parliament and local government. President Susilo Bambang Yudhoyono, the country's first directly elected chief executive, is a member of a smaller Democratic Party but rules in cooperation with Golkar.

golput INDONESIAN Registered voters who stay away from the polls or cast blank ballots. The word is a spinoff from **Golkar**, the longtime ruling party in Indonesia. During the Suharto era of **New Order** authoritarian rule, many people levied a protest by either staying away or casting blank ballots. However, the incidence was a relatively low 10%, presumably because people feared consequences. Now that Indonesia is a democracy, the incidence of *golput* has actually risen, reflecting a certain apathy expressed in the Indonesian phrase *itu itu saja lagi*, or "same old faces running again".

Gomburza FILIPINO acronym for the Fathers Gomez, Burgos and Zamora, three priests who were executed by the Spaniards in 1872 after being arrested in the wake of an anti-Spanish uprising in Cavite, near Manila. They were charged with treason and garroted. Their martyrdom inspired the next generation of Filipino freedom fighters, including the national hero Jose Rizal.

gong A round metal plate that is struck with a padded beater, producing a sound that is very evocative of Asia. The word now common in English comes from JAVANESE, and the instrument figures prominently in the Indonesian *gamelan* and gives the orchestra its distinctive sound.

Gordon, Beate Sirota (1923-2012) American feminist who wrote the article in Japan's post-war constitution guaranteeing women equal rights. Gordon was 22 when she joined Gen MacArthur's staff in Tokyo as a translator. The general was unhappy with Japanese politicians' efforts to write a new constitution, especially in how it portrayed the status of the emperor. In frustration, he ordered his staff to write a totally new one. They had nine days to do it. Gordon was assigned the task of writing the portions of the document dealing with women's rights. Many of her provisions were discarded with the notion they could be corrected later by legislation. Japanese (male) legislators also raised objections to what was included but were overruled. The document was approved in 1946 and went into effect in 1947. It has never been amended. (See also **Article 24**)

goreng INDONESIAN Chicken, bananas, soybean cake and many other food items are cooked in this high-cholesterol fashion as are the national dishes of Indonesia, *nasi goreng* (fried rice) and *mie goreng* (fried noodles). (See *gado gado*)

Gorkha A small town in Nepal, about 136 km from Kathmandu and the home of the ruling family of Prithvi Narayan Shah (1723-1775) who extended his kingdom throughout the Kathmandu Valley and essentially created Nepal. His fierce fighters from the fortress town were known as Gorkhas, from which came the word Gurkhas, the tough mercenaries who have served the British army for two centuries.

Government-General Building A large edifice in Seoul which served as the headquarters for the Japanese Governor-General from 1926, when completed, until 1945 when the Japanese surrendered. In its time it was one of the largest public buildings in Asia and obviously meant to overawe Japan's Korean subjects. It was deliberately placed to obscure the **Kyongbok Palace**, the seat of the last indigenous Korean dynasty deposed by Japan in 1910. After liberation, the building was used for several purposes, including the National Museum. South Korea's first president, Syngman Rhee, took his oath from this building. But there remained a nagging feeling against this prominent symbol of Japanese colonialism, although in the early post-war years Korea was too poor to tear it down. By the time Kim Young-sam had become president in 1993, Korea was rich enough to demolish the building with plenty spare to rebuild many of the Kyongbok Palace buildings that the Japanese had demolished to build their own capitol. However, some other landmark buildings from the Japanese period, such as Seoul City Hall, still exist.

Great Council of Chiefs One of the South Pacific's oldest political institutions was made up of 55 hereditary chiefs in Fiji. It was created by the British in 1876 as a way of sounding out local opinion among the tribal chieftains. The venerable council was disbanded by Fiji's military ruler Voreqe (Frank) Bainimarama in 2012 as being "a product of our colonial past." Fiji is ethnically divided between indigenous Polynesians and Indians imported by the British.

Great East Japan Earthquake Official name for the devastating quake and tsunami that struck off Japan's northeast coastline at 2:47 p.m. on March 11, 2011, in what has been described as Japan's worst disaster since the end of World War II. The quake registered 9 on the Richter Scale and sent a 15-meter tsunami to ravage the coastline, destroying coastal villages, killing more than 20,000 people and precipitating **meltdowns** at three large nuclear power plants on the coast of Fukushima Prefecture about 170 miles north of Tokyo. The nuclear disaster took the better part of a year to bring under control. Other "Great" earthquakes in Japan of recent vintage: the Great Hanshin Earthquake that killed some 5,000 people in Kobe and vicinity in 1995, and the Great Kanto Earthquake that devastated Tokyo in 1923 (see **Big One**).

Great Hall of the People China's parliament building, completed in 1959 and located on the edge of Tiananmen Square. It is the site of government meetings and ceremonial banquets for foreign dignitaries. The Great Auditorium accommodates the 3,000 members of the National People's Congress, which meets every year in March for two weeks spent listening to Chinese leaders giving boring economic reports and then ratifying government decrees passed down from on high. Also the site of the Chinese Communist Party's Congress, held every five years.

Group Representation Constituency (GRC) Singapore's unique contribution to democracy, or the suppression of democracy, depending on your point of view. Instead of choosing members of parliament from single member seats on the British model, up to six candidates run as a team from a single district. One of the team members must be an ethnic Indian or Malay or some other minority. The official purpose was to assure that minorities were represented in parliament, but critics say it was also designed to make it harder for the opposition to field teams of qualified candidates and pay their deposits. As of the 2011 general election, Singapore had 13 GRCs and eight single-member districts. In the 2011 general election the Workers Party became the first opposition party to capture a GRC, thus tripling its representation in parliament overnight. Another Singaporean innovation is the **NMP** or nominated members of parliament, who are appointed to parliament but have no vote. Their function is to serve, in the absence of an effective opposition, as debating foils for the regular MPs.

guanxi MANDARIN If there is one word in Mandarin that every businessman working in China knows, it is *guanxi*, meaning (roughly)

relationships or connections. In the business world the word is understood to mean a network of relationships among various parties that cooperate and support each other. Everything from obtaining cinema tickets to getting a telephone line installed quickly is done through this network. In a country where the rule of law is still weak, using one's *guanxi* often is the only way to get things done. In essence it means exchanging favors, which are expected to be done regularly and voluntarily. In China it is often having the right *guanxi* that makes all the difference in ensuring that a business deal will be successfully concluded. Basically, one has to make oneself known personally before any real business can be conducted.

guqin [goo.chin] MANDARIN for a traditional Chinese stringed instrument similar to a zither. It is one of the oldest musical instruments in existence, tracing its origins back almost 5,000 years and in its present form back for 2,000 years. There are written tableaus available to play music composed hundreds of years ago. The term *guqin* literally means ancient (*gu*) stringed instrument (*qin*). Instruction in playing the *guqin* was considered essential for the proper education of a gentleman throughout Chinese history. Confucius was said to be a master. It features in many Chinese paintings and poetry. The *guqin* is making a comeback in modern China after being sidelined for a while by more modern, imported instruments such as the piano. In 2010 a *guqin* that belonged to Emperor Huizong of the Song dynasty sold at auction for the equivalent of $22 million, the highest price ever paid for a musical instrument. Not to be confused with the *guzheng,* another zither-like stringed instrument.

Gundam The Japanese have been obsessed for years with the idea of giant robots. The Gundam (venerated fighting robot) story developed by famous animator Yoshiyuki Tomino was first launched as an animated television series in 1979 and spawned a virtual industry in sequels and plastic models. The figure of the "Mobile Suit Gundam" has become one of the most recognizable images of modern Japan. An 18-meter-tall model of the muscular robot was erected on the Tokyo waterfront in 2009 and will take pride of place at a robotic theme park. (See *otaku*)

gung-ho English from MANDARIN *gong he* meaning something like cooperation or together. Seems to have entered English during and after World War II to denote an attitude of unquestioning enthusiasm, especially in military ventures.

guru SANSKRIT originally for a Hindu religious teacher, but the word has been incorporated into English for any person who is considered an authority on something. In MALAY *guru* simply means teacher or master, while the equivalent term in FILIPINO is *guro*. JAPANESE *sensei* is similarly used to address a teacher, doctor or religious leader.

gyosei shido JAPANESE for administrative guidance. A phrase that indicated the enormous power that Japan's government ministries had to manipulate the country's economy by "suggesting" that companies and industries take a certain course of action. The greatest wielder of *gyosei shido* was the Ministry of International Trade and Industry (MITI), now known as the Ministry of Economy, Trade and Industry. The heyday of administrative guidance was probably in the 1970s and 1980s and was somewhat discredited by the bursting of the **Bubble Economy** in 1989 and sluggish economic growth since then. The Democratic Party of Japan has campaigned with mixed success against the excessive power bestowed on bureaucrats at the expense of politicians.

H

haenyo KOREAN for "sea women," more specifically the women divers of **Jeju** and Udo islands in South Korea who make their living diving for abalone, sea urchins, octopus and seaweed. It has been an exclusively female occupation for most of the past century, as male divers were discouraged and women thought to be better suited to the job. Many have been trained to hold their breath for two minutes and dive as deep as 20 meters. But it is a dying profession as daughters prefer to move to the cities on the mainland or find jobs in the growing tourism industry. In the 1960s some 30,000 women were *haenyo* and Japan was a big market for their products. But they now number about 5,000 with two-thirds of them over 60. They live and work out of distinctive igloo-like buildings made of black lava rock.

hagwon KOREAN for after-hours cram schools. After spending virtually all day in school, many Korean students have to spend several more hours cramming for national tests in the *hagwon* schools. There is a Korean saying: Four hours of sleep gets you into Seoul National University." Presumably four more hours of sleep means you don't make the cut. South Korea may be the world champion in rote learning and exhausting study. Korean parents shell out the equivalent of hundreds of dollars a month to send their children to the *hagwon*. Japanese have a similar system they call *juku*.

Hai Ba Truong (ca. 40 CE) VIETNAMESE for the Truong Sisters: two Vietnamese women, Truong Trac and Truong Ngi, who led a temporarily successful rebellion against the Chinese who had occupied Vietnam for about a century. Theirs was the first real resistance movement against the

Chinese or any other foreign occupation, and as such they remain national heroes 2,000 years after they died. The sisters are recalled in innumerable streets, postage stamps, schools, monuments and other place names. They rank among history's most formidable women warriors, along with Boudicca and Joan of Arc.

Hakka A group of ethnic Chinese found in southern parts of China as well as the Chinese communities in Taiwan, Hong Kong and throughout Southeast Asia. Hakkas migrated from northern China some 700-800 years ago, and their language has similarities to both Cantonese and Mandarin. An estimated 80 million to 100 million Hakka are scattered throughout the world. An extraordinary number of prominent Chinese were or are Hakka. They include Deng Xiaoping, Lee Kuan Yew, Sun Yat-sen, the extended Soong family, Taiwan's past presidents Lee Teng-hui and Chen Shui-bian as well as present president Ma Ying-jeou. They include Hong Kong film star Chow Yun-fat, democracy leader Martin Lee and three Thai prime ministers, Thaksin Shinawatra, Abhisit Vejjajiva and Yingluck Shinawatra. A center of Hakkas in mainland China is Ganzhou in southern Jiangxi province.

Han A word that has several meanings in Asia. In KOREAN it is the name for the people and country. The formal name for South Korea is Daehanminkuk, meaning literally the Nation of the Great Han People (Hankuk for short). The Korean alphabet is naturally **Hangul** (but the Han River that flows through Seoul is a homonym with a different meaning). North Korea prefers to call itself Chosun, an ancient name for Korea. Han is also used to distinguish ethnic Chinese from the numerous minority peoples like Tibetans in the PRC. The Han Dynasty, one of the golden eras of Chinese history, ran roughly parallel in time with the Roman Empire.

Hanbok KOREAN Literally "Korean clothing". For women, it consists of a long-sleeved blouse and a heavy wrap-around skirt fastened high on the chest, using much material and often sporting vivid colors. It is one of the most recognizable and appealing aspects of Korean culture.

In North Korea it is known as Choson-ot, though not many women apparently can afford it.

hanryu KOREAN for the "Korean Wave". It is the name given to the remarkable popularity of Korean cultural exports, especially television dramas but also popular music, food and other Korean products. South Korea has become the Hollywood of East Asia, producing dramas watched by millions of fans from Japan to Indonesia. Popular Korean actors have become the highest-paid performers outside of Hollywood, with heart-throb **Yonsama** earning about $5 million per film. The wave began rolling in the late 1990s with the extraordinary popularity of the Korean tear-jerker *Winter Sonata* in Japan. Originally, the dramas were watched mainly by middle-aged women, but the audience has since expanded to all generations. The operator of Japan's largest DVD and bookstore, Tsutaya, says that the rental frequency of Korean dramas exceeds those of Hollywood and Japanese films. Some nationalists in Japan and China consider the Korean wave phenomenon unpatriotic and have organized protest marches against television stations.

Hang Tuah A Malay warrior who lived during the 15th century, before the European incursion into Asia, and served as an admiral for the Sultan of Malacca. He is arguably the most illustrious warrior figure in Malay culture. His life, actual and legendary, is grist for enough tales of duels, loyalty, revenge, and love to fill a dozen books that echo down to this day. Several movies have been made about his life. His purported words: "*Takkan Melayu Hilang di Dunia*, Malays will never vanish from the face of the Earth" is a nationalist rallying cry. Both the Malaysian and Indonesian navies have frigates named *Hang Tuah*. (See **Naresuan, King**)

Hangul KOREAN writing script. An alphabetic script created by King Sejong, the fourth ruler in the Yi Dynasty (the dynasty the Japanese displaced in 1910) and revealed in 1446. The script originally consisted of 28 letters, 17 consonants and 11 vowels, but was simplified in 1933 with the dropping of several letters. It fits the Korean language in a way that borrowed Chinese characters never could. The script can be learned in a day and has contributed to the high literacy rates in both Koreas. South Korea may be the only country that actually has a holiday to celebrate its language – October 9 is "Hangul Day", a token of the exceptional pride that Koreans take in their script. The Hunminjeoneum Society (to use the original name) promotes the use of Hangul worldwide as an alternative to Roman script, with special attention to small tribal languages that have no written form.

Harajuku Technically, Tokyo's prime gathering spot for the younger generation does not exist as an official place. The area stretching along Omote-sando Avenue from the Meiji Shrine is identified on maps as Jingumae (below the temple). There is a Harajuku station on the Yamanote Line with an attractive Tudor-style façade. But the real Harajuku is a state of mind that conjures up youth fashion and a kind of tame rebellion associated with outlandish clothes and colored hairstyles. Harajuku began to attract young people because of the local American ambience stemming from the nearby Washington Heights military housing district – now Yoyogi Park. At the same time, in the 1960s, young people were beginning to acquire some spending money. The habitués are the *Harajuku-zoku*, or Harajuku Tribe. On New Year's Day tens of thousands visit the Meiji Shrine to pray for a propitious new year.

harubang KOREAN, also called *dol harubang,* are statues made out of volcanic rock that are unique to South Korea's southern island **Jeju**. They stand about three meters tall with a kindly, grandfatherly visage. Like the famous Easter Island statues, their origin and purpose are obscure. They probably acted as guardians of villages or possibly part of shamanistic fertility rites. The many Korean honeymooners who descend on Jeju in droves put their fingers in statues' nostrils, an act which supposedly improves the chances of having a son.

hashi JAPANESE for what the English-speaking world calls chopsticks. They are ubiquitous eating utensils in East Asia (but not Southeast Asia where people tend to eat with spoons and forks, or sometimes their fingers). They originated in China as far back as 1700 BC, when they were made of bamboo, ivory and even precious metals. Nowadays they are mass-produced in wood or plastic. Every Japanese restaurant has a jar full of the wooden *waribashi* partially split and enclosed in a paper wrapper. After eating they are thrown away, to the consternation of environmentalists who complain about the number of trees – about 25 million annually in China – that have to be felled to keep Asia in chopsticks. The origin of the English term is obscure, but probably is related to pidgin Chinese "chop chop" for quick, quick, although there is another expression in Cantonese for quick, quick. (See ***fai di, fai di***)

hatarakibachi JAPANESE for "workaholic," except it is not widely used in Japan, where everyone is presumed to be a workaholic.

Hatoyama, Ichiro (1883-1959) Influential Japanese politician in the early post-war years, serving as premier from 1954-1956. He was instrumental in the merger of the Liberal and Democratic Parties into the Liberal-Democratic Party, which ruled Japan almost unbroken for 40 years (see **1955 System**). Ironically his grandson, Yukio, became the first prime minister from an opposition party after the 2009 general election. He served less than one year.

Hatta, Mohammad (1902-1980) One of the most important but now almost forgotten leaders of independent Indonesia. He was imprisoned by the Dutch for his youthful nationalist activities and not freed until the arrival of the Japanese. Immediately after Japan's surrender, he and Sukarno declared Indonesia independent. He served as Sukarno's first vice-president and prime minister, though he resigned his posts over policy differences. He later became a confident of Suharto. He is remembered in the Soekarno-Hatta International Airport that serves the capital, Jakarta.

Hawala HINDI from Arabic, meaning an informal method of transferring money, widely used in India and other parts of South Asia and the Middle East. It operates a little like Western Union in that one broker accepts money and calls another broker, who arranges for the payment. There are no promissory notes involved; the system relies on the honor of the brokers. It predates the modern banking system in much of the region and has flourished in India in particular because of the onerous paperwork and fees required to transfer money through the normal banking system. The broker is called a *hawalawadeer* or sometimes a *hundiwala*. The practice has come under more scrutiny since the rise of Islamic terrorism.

Hayabusa The name for a Japanese space vehicle which in 2010 returned to Earth following a seven-year round trip to the asteroid Itokawa, 300 million kilometers there and back, thus becoming the first space vehicle to visit another world and return to Earth since the Apollo moon flights. Taking 2,542 days, it is the longest round-trip space voyage on record, eclipsing the American "stardust mission" of 1999-2006, which collected space "dust" but did not land on another world. The asteroid, discovered only five years before the mission began, was named for Hideo Itokawa, generally considered the father of Japanese rocket development.

hay fever People in Tokyo know that when the plum trees blossom in early spring, it is time to stock up on antihistamine tablets, eye drops, herbal medicines, allergy shots and face masks. Tokyo is the world capital for hay fever, known to the Japanese as pollen sickness. During the hardscrabble years after the war, Japanese denuded forests of timber to rebuild burned-out homes and make charcoal for heating and cooking. In the 1950s and 1960s the government undertook a successful reforestation program, planting millions of cedar trees. They were cheap, fast-growing and prodigious producers of pollen. When the cedar tree pollution abates, cypress trees kick in. So for those who suffer from hay fever there is an unbroken period of sniffling through April. Tokyo municipality has begun a program of gradually replacing cedars with broadleaf trees that produce less pollen. (See **yellow dust**)

haze A thick blanket of smoke that covers much of Southeast Asia every year, resulting from fires, legal and illegal, on the islands of Sumatra and Kalimantan, causing schools to close, aircraft to divert and even Formula 1 automobile races to be delayed (as the drivers can't see far enough ahead to race safely). The smoke originates from fires in Indonesian rainforests, some set by lightning but most by people wanting to clear the land to create more palm oil plantations. It is a perennial complaint by Malaysia and Singapore that often bear the brunt of the smog, but their complaints usually come to nothing. The Indonesian forestry ministry makes a lot of money issuing burning permits. The fires help make Indonesia the world's third-largest producer and emitter of greenhouse gases.

Heisei JAPANESE The current era name in Japan, which began on January 8, 1989, following the death of the Emperor Hirohito and ascension of his son Akihito. The name was carefully chosen following research into Chinese classics and is intended to mean "peace everywhere." For such a modern nation, it is odd that Japan still measures the calendar by reign years. Hence the year 2015 is Heisei 25, with the new year beginning on

January 8. Previous reign names in the modern era include Meiji (1868-1912); Taisho (1912-1926); and Showa (1926-1989).

Hengdian World Studios The largest movie lot ever built, located in China's eastern Zhejiang province. The studio is said to be 27 times bigger than Hollywood's Universal and Paramount studios combined. On any day, on average, 20 movies or television dramas are being filmed on the massive lot. The studio got its start in 1996 filming the *Opium War*, an epic that was scheduled for release to accompany the handover of Hong Kong in July, 1997. Since then it has expanded enormously, recreating some of China's famous buildings, including the Forbidden City, various Ming and Qing Dynasty palaces, the Yan'an Caves, Shanghai Bund – all designed as backdrops to help satisfy China's endless appetite for historical dramas. Indeed, it also serves as a kind of theme park, and the Hengdian Group (a private company), which owns the lot and just about everything else in the township, makes much of its profits from tourists. Most of the productions are unknown outside of China, but **Zhang Yimou's** 2002 martial arts epic *Hero* was partially filmed at Hengdian.

heping jueqi MANDARIN for peaceful rise. It is how China and its leaders would like the rest of the world, including its Asian neighbors, to view its rise from the depths of colonialism and the depredations of early communist rule to become a world powerhouse. China's leaders thought the term "rise", by itself, sounded too menacing. Unlike past emerging powers, whose might could cause shockwaves, China would threaten no one even as it emerged to become a great power, or *daguo*. "China's rise will not come at a cost to any other country ... or threaten any other country," declared Premier Wen Jiabao in 2003. (See **Confucius Institute**)

Heung Yee Kuk Officially sanctioned political group purporting to represent the interests of pre-colonial period rural residents of Hong Kong's New Territories. It is often seen as a conservative drag on modern Hong Kong as it opposes such things as allowing women to inherit property. The Kuk has a guaranteed seat on the Legislative Council.

hibakusha JAPANESE This is the term for survivors of the atomic bombings at Hiroshima and Nagasaki. Literally, it means "explosion-affected people" or "those who were bombed." The term denotes people who were within 2 km of the epicenter for at least two weeks. A surprisingly large number of *hibakusha* are living. As of 2011 there were more than 200,000, most of them in their seventies. The government provides an allowance and medical care for those suffering from radiation-induced illnesses. Recently, attention has centered on *niju hibakusha* or double survivors, meaning people who survived the Hiroshima bombing and fled to Nagasaki only to be hit again. There are now about 100 double *hibakusha*. The official death toll in the bombings was 66,000 in Hiroshima and 30,000 in Nagasaki.

hikikomori JAPANESE Literally "pulling away" or "confined", the term *hikikomori* refers to the phenomenon of complete social withdrawal. The *hikikomori* may spend months, even years, never leaving the confines of his or her small bedroom. Many Japanese young people live even beyond adolescence with their parents to save on money, but the *hikikomori* take things to the extreme. Numerous social anomie arguments have been put forth to explain the phenomenon, such as bullying in school, extreme pressure to do well in exams, and a lack of stimulating careers. The victim often retreats following some traumatic incident or academic

failure. Generally thought to be a Japanese phenomenon, cases have been reported in Taiwan, China and Korea.

Hindutva "Hinduness" – a word coined in 1923 to denote a feeling of Hindu nationalism, encompassing native religions such as Buddhism, Jainism and Sikhism but not Christianity or Islam, which are considered foreign, polluting influences. One of the first and more enduring institutions to embrace *Hindutva* was the extreme nationalist Rashtriya Swayamsevak Sangh, better known by its initials RSS. Its modern political wing is the Bharatiya Janata Party (BJP) which was in power as India's governing party from 1998-2004. Hindu nationalism got a major boost in the dispute over the 16th-century Mughal Babri Mosque at Ayodhya. A huge number of Hindu nationalists from all parts of India razed the mosque in 1992, causing nationwide communal riots. The razing of the mosque and the conflict it spawned lifted the BJP to national prominence and gave a tremendous boost to *Hindutva*.

hinkaku JAPANESE A vague word indicating a kind of athletic dignity. It became controversial in the 1990s when Sumo authorities decided not to bestow the coveted rank of *yokozuna* on the Hawaiian-born wrestler who went by the name Konishiki, allowing him to become the first foreign-born grand master. He had won the required number of tournaments, but doubts were raised over whether he had enough of that ineffable quality known as *hinkaku*. Konishiki didn't help his cause by complaining to *The New York Times* that he was being discriminated against. It fell to another Hawaiian, Akebono (nee Chad Rowan), to become in 1993 the first foreign grand champion. Konishiki retired from the ring and became a television personality.

Hinomaru JAPANESE Literally the sun disc flag, or the name of Japan's national flag, descriptive in the way that the "Stars and Stripes" is for the flag of the United States. The simple design with a round red disc representing the rising sun against a white background has been used since 1870, although it was not officially designated the national flag until 1999. An alternative design showing sunrays extending from the slightly off-center red disc appears in documentaries of World War II and is often thought to be a special war flag, like the red-and-black banner of Nazi Germany. In fact, it is simply the naval ensign and is used even today on warships of the Maritime Self Defense Force. The *hinomaru* is displayed in front of government offices, but it is seldom seen in front of private homes, businesses or on taxi cabs. Some on the political left still object to its display, claiming it represents militarism, even though its design dates back well before the emergence of Japanese militarism and aggression in the 1930s.

Hinomaru Oil Name for petroleum reserves abroad owned by Japanese companies. Japan is totally dependent on imported petroleum, so it is not surprising that it seeks to acquire rights to petroleum deposits in the Middle East and elsewhere, often in competition with China. The policy has often brought Tokyo in conflict with Washington's priorities, especially concerning Iran. Japan's withdrawal from the Azadegan field in Iran near the border with Iraq in 2010 came after steady pressure from the United States. Japan had considered it one of the few stable sources of crude it could tap to make up for losses in Saudi Arabia. But Tokyo eventually divested its ownership for fear that its companies might be sanctioned for dealing with Tehran. Japan has stakes of 10 to 30 percent in Azerbaijan, Abu Dhabi, Kazakhstan, and other countries.

Hluttaw BURMESE for Myanmar's national parliament, created in 2010. The assembly is composed of 664 members in two houses, with a quarter of the seats reserved for the military in the manner of the Indonesian parliament which has since abandoned the practice. Political parties associated with the army dominate for now, but in 2012 the National League for Democracy, including one of its leaders, Aung San Suu Kyi, entered parliament with a strong mandate. The assembly meets in a sprawling, low-rise complex in the new purpose-built capital **Naypyidaw**. It has 31 spires said to represent the **31 planes of existence** in classical Buddhism. The buildings were planned by former dictator Than Shwe, a devout Buddhist fascinated with numerology. The word refers to ancient royal councils, and there are other *Hluttaw* buildings in Myanmar, including the imposing pagoda-style edifice in Mandalay.

Hmong A tribal group found in Laos, Thailand and Vietnam previously known as the *Miao* or *Meo*, which is a derogatory Chinese term meaning "savage". The Hmong were recruited by the French to fight the Vietnamese communists and later by the Americans under CIA-backed General Vang Pao to fight the Laotian communists known as the Pathet Lao. With the Pathet Lao's victory in 1975, the Hmong fled Laos in large numbers, many going to the United States. Vang Pao (1929-2010) became a leader of the exiled community in the US. In 2007 he was indicted under the Neutrality Act for allegedly plotting to overthrow the Laotian Government. Charges were dropped under pressure from influential Americans, citing his services during the Vietnam War. The Hmong are divided according to their dialect and dress into Black Hmong, Blue Hmong, White Hmong and others.

Hodori KOREAN The name of the tiger mascot for the 1988 Olympic Games held in Seoul. "Ho" comes from *horangi* (tiger) and "Dori" is a generic boy's name. Koreans regard the tiger as their national animal, even though they are almost certainly extinct in Korea. The government had to import a pair especially for the Games. (See **Siberian Tiger**)

Hongbaoshu MANDARIN for the Precious (or Little) Red Book, also known as *Quotations from Chairman Mao*. The red-colored, pocket-sized booklets became an indispensable holy book during the Cultural Revolution, and some 740 million copies were printed between 1966 and 1968. No *Hongweibing* or Red Guard (the name for the fanatical students determined to prevent China from deviating from Mao thought) was without his copy. They are now mostly found in flea markets. *Hong* by itself means red, which is the favorite color of Chinese as well as communists, and it appears in many other contexts such as *Dongfang Hong*, a revolutionary song known in English as *The East is Red,* in revolutionary drama such as *Hongse Niangzijun, The Red Detachment of Women*, one of the few Chinese "operas" allowed to be performed during the Cultural Revolution, and in classical literature such as *Hongloumeng* or *Dream of the Red Chamber*, the great 18th-century Chinese novel.

Hong Kil Dong The Korean version of Robin Hood who was said to be a scourge of greedy landlords, corrupt officials and venal monks. He was the most famous of Korea's *hwalbindang*, a term for roving bandits who stole from the rich to give to the poor.

Hong Kong dollar peg Mention "the peg" in Hong Kong and everyone immediately understands that you are referring to the link between the local currency and the U.S. dollar. For nearly 30 years the Hong Kong dollar has been valued at a ratio of 7.8 to the American dollar. From 1974-1983 the dollar was allowed to float, but a confidence crisis caused by the impending return of Hong Kong to China prompted the government to create the peg. It is maintained through the operation of a currency board system in which the Hong Kong Monetary Authority, supplied with a pot of money, buys and sells the currency to keep it within a designated range. Over the years, the peg has become almost sacrosanct. From time to time various financial experts in the territory suggest dropping the peg and either floating the dollar or linking it to another currency, possibly the *renminbi*, the official currency of China. The financial secretary is usually quick to deny any such intention.

Honiara The capital of the Solomon Islands and situated on the largest of them, Guadalcanal, the site of fierce battles between Americans and Japanese during World War II. The city grew out of the former American base, and the principal airport is still called Henderson Field.

Horie, Takafumi (1972-) Controversial Japanese entrepreneur who created a website, Livedoor, and parlayed that into a fortune. His "un-Japanese" business methods, such as promoting unfriendly takeovers, not to mention a brash personal style, alienated much of the establishment. Horie was the quintessential "nail" that stuck out, and he got "hammered." In 2006 he was convicted of securities fraud and sentenced to two years in prison. In 2005 Horie ran for parliament in the postal rebellion snap general election. He had the backing of Prime Minister Junichiro Koizumi but narrowly lost to one of the main postal rebels. (See "**assassins**")

Horyuji The oldest surviving temple in Japan, located near Nara. Horyuji was built in 607 by Prince Shotoku, and it houses some of the world's oldest wooden structures. A bone of the Buddha is supposedly buried underneath the temple pagoda's main pillar.

Htamane BURMESE Myanmar's festival of the harvest, held in February. At this time, paddy fields are harvested, food offerings made to monasteries and feasts held. (See ***Chusok***)

huang MANDARIN for the color yellow. While red is auspicious in China, yellow is associated with decadence and obscenity. Porn movies are called "blue movies" in the West, but the Chinese call them *huangse dianyung* (yellow movies). The name for what the rest of the world calls the Yellow River, China's second longest, is Huanghe. However, in Thailand yellow is associated with a popular monarch, and in the Philippines was the color of People Power.

hudud ARABIC In the West, *hudud* is often confused with **sharia** or Islamic law. *Hudud* is a subset of Islamic law and refers to a class of severe punishments for certain crimes against God, such as theft, fornication, drinking alcohol and apostasy. They include execution by sword, stoning, amputation of hands or feet and flogging – 40 strokes for the first alcohol offense and 80 for the second. In Asia, most Islamic countries shun the strict application of *hudud*. Malaysia, for example, may punish Muslims for drinking alcohol but not with the prescribed 40 lashes. One Malaysian state, Kelantan, controlled by the Islamic *Parti Islam SeMalaysia* or **Pas**, has enacted the State Syariah [Shariah] Criminal Law using *hudud* penalties, but the national government, which has jurisdiction over criminal prosecutions, does not choose to enforce it.

Hukbalahap FILIPINO for communist rebels in Luzon, more commonly known as Huks. The guerrilla group has a history going back to World War II, when it was formed to fight the Japanese. They succeeded in taking over much of central Luzon. The Huk rebellion was mostly suppressed by popular President Ramon Magsaysay in the 1950s. Remnants struggle on under the banner of the New People's Army.

hukou MANDARIN for a residency registration system used by the Chinese Communist Party since 1958 to minimize the movement of people from the farms to the cities. It is similar to the Japanese *koseki* family registry except in one important detail. The family is listed as being either "rural" or "urban". A person who moves from the farm to take a job in the city must petition the authorities to change his *hukou* designation or stay, as many do, as a kind of illegal immigrant. With China's economic reforms and the prosperity of the coastal cities and their need for labor, the *hukou* system is breaking down, but has not been eliminated entirely.

Hung Vuong Mythical founder of the first Vietnamese dynasty according to ancient records (not supported by archaeological evidence). Hung Vuong established the state of Van Lang in the 3rd millennium BC. The kingdom lasted 18 generations before being overthrown.

I

ianfu JAPANESE for "comfort women," a euphemism for women of various nationalities from the countries conquered or administered by the Japanese Imperial Army who were drafted into providing sex for Japanese troops. The issue began to haunt Tokyo in the early 1990s, when many of the women came forward publicly to rebuke Japan and seek some kind of reparations. In 1990 South Korea, where the issue is particularly burning, protested to Japan on behalf of Korean comfort women. Conservative nationalists in Japan usually deny that any women were forced into prostitution but did so willingly. Prime minister Shinzo Abe opened a bucket of worms in 2007 when he publicly denied any "hard evidence" that the army had coerced Asian women into being comfort women. Thus he undercut the goodwill he had won with China by not visiting the Yasukuni Shrine, like his predecessor Junichiro Koizumi.

ice cream In Asia, local tastes have resulted in ice cream flavors not usually found in the West. The Japanese like green tea-flavored ice cream. Red bean ice cream is popular in Hong Kong and Singapore. Durian is a flavor of the month in Malaysia and Indonesia, while the Filipinos like **macapuno** (a kind of coconut) ice cream. Of course, no New Zealander would be happy without his hokey pokey ice cream, a concoction of vanilla with lumps of toffee inside. Premium ice cream purveyors such as Baskin Robbins and Haagen-Dazs (founded in New York, not in Europe) are popular throughout the region, and often boast the world's top-selling shops.

Ichifu JAPANESE What people working at the plant call the Daiichi Fukushima nuclear power plant: a combination of "*ichi*", or number one, and *Fu*kushima.

Ichiro Suzuki (1973-) Famous Japanese baseball player, who usually goes by his first name alone. After a distinguished career with the Orix Blue Wave team in Kobe, Ichiro joined the Seattle Mariners in 2001, becoming the first Japanese to regularly play a position (as opposed to pitching) in the Major Leagues. He holds a number of records, including the most hits (262) in a single season and the only player to hit at least 200 in 10 consecutive games, breaking a nearly 100-year record held by Wee Willie ("I hit 'm where they ain't") Keeler. He has played in 10 All-Star Games but, alas, never in a World Series, as his team, the Mariners, has never won a league championship. That honor belongs to his fellow countryman **Hideki Matsui**, who helped power the New York Yankees to World Series victory in 2009. Ichiro is almost certain to become the first Japanese inducted into the American Baseball Hall of Fame (he's already in the Japanese version.)

Idul Fitri INDONESIAN name for the three-day holiday following the end of the Muslim month of fasting. It is more widely known from the ARABIC as **Eid ul Fitr**. Eid is the most important holiday in Indonesia and Brunei and also widely celebrated in Muslim Malaysia and in Singapore, where Muslims make up a significant minority. The celebration is usually called *Hari Raya Puasa* in Malaysia, Singapore and Brunei. In Indonesia, where it is also known as **Lebaran,** it is a time for family visits and distribution of annual bonuses. In 2002 the Philippines made Eid a national holiday in deference to its restive Muslim minority.

Ilustrado FILIPINO from Spanish, meaning "enlightened", for the educated middle class that emerged in the Philippines during the latter part of Spanish rule. The *Ilustrado* were the source of much anti-colonial agitation and produced many nationalist leaders, including Jose Rizal.

Imlek INDONESIAN word for Chinese New Year, once highly controversial but now becoming an accepted part of Indonesian life, with the usual New Year festivities such as lion dances and Chinese folk rituals. Under the New Order (which came into power following a coup designed to head off a communist takeover, largely thought to be Chinese-inspired), any New Year celebration plus other expressions of Chinese ethnicity, even writing, were outlawed. That relaxed after the fall of Suharto. In 2000, President Abdurrahman Wahid declared *Imlek* an optional national holiday. At the same time, Confucianism was restored as an officially recognized religion.

Internal Security Act Laws in Malaysia and Singapore which permit the government to detain individuals for up to two years without trial. The home minister in each country has the option to increase the term at two-year intervals virtually indefinitely. Both countries trace their laws to regulations enacted by the former British colonizers during the **Malayan Emergency** which the leaders of independent Malaysia and Singapore have found convenient to retain. Over the years hundreds of political opposition leaders, human and religious rights activists and

others suspected of being communists (or more recently Jihadists) have been detained under the ISA. In 1998 former Malaysian Prime Minister Anwar Ibrahim was briefly detailed under the Act before being tried for sodomy. The longest detainee was Chia Thye Poh, of Singapore, who was detained from 1966 to 1998. Indonesia and Thailand seem to manage without their own versions of the ISA.

Ipoh The capital of the northern Malaysian state of Perak and the country's second-largest city. It is named after a tree from which the indigenous people extracted a poisonous resin used for hunting. Ipoh is the center of Malaysia's tin mining industry, and many of its population descend from Chinese laborers who once toiled in the tin mines.

iron rice bowl This term refers to an occupation with guaranteed job security. In Mao Zedong's time, just about every urban Chinese had lifetime employment and care working in one of the state-owned enterprises and belonging to a **danwei**. Rice, of course, has been the staff of life in China for generations and so is symbolic of sustenance. The iron in the phrase means it can't be broken. But in fact Mao's successors set about smashing iron rice bowls right and left through massive privatization of the former SOEs. (See **lifetime employment**)

Irrawaddy Storied river that runs north and south the full length of Myanmar and is probably the most significant geographical feature of the country. Unlike the **Mekong**, which originates in China and traverses several countries before draining into the sea, the Irrawaddy is virtually entirely contained in Myanmar. As it travels about 2,000 km south from its headwaters in Kachin state through the country's heartland, it carries nutrients to the partially arid central region and ultimately fans out into a huge delta at the Bay of Bengal, an area of rice paddies so fertile that it once fed large stretches of the British Empire in Asia. Only one bridge spans the river, near Mandalay. Also the name for a Burma-watching news magazine published in Chiang Mai, Thailand. (See **Cyclone Nargis**)

Isan (also Isaan, Esarn) A term for the northeastern third of Thailand, an area about the size of England and Wales but generally considered the poorest part of the country. The word comes from SANSKRIT *Ishan* meaning northeast. The people are ethnically Lao and speak a version of the Lao language.

isei JAPANESE Meaning first generation, followed by *nisei*, second generation and *sansei*, or third generation. Used mostly among Japanese-Americans to denote their pedigree in America. An *isei* may have some trouble speaking English; a *nisei* may be bilingual, while the *sansei* would probably struggle to speak Japanese. Nobody counts much past the third generation. In the 1940s there was a fourth category, *kibei*, (literally "go home to America") which denoted Japanese-Americans born in the US, educated in Japan, and returning to the US. Many served as language instructors during World War II. The designation has fallen out of use, as relatively few Japanese-Americans seek higher education in Japan unless they have a special interest in Japanese culture.

Ishikawa, Ryo (1991-) Probably Japan's most famous golf prodigy, Ishikawa won his first Japan Golf Tour tournament as an amateur when he was 15. He turned professional in 2008. The youthful heart-throb has dominated Japan's pro golf tournaments but has not yet lived up to his billing in international events. In 2011 he had to receive a special exemption to play in the Masters Tournament, as he did not quite rank in the world's top 50. But he has a long career ahead of him. Japanese are among the world's most avid golfers, although the game's popularity is spreading rapidly throughout Asia, including China, where it was once disdained as bourgeois. During the Bubble Economy years, prices of golf memberships in Japan soared along with property, stocks and art to the point where they were traded like so many gilt-edged securities. Prices have fallen considerably but are still pricey, which is why many Japanese travel to Thailand and other countries, including the US, to play golf.

Ishin JAPANESE for restoration or renewal. The most famous Ishin in Japanese history, of course, is the Meiji Ishin, or Meiji Restoration, which overturned the Tokugawa Shogunate and pushed Japan into the modern world. Given its recent troubles, many Japanese yearn for another Ishin to overturn entrenched bureaucracy and help solve other ills. Popular Osaka mayor Tory Hashimoto named his political party the *Osaka Ishin no Kai* (Osaka Restoration Party) in an obvious reference to the Meiji Restoration. South Korean dictator Park Chung-hee appropriated the word, slightly Koreanized as **Yushin**, for his program of industrial modernization.

J

jaipong One of the traditional dance forms from Indonesia. It was essentially created in the early 1970s by Indonesian artist Gugum Gumbina after then-president Suharto banned rock and roll and other Western forms of popular music and dance in Indonesia. The dance is fast and energetic with the dancers employing castanets. Though created as an indigenous substitute for provocative Western dance styles, it has come under fire from conservatives who urge dancers to tone down the erotic moves.

jan-ken-pon JAPANESE for rock, paper, scissors, a way of settling differences similar to flipping a coin or drawing straws. The "rock" is a clenched fist; "paper" an open hand; and the "scissors" two fingers extended. In the game, rock breaks scissors; paper defeats, that is covers, rock; and scissors cut paper. In the game, two players (there can be more)

shake their hands twice, chanting *jan-ken-pon*, then reveal their choice. If they have the same gesture, they do it again. More than mere chance, as in flipping a coin, there is an element of skill and psychology involved, and there are such things as international tournaments. The game traces its history as far back as Han-dynasty China and has become widespread. Occasionally, serious matters are settled in this way. In at least one case, an American judge ordered the contestants in a trivial lawsuit to settle their case with *jan-ken-pon*. One Japanese tycoon wanting to sell off a collection of French Impressionist art, and finding little to choose from between the two main auction houses, Christies and Sothebys, had them settle the matter with *jan-ken-pon*. Christies won the right to sell $20 million in paintings.

jangmadang KOREAN A North Korean term for free markets, part of Pyongyang's on-again, off-again market reforms. Originally meant to sell farm products, the *jangmadang* were considered critical in preventing starvation during the country's periodic famines. Among the most popular items sold at these markets, according to *North Korea Economy Watch,* are "rice in artificial meat" (basically fried tofu with a rice filling), car battery lights to see by when the power goes off at night, South Korean-made Cuckoo rice cookers, and men's dressy shoes for festivals and political rallies. Periodically, the government, which has never quite embraced market reforms, cracks down on the kinds of things that can be sold at *jangmadang*.

Japan bashing A phrase invented in the late 1980s in America to describe people who were criticizing Japan unfairly, especially at a time when that country's seeming economic onslaught in the form of automobile exports and sale to Japanese investors of such icons as Rockefeller Center were hurting American jobs and pride. It was fundamentally a verbal weapon in Washington over trade policy rather than an expression of overt racism, such as in the now-obsolete term "Yellow Peril". The phrase was inspired by the then-current British term "Paki-bashing" although it had less of a racial element to it and more economic anxiety. As Japan entered its lost decades, the term fell out of fashion in the US but was retained by the Japanese press who used the same words, *Nihon tataki* in JAPANESE, to describe foreign criticism over such things as automobile recalls and whaling. As more Americans turned their attention to China, ignoring Japan, another term, "Japan passing", entered the language. China's rise and disputes over currency valuation and other trade matters has not given rise to the term "China bashing", yet there has risen a new term, **panda huggers**, for those who are thought to be overly eager to engage China and direct its rising power in constructive channels rather than view the country as a threat.

Jatukam A Buddhist amulet which became hugely popular in Thailand in 2007. The Jatukam amulets were first made in 1987 under the auspices of Nakhon Si Thammarat's Holy Pillar Shrine. Sales of amulets in Thailand are not new, but the Jatukam phenomenon took things to a new level. The amulets, like many others, were bought and worn to ward off bad news and to bring good fortune, but on an unprecedented scale. The name is thought to be a corruption of Khuttugama Ramadeva, two Hindu figures who stand by the entrance to the Wat Maha That Woramaha, the oldest and most important Buddhist temple in southern Thailand. Another theory holds that the name comes from two princes of the Srivijaya Kingdom (757-1257), of which Nakhon Si Thammarat was the center.

Javan rhinoceros A member of the rhinoceros family that once ranged throughout Southeast Asia and even into India and China but is now almost extinct. The last Javan rhinoceros in Vietnam was killed by a poacher in 2011 in the Cat Thien National Park, supposedly a protected area, leaving only a population of 40 to 50 in the Ujung Kulon National Park at the western tip of Java. It is generally considered the rarest large animal on Earth. The decline is mainly attributed to poachers seeking their horns because they are valued by traditional Chinese medicine. There are no Javan rhinoceroses in captivity.

Jayavarman II (circa 770-850) Cambodian king who founded the Angkor Empire in 802 AD. The empire lasted about 600 years and at one time covered most of the territory defined by today's Cambodia, Laos, and Thailand. Little is reliably known of this important period, since most of the information is taken from inscriptions on temple stones, sort of like the Mayan Empire in Central America. At one time the seat of the empire, Angkor, was the largest city in the world with about a million inhabitants. There are numerous Angkorian temples throughout the region, including the great Angkor Temple, better known to the world as Angkor Wat. The most reliable surviving account of life in that era came late in the empire when Chinese writer Zhou Daguan visited in 1295.

jeepney Though declining in use, jeepneys are still the most common form of public transportation throughout the Philippines. The name comes from the fact that the original jeepneys were built on war-surplus US Army jeeps. They are known for their extravagant decorations, and as such they have become one of the most universally recognized expressions of Philippine culture. They are feeling the pressures of government regulation and cost because they are gas guzzlers, weighed down by excess steel used in making the decorations.

Jeju Strategically placed island province off South Korea's southern coast. The Mongols occupied the island from 1273 to 1374 and the Japanese from 1910 to 1945, capitalizing on its strategic position vis-a-vis China. It is increasingly popular for Chinese tourists for its beaches, food and three World Heritage sites. But the island has had a strained relationship with the mainland, as shown in the Korean drama *Tamra: the Island*, which depicts tensions between the island's divers (see *haenyo*) and farmers and the Confucian elite in Seoul. The most recent issue related to the **4.3 Incident**. The date refers to a rebellion, probably stoked by the communist Workers' Party (now the rulers of North Korea but banned in the South), that broke out on April 3, 1948. The army put the rebellion down but it is estimated that 14,000 to 60,000 people were killed. Since then South Korea's military has not been particularly welcome on Jeju.

jeong KOREAN An ambiguous term that encompasses emotions that bind people. It could be described as empathy for others or some kind of collective feeling. South Korea's President Park Geun-hye is said have a unique bond with older Koreans of the **"50/60" generation**, meaning those over 50 years old who now have nostalgic memories of her father Park Chung-hee. It exists in other Confucian cultures, including Japan and China, and may even be said to apply in the West. Former US President Bill "I feel your pain" Clinton had *jeong*.

Jeyaretnam, B.J. (1926-2008) The first opposition member of the Singaporean Parliament since the republic's founding in 1965. He won his seat in 1981, defeating a candidate of the ruling People's Action Party (PAP). He had a tumultuous parliamentary career that brought him into constant conflict with the country's founding prime minister Lee Kuan Yew. Eventually he was declared bankrupt, and thus ineligible to serve, when he fell behind in some large damages payments brought on by libel suits filed by PAP leaders. Since 1981 the parliament has never been without at least one opposition member, and in the 2011 general election, Jeyaretnam's Workers' Party captured a **Group Representation Constituency** (GRC), thus tripling its representation overnight.

J-Horror Short for Japanese horror, a modern style of popular horror fiction with roots going back to ancient ghost stories or *kwaiden*. The style downplays gore and puts the emphasis on a quiet psychological buildup. One of the more popular J-Horror stories is *Ring,* written by Koji Suzuki, which was made first into a hit Japanese film of the same name and transferred to the English-speaking world through the film *The Ring*. A leading practitioner of J-Horror is director Kiyoshi Kurosawa, whose most famous film, *Cure,* screened in 1997.

Jiang Qing (1914-1991) Mao Zedong's third wife and the most prominent member of the **Gang of Four**, which took charge of the power organs of China in the latter stages of the Cultural Revolution. Jiang was a B-grade actress when she insinuated herself into Mao's entourage in Yan'an in 1937 assisted by Kang Shen, Mao's sinister secret police head.

She and her supporters used their power to persecute their enemies until they were overthrown in a "coup" in 1976, shortly after Mao's death. They were tried for treason and given long prison sentences. She allegedly committed suicide in 1991.

jiban, kanban, kaban JAPANESE The three indispensable requirements that every budding Japanese politician must have to succeed: namely a support base (*jiban*), name recognition (*kanban*) and lots of money (*kaban*). It is the main reason why so many members of the Diet are the sons or, in a few cases, the daughters of former members who pass their seat on like an inheritance.

Jikji Simgyong The oldest existing book fragment, a Zen Buddhist text, published using moveable metallic type. It was printed in 1377 at the Heungdok Temple in Korea, which means it is about 70 years older than the Gutenberg Bible, the oldest printed book in the West (1450). The oldest "printed" book is the Diamond Sutra discovered on the old Silk Road by Hungarian explorer **Aurel Stein**, but it was composed by a carved woodblock. The Chinese are believed to have invented the first moveable type using ceramic blocks. The Koreans improved on this by making metal type. The *Jikji* is currently displayed at the National Library of France (a Frenchman having purchased the original manuscript). The Koreans would like to have it repatriated. (See **Uigwe**)

jilbab ARABIC The term refers to any long, loosely fitting garment worn by Muslim women in India and other parts of Muslim Asia to comply with Islamic law and tradition. The long overcoat covers the entire body except for hands and the face, which is not covered like a *burqa*. In Indonesia *jilbab* mostly refers to a headscarf rather than the long, baggy over-garment. The stricter dress codes of the Middle East are not generally practiced in Indonesia, not even in especially pious Aceh. A new type of *jilbab* developed by Nike allows Muslim women to compete in international sporting events while still respecting traditional clothing.

Jindo (also **Chindo**) A Korean breed of dog, the only breed wholly peculiar to Korea, that was bred on the southern island of **Jeju** for hundreds of years but only recently recognized as a legitimate breed by international kennel associations. It is a medium-sized dog similar to the Akita, usually with a white coat, smooth fur and perked ears and famous for its loyalty. It is officially listed as a National Protected Resource.

jinshin jiko JAPANESE for "human accident," a euphemism for suicide by throwing oneself under the wheels of an express train. Suicide is remarkably common along Tokyo's extensive subway and rail system. Approximately one person a month throws himself before one of the trains of the popular **Yamanote Line**, and it is just one of dozens in the vast Tokyo conurbation. Commuters who hear the announcement "We regret to inform you that this train has been delayed by a human accident" and who are not having to get anywhere in a hurry repair to a local coffee shop to wait out the delay, which normally takes about 30 minutes. More than 30,000 Japanese commit suicide each year, but only 2-3 percent do so by throwing themselves in front of moving trains or other vehicles.

Jogjakarta (Yogyakarta) Major Indonesian city and the center of Java's ancient Buddhist-Hindu heritage. It is known to everyone as "Jogja". One of the early kingdoms centered on the city built the world-famous **Borobudur** temple complex. Jogja was also the capital of Indonesia from 1945-49. Since 1755 a dynasty with the long name of *Hamengkubuwono* has resided in the *kraton*, or royal palace, in the center of the city. The widely respected and popular ninth Sultan actively supported the war of independence and served as a cabinet minister and vice-president in the republic's early years. When he died in 1988, multitudes turned out for his funeral. He was succeeded in 1989 by the tenth holder of the name.

Ju-jitsu Although the differences are fairly subtle to those not schooled in the martial arts, ju-jitsu is not the same as judo. Its practitioners insist it is a separate sport altogether. Ju-jitsu has deep roots in Japan, going back at least to the fighting techniques of samurai warriors of the 16th century.

Judo evolved from ju-jitsu at a later date. Both manipulate an opponent by using his force against him, but judo puts more emphasis on throws. It was a demonstration sport in the 2009 Asian Games but has so far not been made a medal sport.

jun ai JAPANESE Pure love, a term that has a special meaning in Japanese melodrama. A *jun ai* couple would face many obstacles contrived to keep them apart and pine for a romantic reunion. Compare with *koi,* a term used in Japan for a sexual relationship free from the melodramatic trappings of love. Best exemplified in the South Korean tear-jerker *Winter Sonata*, which captivated Japanese as well as other Asian audiences in 2001, thrusting a previously obscure Korean actor named Bae Yong-joon (known in Japan as **Yonsama** using the honorary suffix for screen idols with the soft good looks and killer smile) to superstardom. (See also ***hanryu***)

junk The English name for offshore vessels stems from the JAVANESE term *djong,* later corrupted by the Portuguese as *junco.* It describes Chinese ships first developed during the Han dynasty but still used today, perhaps most famously in Hong Kong. The vessel was known throughout two millennia for the sturdiness of its construction and the simplicity of its rigging. Sailing junks have virtually disappeared save for hobbyists and tourism promotion boards, but motorized junks are still common in Hong Kong and are popular with expatriates who sail them to outlying islands for picnics (known as junk parties) on Sundays.

K

K-pop Korean popular music has rapidly climbed the charts throughout Asia and North America. It is part of the overall Korean cultural exports known as *hanryu*. Beginning in the 1990s, Korean films and especially television dramas became hugely popular throughout Asia. Music lagged behind until the advent of social media, after which it really took off, as Korean groups with strange names like 2NEU or SHINee became global household names with the older teenage set. The basic formula combines synthesized music, video art, fashionable outfits and a teasing sexuality, mixed with doe-eyed innocence.

Kabaddi An indoor sport in which two teams send players ("raiders") into the opposing side and win points by touching some of the opposition players. It is highly popular in India, Bangladesh and Iran. It may have peaked as a global sport in 1936 when it was a "demonstration sport" at the Berlin Olympics. A World Cup is held, invariably won by the Indian team. Although Kabaddi never became an Olympic sport, it is recognized in the Asian Games.

Kaharingan A purported form of Hinduism practiced by indigenous peoples known as **Dayaks** in Kalimantan, the Indonesian portion of Borneo. It is said to comprise mostly long-lost traditional beliefs that were suppressed during the Dutch colonial period now dressed up as a form of Hinduism to comply with Indonesian religious law. The principles of *Pancasila* require belief in God and adherence to one of six approved religions, of which Hinduism is one. Although these people are considered Hindus by the government, they do not seem to be familiar with any Hindu gods such as Shiva or Vishnu, traditional rites or even such concepts familiar to many non-Hindus such as karma. Traditional Hinduism is practiced mainly on the island of Bali.

kaiten zushi JAPANESE for conveyor belt sushi. Customers sit at a brightly-lit counter watching as sushi glides by, two pieces to a plate. No words are necessary; you see what you like and reach out and grab it. The customers pay by the number of empty plates stacked up in front of them when they are sated and ready to leave. When *kaiten zushi* shops first appeared in Tokyo in the late 1980s, they were seen as a kind of gimmick. How could they compete with traditional sushi establishments? However, they have stayed and prospered and account for almost a third of all sushi sales in the capital.

kakuseizai JAPANESE for "speed" or meth, the drug of choice in Japan and a major source of income for gangsters known as the yakuza. *Kakuseizai* was a legal drug for years, sold under the brand name of Hiropon, and it was distributed to soldiers during the war to keep them alert and fighting. As the side effects of the drug became more widely understood and as the number of addicts grew, it was banned in 1951. The yakuza stepped in to keep the now illicit trade going.

kalae THAI for a pair of crossed boards at the top of the sharply peaked roof of a traditional Thai house. It is said to represent horses and water buffalo. *Kalae* are found most commonly in northern Thailand, especially its main population center, Chiang Mai. There they are seen everywhere, even on modern buildings, almost a symbol of this region formerly known as the **Lanna Kingdom**. The word sometimes applies to the whole house.

Kampong Ayer MALAY Kampong Ayer literally means water village, or a village built on stilts. By far the largest, most ancient and extensive Kampong Ayer anywhere is located on the Brunei River in Bandar Seri Begawan, capital of Brunei. Everything is built on stilts, including homes, stores, schools, mosques and hospitals, all connected by boardwalks or water taxis. It currently has about 40,000 people. Brunei's Kampong Ayer goes back centuries, and was noted as being a busy entrepot by European visitors in the 16th century. It is not the name for the community, which is divided among several separately named villages. It is considered a valued part of Brunei's cultural heritage as well as an important tourist attraction.

Kampot pepper A kind of boutique pepper grown only on Cambodia's southern coast (in Kampot and Kep provinces) now being marketed as the "world's best pepper." The origins of pepper cultivation in Cambodia lie in the 19th century when Aceh, then supplying half of the world's crop, cut back production for fear of attracting European imperialists who were fanatical about pepper. Cambodia filled this gap with a pepper that astonished buyers for its flavor. By 1900 millions of kilograms were being exported. Production collapsed under the ruinous rule of the Khmer Rouge and lingering civil war and is only now being revived.

Kanchipuram A famous conglomeration of ancient Hindu temples in the northern corner of India's Tamil Nadu state, also known as the "city of a thousand temples." Its history can be traced back several centuries before Christ. It has flourished as a center for Hindu, Buddhist and Jain learning for generations. The founder of Zen Buddhism, Bodhidharma, was reputedly born there. Kanchipuram reached its peak in the 9th century as the capital of the Pallava Empire and later as an important city of the Vijayanagar Empire. The city is off the beaten path and is relatively unsoiled by tourists. Its temples are scattered around, interspersed with streets and alleys dotted with inexpensive restaurants and silk *saree* shops for which the city is also famous.

Kangmei Yuanchao Zhanzheng MANDARIN: War of Resistance Against America and Support of Korea – what the Chinese call the Korean War.

kanji JAPANESE word for Chinese characters used in their complicated writing system. Imported from China, they alone do not accurately convey the Japanese language, so the Japanese devised a supplementary script called *hiragana*. The latter is an alphabet and sufficient in itself to convey meaning, but the Japanese still insist on mixing the writing with *kanji*. Another alphabet called *katakana* is used to convey foreign words. It is not unusual to find all three scripts in a single sentence.

kasepekang BALINESE A form of ostracism that is considered a traditional punishment in Bali. Anyone who breaks customary law is subject to a sliding scale of punishments at the hand of local communities acting through councils called *banjar*. They start with fines and ultimately exile. *Kasepekang* has grown with the resurgence of traditional practices that were suppressed under Suharto. On the other hand, some critics consider *kasepekang* a form of oppression and control.

Kasumigaseki Literally, the slope of the barrier mist – the district in Tokyo near the Imperial Palace where Japan's government ministries have their offices and where the fabled civil servants roost. The word is used in a way that is similar to Whitehall in Britain.

karaoke Timeless, classical songs mangled by howling drunks in countless dark bars across Asia. The karaoke machine may be the most ubiquitous post-war Japanese invention since instant ramen noodles. The machine was invented in 1971 by one Daisuke Inoue, a nightclub piano player looking to provide music for a customer who wanted to sing on a business trip. It has since turned into a multi-million industry.

Kanchanaburi A small Thai province of about 50,000 people located west of Bangkok on the border with Myanmar. It is famous as the location of the Kwai River and with it the ***Bridge on the River Kwai***. The people of Kanchanaburi make a good living out of the bridge and the novel and movie that made it famous. The bridge was important in the Japanese plan to link Bangkok with Rangoon during World War II, and thousands of British and Australian POWs from the Malaya and Singapore campaigns and many Asian slave laborers worked and died to build it. The bridge itself is an unremarkable ensemble of concrete stanchions and iron trusses (not timber and bamboo as in the film). The bridge was put out of commission by Allied bombers and restored after the war.

***kariyushi* shirts** The Okinawan version of Hawaiian aloha shirts – the word *kariyushi* is OKINAWAN for happiness. The colorful shirts with Okinawan themes printed on them were introduced in the 1970s by hotel owners to promote Okinawa as a tropical tourist destination similar to Hawaii. Later they were adopted by businessmen for casual workdays and to show determination to cut down on air conditioning. (See **cool biz**). In 2000 all heads of state posed in *kariyushi* shirts at the G-8 meeting held on Okinawa. The fashion is gradually migrating to mainland Japan. The term *kariyushi* is trademarked by the Okinawa Industrial Joint Association.

Karuizawa A small town in the mountains of central Japan which has the distinction of being the only town in the world to host events for both the summer and winter Olympic Games – equestrian contests for the 1964 Tokyo Olympics and curling for the 1998 winter games in nearby Nagano. The town was essentially founded by Christian missionaries seeking surcease from hot weather, and boasts some attractive and historic churches. Its pine forests are now dotted with secluded summer retreats for wealthy Japanese. The current emperor, Akihito, famously met his empress at the town's posh tennis club. (See **Baguio**)

kathoey THAI for transvestites, or "third gender", usually rendered as "ladyboy" throughout much of the region. All countries in Southeast Asia have transvestites (see ***ah quah***), but nowhere do they seem so much part of the culture or as accepted as they do in Thailand. The *kathoey* dress as women and adopt some feminizing medical procedures but are still considered legally to be men. Dressed in gorgeous costumes, they take part in lavishly staged revues and in beauty pageants where the winners' names are often published in the newspaper. Despite this tolerance, men are not allowed to legally change their gender to female as they are in the West.

kawaii JAPANESE for cute. But it is more than a word; it is a syndrome covering an array of Japanese popular cultural objects and attitudes. It can mean "cool", "charming", even "groovy". The epitome of *kawaii* is Hello Kitty, the kitten with the featureless face which first appeared in 1974 and continues to make money for its creator, the Sanrio Co., which licenses the image for handbags, stickers, pencils, pen sets – the list goes on and on. The company has two Hello Kitty theme parks in Japan and plans to open another in China and perhaps later in Taiwan and Malaysia. (See *zakka*)

keitai JAPANESE for mobile or cell phones, which are virtually universal in Japan. Every high-school girl and young woman in Japan owns one. Enter any commuter train and one can see a whole bank of them, busily text-messaging. According to one government study, high-school girls spend an average of two hours a day on their *keitai*, with high-school boys clocking in at 90 minutes a day. An industry study showed that the 127 million Japanese now own 100 million phones, which is a lot of button-pressing. It is sometimes an occasion for handwringing over the new "thumb culture" as the two hours spent text-messaging is two hours that could be used in real face-to-face relationships, not to mention reading, studying, playing sports or doing something else that is useful.

keitai shosetsu The cell phone novel: possibly the first literary genre to emerge, unfiltered and unedited, from the cellular age. Most of the stories are written and read by women and revolve around true love, or more precisely the obstacles that have stood at the core of romantic fiction – rivals, triangles, incurable diseases – from time immemorial. Maho i-Land, which is the largest cell phone novel site, carries more than a million titles, most of them from amateurs writing under screen handles and available for free. (See *jun ai*)

kendama JAPANESE A traditional Japanese wooden toy, consisting of a "sword" (*ken*) and a ball (*tama*), connected with a string. The *ken* has two cups and a spike. The object is to catch the ball in one of the cups or impale it on the spike extending out from the handle (sword). The experienced player can perform all kinds of juggling tricks with the *kendama*. It is thought to have been imported into Japan from Europe in Edo times through the port of Nagasaki.

ketuanan Melayu MALAY meaning Malay supremacy or dominance. The implication is that Malays are the master race in Malaysia even though they barely constitute a majority. The large numbers of Chinese, Indians and indigenous peoples are tolerated interlopers. The notion of Malay supremacy tends to wax and wane depending on the political climate and whether the Malay majority feels threatened. (See ***The Malay Dilemma***)

Khabarovsk Trials A series of war crime trials held in 1949 in the Russian city of Khabarovsk, which were singular in that they accused members of Japan's Kwantung Army of manufacturing and using biological weapons in World War II. It was significant as it confronted the issue of **Unit 731**, which had been ignored at the more famous Tokyo Trials. Twelve officers were found guilty and sentenced to long stretches in labor camps, but were released and repatriated to Japan, like other POWs, in 1956.

khoomei TUVAN A style of singing in which one or more pitches are made simultaneously, commonly known as throat singing. Properly sung, *khoomei* sounds like the singer has ingested a set of bagpipes. The sounds are said to imitate those in nature such as rivers or birds. Several versions are found in Central Asia, but the most popular is in the Tuvan Republic, a part of the Russian Federation in southern Siberia. The most famous practitioner of Tuvan throat singing, Kongar-ol Ondar, died in 2013 at the age of 51.

kimchi KOREAN Probably the most easily recognized Korean food, *kimchi* is a pungent mixture of fermented vegetables. The most common is cabbage, but there are innumerable variations. The dish has deep roots in Korean history, going back centuries. In ancient times *kimchi* was made of greens, pickles or salt. Over the years, other ingredients were added. Large quantities are fermented in November so they can be eaten over the winter months.

Kimjongilia Literally the "flower of Kim Jong-il". It is a hybrid of the begonia family, originally bred by Japanese botanist and Kim admirer

Motoderu Kamo to honor the North Korean leader on the occasion of his 46th birthday in 1988. It is said to be widespread now across North Korea and bred to blossom each year on February 16, the late dictator's birthday. Banks of *Kimjongilia* surrounded the bier as Kim lay in state in Pyongyang following his death on December 17, 2011. During a 1965 state visit to Indonesia, President Sukarno named an orchid after Kim Il-sung – *Kimilsungia*. A *Kimilsungia* flower show is held annually in Pyongyang to honor the Great Leader. Foreign embassies present bouquets of the flower. Neither *Kimjongilia* nor *Kimilsungia* is North Korea's official flower. The national flower is the magnolia.

Kiwi fruit This famous fruit originated in China – hence its former name Chinese gooseberry – but was planted in New Zealand, where it grew to be the country's iconic product and a major export earner. Sales took off when, in a brilliant marketing move, New Zealanders dropped the older name and adopted the name Kiwi fruit. Growers were spurred to action in the 1950s when major importers in the US complained that the old name lacked sex appeal and made people think that it came from **Red China**, a stigma that most Americans in the 1950s wanted to avoid. They suggested that the growers adopt a Maori name that connoted New Zealand, but the major grower, Turner & Growers of Auckland, hit on the idea of marrying the word Kiwi, a colloquial term for New Zealanders, to fruit. Sales took off.

kizuna JAPANESE for a bond or connection between people, or in the context of 2011, a sense of solidarity or unity in the face of the March 11 triple disaster. When nine **Diet** members broke away from the Democratic Party of Japan over the consumption tax issue, they named their new splinter group Kizuma. The women's world champion soccer team also stressed *kizuma* or unity in achieving their success. The word was named the Kanji of the Year for 2011 (the more downbeat runner-up was *wazawai*, or disaster).

Klai Kongwan THAI The name for the summer palace of the Thai royal family that delightfully translates into English as "Far From Worries", a place to get away from the cares and worries of Bangkok. It is located on the Gulf of Thailand coast in the small town of Hua Hin, about 200 km south of Bangkok. It was a small fishing port until it was discovered in the 1920s by the royal family and other members of the Thai aristocracy who built summer cottages there. The Klai Kongwan palace was built by King Rama VII as a getaway. King Bhumibol lived there almost permanently in the latter years of his reign until ill health forced him to move to a Bangkok hospital.

koban JAPANESE for police box. An essential element in Japanese community policing, they are small buildings housing one or two uniformed cops, scattered throughout the country. By some estimates Japan has about 6,000 *koban*. Perhaps the best known *koban* is the one in the Ginza next to the Sukiyabashi scramble crossing. The policemen there spend a lot of time answering questions from foreign tourists. The policemen occasionally leave their box to patrol on foot or bicycle, living up to the Japanese name for policeman, *o-mawari-san*, or Mr. Walking Around Man.

Kogaryo (Goguryo) In the first centuries of the common era, several rival kingdoms fought to dominate the Korean peninsula and adjacent territory now in China. Kogaryo, Silla and Paekje were the most powerful contenders. Before being conquered by the Silla, the Kogaryo kingdom dominated the northern peninsula and parts of present-day trans-Tumen River China, known as the ethnic Korean-speaking **Yanbian Autonomous Region**. Though it passed from history in the 7th century, Kogaryo still resonates today. Some Chinese historians claim that Kogaryo was a Chinese kingdom, and thus it could be argued that the true border with Korea should be further south in what is now North Korea. If it was a Korean kingdom, then the natural border should extend further north into what is now China. The current border was demarcated in 1909 between Japan and China and is thus illegitimate to extreme nationalists. However, it would be hard to find a more natural physical border than that provided by the Yalu and Tumen Rivers.

Kopassus An elite special forces unit of the Indonesian Army, which is widely known from its Indonesian initials as the **TNI** (*Tentara Nasional Indonesia*). Kopassus was formed in 1952 with the special mission of suppressing regional rebellions which were rife on the archipelago in years immediately after independence, most notably the long rebellion in **Timor Leste** and the long-running insurgency in Aceh. Kopassus has been accused of using torture and other abuses in its efforts to suppress rebellions, which has impeded military cooperation between the US and Indonesia. As rebellions have faded into history (with the exception of a sputtering insurgency on Papua), Washington has moved to improve its contacts, training and other assistance to the TNI. (See **Detachment 88**)

Korematsu, Fred (1919-2005) Japanese-American who was interned along with 120,000 others during World War II and fought his internment all the way to the US Supreme Court. In doing so he became a hero to Japanese-Americans and a symbol for civil rights to all Americans. It took 30 years but in 1983 a federal court judge overturned his conviction. In 1988 President Ronald Reagan formally apologized, and Congress authorized payment of $20,000 in compensation to surviving internees. Korematsu himself received the Presidential Medal of Freedom in 1998. While in his 80s, Korematsu filed a friend-of-the court brief concerning the Guantanamo detention center, arguing that "the extreme nature of the government's position is all too familiar." (See **Executive Order 9066** in *Numbers*)

koseki JAPANESE for family registry. This document, maintained by local authorities, serves as a combination birth certificate, death certificate and marriage license in Japan. It originated in its present form in the early years of the Meiji period as a way of keeping track of people. At the same time, all Japanese were required to adopt family names as well as given names. Married couples are required to enter only one family name on the *koseki*. It can be the wife's family name, but it must be just one name. This is a sore point with feminists in Japan, who want the right to retain their maiden name. They have argued, so far unsuccessfully, that this denial violates several provisions of the constitution. It is similar to the Chinese *hukou*, except that registration is not linked to a specific place, which means Japanese are free to move to different parts of the country. South Korea abolished its *koseki* system in 2008.

Koshien High-school baseball is to Japan what high-school football is to Texas, an obsession. For two weeks in the spring and later in the summer, Japanese turn their attention away from professional baseball, and a lot of other things, to watch the high-school championships. Four thousand schools are winnowed down to 49 that face each other in Koshien Stadium, the grand cathedral of Japanese baseball located near Osaka and normally the home field for the pro team Hanshin Tigers. The final games are televised nationally and draw some 800,000 fans to the various venues, a kind of attention that surpasses anything the pros do. Several big-time players, such as pitcher Yu Darvish, made their name in the Koshien. Players pinch some of the holy dirt of the infield to keep as a lifetime memento.

kotatsu JAPANESE A charcoal brazier covered by a wooden frame and quilt. Although it warms little more than the hands and feet, the *kotatsu* was once almost the only heating device in the average Japanese home. Families used to gather around the *kotatsu* in winter. The warmth came from the *hibachi*, the traditional Japanese charcoal stove, placed in a recess in the floor around which inhabitants gathered. More modern versions replace the charcoal bowl with an electric heater, which cuts down on the danger of carbon monoxide poisoning and the threat of fire immediately after earthquakes. Toppled *hibachi* contributed to the death toll from fire during the Great Kanto Earthquake of 1923. In recent years, however, it has come into disuse as more Japanese discover the delights of central heating and have the means to pay for it.

kretek INDONESIAN A type of cigarette in which tobacco is blended with cloves, invented and largely smoked in Indonesia. About 68 percent of Indonesia's male population (but only 5 percent of women) smokes, and they overwhelmingly choose *kretek* cigarettes that are manufactured by a local industry that employs about 180,000 people. It is a source of friction with the United States, which in 2009 adopted the Family Smoking Prevention and Tobacco Control Act which prohibits the sale of flavored cigarettes, save for mentholated smokes, even though *kretek* sales are minuscule in the US. Jakarta considers the ban sheer protectionism, as it leaves untouched menthol, which is added to a large percentage of American-made cigarettes. In 2010 Jakarta filed a trade complaint with the World Trade Organization.

***Kwangbok* supermarket** North Korea's first real shopping mall, known officially as Pyongyang Department Store No. 1 but unofficially from the Kwangbok neighborhood where it is located. It is a joint venture between China's Feihaimengxin International Trading Company and the Korea Taesong Trading Co. and is filled with Chinese products such as cell phones, laptop computers, rice cookers and even karaoke machines. Strangely it is the one place in North Korea where one can buy vintage American products such as Pabst Blue Ribbon beer or Skippy peanut butter (by way of China; direct trade is banned). Dear Leader Kim Jong-il toured the store two days before he died. Can a Pyongyang Walmart be far behind? (See **Rason**)

kwangliso KOREAN for "holding place" or, more accurately, concentration camp. North Korea runs half a dozen of these camps, which are mainly designed to hold political prisoners. By some estimates the population of this Korean gulag runs to 200,000. Inmates are sent there with no pretext of a judicial review and are usually forced to work in coal or iron mines, sometimes for the rest of their lives which, given the conditions, are usually pretty short. Another word, *kyo-hwa-so,* meaning "place to make a good person through education", in short a re-education camp, is a separate place where political dissidents are sent to have their thoughts changed.

L

Lapu-lapu (1401-1542) The ruler whose soldiers famously killed Ferdinand Magellan during his milestone world-circling voyage. Lapu-lapu was the *datu,* or ruler, of the Visayan island of Mactan, where the Battle of Mactan took place on April 27, 1521. He is now regarded as the "first Filipino hero" and the first Asian to successfully resist the European invasion of Asia. His image is depicted on statues, old coins and is the name for a city.

Lanna Name for a kingdom that dominated what is now northern Thailand and once stretched from China to Luang Prabang in Laos, with its center in Chiang Mai. Originally called Lan Na Thai, the name means "millions of rice fields". The kingdom was annexed to Siam in the early 20th century. The Thai kings, anxious to build a unified Thai state and culture, initially allowed the Lanna culture to slowly erode. The most visible elements of what remains of Lanna culture are its monuments, including many of the temples.

laogai MANDARIN for "reform through labor", China's system of prison farms, detention centers and re-education camps. It was created by Mao Zedong and modeled after the Soviet Gulag but endures to this day. Some inmates are convicted of actual crimes; others of non-crimes or economic crimes. For the North Korean gulag, see *kwangliso*.

Leal Senado PORTUGUESE for Loyal Senate. The Portuguese community in Macau ruled itself through its local senate. King Joao VI conferred the title "Loyal" in 1810 honoring its fealty to the Portuguese monarchy even during the period in the 17th century when the Spanish and Portuguese crowns were united. The words "Leal Senado" were emblazoned across the front of the senate building until shortly before the 1999 handover to China, when they were removed. It is now known more prosaically as the Municipal Council, responsible for picking up the garbage and repairing the streets in peninsular Macau. The outlying islands of Taipa and Coloane are administered separately.

Lebaran See **Idul Fitri**

Leeson, Nicholas (1967-) The self-proclaimed "original rogue trader." He was a British derivatives trader who in February, 1995, engineered what was then the greatest loss in financial history. Believing he was in a serious financial fix, he made a desperate play to recoup through a series of complex trades on the Singapore and Tokyo stock exchanges. Unfortunately for him, the Kobe earthquake struck the very next day, sending Tokyo (and other markets) into a tailspin. Losses totaled $1.4 billion, and a few weeks later Barings, the oldest British bank, was declared insolvent. Leeson was convicted of fraud in Singapore, served a couple of years in Changi prison and now makes a living on the lecture circuit. He has since been superseded in the trader hall of shame by Yasuo Hamanaka, who lost $2.6 billion trading copper for Sumitomo Corp, and Jerome Kerviel, who lost $6.7 billion for Societe Generale.

Lei Feng (1940-1962?) A possibly mythical soldier in the People's Liberation Army who, following his death, was turned into the model Communist and subject of a nationwide Mao-inspired campaign to "learn from Comrade Lei Feng". He was only 22 when he was killed when a telephone pole hit him while he was directing his transport unit, a rather ignominious death for somebody who would be turned into a cultural hero. **Lin Biao**, who would later die in a mysterious airplane crash in Mongolia, got the cult moving when he published what was purported to be Lei Feng's diary, full of praise for Chairman Mao and other selfless thoughts. His birthplace in Hunan province was named Leifeng in his honor, and there are museums and memorials dedicated to him in other parts of China. An effort in 2012 to revive his value as a communist icon on the 50th anniversary of his death failed as China's new armies of bloggers took turns poking holes in the Lei Feng story.

Lenovo China's leading computer maker and the third-largest in the world. It was founded in 1984 by 11 scientists at the Chinese Academy of Sciences, a government agency for the purpose of commercializing its research. It is now probably China's most recognized global brand. Originally known as Legend, the company adopted a new name and logo as it expanded abroad because the name Legend was too common and already trademarked in the West. It is a combination of the first syllable of Legend and "novo", a Latin word meaning new or novel. In MANDARIN the name remains *Lang Xiang*, a transliteration of Legend.

Leonowens, Anna A British woman of uncertain background who for a time worked as a language teacher in the Bangkok palace of **King Mongkut** (Rama IV). She wrote several memoirs which Margaret Langdon turned into a 1943 best-seller, *Anna and the King of Siam*, which in turn was the basis for the fabulously successful 1950 Rodgers and Hammerstein musical comedy *The King and I*. Most historians doubt that Leonowens developed anything like the influence as depicted in the musical. She was a relatively low-ranked foreign employee whom the King probably hardly knew. Most Thais deplore the musical's depiction of King Mongkut, who was one of the most sophisticated and revered monarchs in modern Thai history. For many years the play has been banned there (see *lese majeste*).

Lese majeste From FRENCH, meaning an insult to the monarch. It refers to draconian laws in Thailand that make it a crime punishable by up to 15 years in prison for insulting the monarchy or members of his family. Filing *lese majeste* charges begins with a complaint lodged by any citizen to the police about an alleged act or words committed by another that supposedly tarnishes the reputation of the King. The charges are filed frequently, often against political opponents. Foreigners are not immune, and several high-profile cases have blemished Thailand's image. The King usually pardons foreigners, but only after they have spent some time in detention awaiting trial.

Life and Death in Shanghai A graphic autobiography about life in China during the Cultural Revolution. The author, Nien Cheng (1915-2009), was imprisoned and tortured for six years beginning in 1966. A few years after her release, she moved to Canada and then to Washington, where she wrote *Life and Death* in 1987 and where she died. She never returned to China. Her privileged background made her an obvious target for Red Guards. She had three strikes against her in that brutal era: she was educated abroad; the daughter of a Kuomintang official (albeit one who elected to stay in China and not flee to Taiwan); and the wife of an executive at Shell, one of few multinational corporations that stayed in China after the communist victory.

lifetime employment Japan's equivalent of the "iron rice bowl". After leaving university, many Japanese join large corporations where they expect to spend their entire working lives and enjoy amenities and protections not accorded other Japanese. For example, many large Japanese companies maintain dormitories for workers, at least until they are married. Remuneration is usually based on seniority, not necessarily merit. The main difference between lifetime employment and the iron rice bowl is that the companies providing these "lifetime" benefits are private corporations with stockholders, and the employees are free to leave to follow other ambitions if they choose to do so, though most do not. Of course, "lifetime" employment was never actually for life, since most companies maintain a relatively young mandatory retirement age of 55. Considering that Japan is famous for longevity, most ex-**salarymen** could probably look forward to another 30 years of post-employment life. If they happen to retire after achieving a position of power in the company, then other lucrative options, such as board memberships, are open to them. For the rest, it means years of playing *go* or just trying to keep from getting on their wives' nerves as they stay home. And it was never something extended to women. Most women were expected to spend a couple of years in a corporation making tea and photo-copying documents as office ladies or "**OLs**" until they got married and left the company to raise a family. Even in its glory days of rapid growth in the 1960s and 1970s, millions of farmers, supermarket checkers, owners of small noodle shops and managers of bath houses had no such lifetime protections.

Lim Wee-chai (1958-) Chinese-Malaysian entrepreneur. In Malaysia, rubber and latex gloves go hand-in-hand, and nobody has prospered more from this happy synergy than Lim Wee-chai, founder and CEO of Top Glove Corp Berhad. Malaysia supplies some 60 percent of the world's rubber gloves, and Top Glove leads the pack with a global share of around 25 percent. Lim and his wife founded Top Glove in 1991 with about $50,000 in savings, one factory and three production lines. In 2008 he was named "Entrepreneur of the Year" at the Asia-Pacific Entrepreneurship awards.

Lin Biao (1907-1971) Lin was a celebrated Red Army general during the Long March and later against the Japanese and the Kuomintang. In 1959, Mao Zedong named Lin defense minister and his anointed successor. He took a leading role in the Cultural Revolution, but Mao's favor began to falter as he began to suspect that Lin was plotting to overthrow him. In September, 1971, Lin fled China with his wife and son by aircraft, crashing to a fiery death in Mongolia.

Line of Control A *de facto* ceasefire line between India and Pakistan in disputed Kashmir, roughly following the front line as it existed after the first Indo-Pakistan War of 1947, and later formalized by the Simla Agreement. It is not an internationally recognized boundary, merely a practical demarcation until a time, presumably in the far distant future, when the Kashmir question is resolved. The line more or less dissects the old princely state of Kashmir. The Indian portion is known as the state of Jammu and Kashmir, while the two Pakistani enclaves are Gilgit Baltistan and Azad Jammu and Kashmir. Artillery duels occasionally break out along the Line. (See **princely states**)

When things are under control, here could be heaven on earth.

Kashmir

Line of Control

Little Emperors See *Xiao huangdi*

liurai TETUM for the traditional tribal leaders in **Timor-Leste**. The Portuguese, who ruled East Timor until 1974, generally administered the colony through these local leaders who formed a kind of administrative class.

liu si MANDARIN for the numerals 6/4, which is shorthand for June 4, the date in 1989 when Chinese troops swept into Beijing to put down the student demonstrations (see **Tiananmen Massacre**). It reflects a typically Asian penchant to soften traumatic events with numeral euphemisms. On February 28, 1947, the Nationalist government of Chiang Kai-shek suppressed Taiwan-wide rioting, killing thousands; many more, probably, than died in Beijing. It is known today even in Taiwan simply as the "2/28 Incident." Japanese refer to the bloody coup attempt in Tokyo in 1936 as the "2/36 Incident." For that matter, they refer to the years the Japanese army rampaged through China, killing millions, as the "China Incident." It is, of course, not just an Asian penchant. Americans habitually refer to the attack on America on September 11, 2001 as "9/11".

Liu Xiang (1983-) Chinese hurdler who rocketed to fame when he won China's one and only gold medal in track and field in the 110 meter hurdles event at the 2004 Olympic Games in Athens (he also set a world record in the event in 2006). Up until then, China had been accumulating an impressive number of gold medals in such events as table tennis and shooting, but never in the marquee track and field competition. Some had wondered if Chinese possessed the physique to compete in running and jumping. Chinese were looking forward to a repeat performance on home ground at the 2008 Beijing Olympics, but Liu had to pull out due to an Achilles tendon injury. Ditto the 2012 Olympics. One of the most famous athletes among his countrymen, Liu earned enough from endorsements to donate the equivalent of more than $300,000 to disaster relief following the 2008 Sichuan earthquake.

lokpal HINDI In 2011, all of India was captivated by a latter-day Gandhi named "Anna" Hazare. He promised to "fast to the death" until parliament passed the Lokpal Bill, the anti-corruption law in India long sought by activists. The literal meaning of *lokpal* is something like "protector of the people", but it is usually translated as "citizens' ombudsman". First introduced into the Indian parliament in 1968, the Lokpal Bill had been reintroduced and defeated nine times until in the summer of 2011 it became the goal of a massive protest movement led by Hazare, who seemed to tap into a nostalgia for purer days in the struggle for independence. Despite his efforts, however, it was defeated once again.

longyi BURMESE The *longyi* is a single sheet of cloth wrapped around the waist, usually extending to the feet or sometimes below the knees. It is worn by both men and women, although there are subtle differences in the way the skirt is secured. It could be considered an integral part of Myanmar's native dress, although variations are found throughout South Asia. The *longyi* can be made from cotton for everyday use or silk for formal occasions. Women's *longyi* sport many designs, stripes, zigzags and flowers.

longkong A fruit grown in Southeast Asia. It comes in bunches, sort of like grapes, although they are as big as walnuts and have a leathery brown skin. The interior is like a lychee nut, but has a slightly sour taste. It is Thailand's second-largest fruit export after durians, far ahead of third-placed export lychee.

Lop Nur An area in China's far western Xinjiang province, best known as China's version of the Nevada nuclear weapons test site. The first Chinese atom bomb was tested at Lop Nur in 1964. Between 1964 and 1996 the Chinese exploded 45 nuclear weapons, most of them in the atmosphere. *Nur* is MONGOLIAN for lake and describes the region's characteristic salt lake marshes. The area was once the center of a thriving culture, and numerous tombs have attracted the attention of archaeologists. (See **Second Artillery Force**)

Lost decades A journalistic term for the years of sluggish economic growth in Japan following the end, in 1989, of the period of wildly inflated real estate and stocks and Western art acquisitions known as the Bubble Economy. In fact, the economic conditions were never as dire as many scare stories would have it, although it certainly seemed anemic compared with the previous years of extravagant and conspicuous spending. On the other hand, Japan never slipped into a real depression, hardly even into a recession.

Lugouqiao The Lugou Bridge, better known outside China as the Marco Polo Bridge. Here on July 7, 1937, Japanese troops clashed with Chinese troops. It is considered to be the start of the Second World War, which lasted until Japan's surrender in 1945. The granite bridge itself, located about 15 km from Beijing, is architecturally as well as historically significant. It was completed during the Ming Dynasty in 1192 and is composed of 11 arches with lion carvings. Marco Polo mentions the bridge – "a very fine stone bridge" – in his travel writings, which may be why it is known as the Marco Polo Bridge in the West. There is a nearby museum that chronicles China's struggles with Japan.

Luk Thung THAI A form of Thai music which originated in central Thailand just north of Bangkok in the 1950s. It has been likened to American country and western music as it conveys ballads that evoke the hardship of everyday life in rural Thailand. If you want to hear what it sounds like, just take a Bangkok taxi ride, since most drivers come from the country and have their car radios constantly tuned to popular *Luk Thung* stations. The Nashville of *Luk Thung* is Suphanburi, which has nurtured some of the more popular balladeers.

M

Macanese A small but distinct ethnic minority in Macau descended from Portuguese settlers and their Chinese or Malay wives. Formally educated in Portuguese and learning Cantonese from the street, they became the natural intermediaries between the thin Portuguese administration at the top and the bulk of the people. The Macanese over the centuries developed their own special cuisine and a separate dialect, the *patua*, though it is not widely spoken. Not to be confused with the dominant Cantonese majority.

Macau (alternative American spelling **Macao**) Small territory boasting the only legal casinos in China and invariably called an "enclave", at the tip of the Pearl River Delta. Formerly a Portuguese trading outpost, then colony, then province, then "Chinese territory administered by Portugal" and since December 20, 1999, a Special Administrative Region of China. Its origins are obscure, there being no treaty or other accord giving the territory to Portugal until it was 300 years old. The Portuguese began to settle there around 1557. At the time only three Chinese villages dotted the peninsula, along with a few temples, including the A-Ma Temple which gives Macau its name (from A Ma Gao, or the Bay of A Ma). It has other names. In Cantonese it is *O-mun*. In Mandarin it is *Aomen*, and since 1586 it has been officially styled The City in the Name of God in China.

Magsaysay Award Probably Asia's most prestigious award, sometimes called the Asian Nobel Peace Prize. It is awarded each year in August to Asians in six categories, including public and community service and the arts. It was created in 1957 to honor the memory of Philippine president

Ramon Magsaysay, who died in an air crash that year. The award carries a stipend of $50,000 as of 2011.

Mahbubani, Kishore (1948-) Singaporean diplomat, educator, author and leading proponent for Asian Values, the proposition that Asian countries are ascending and Western democracies are declining and that Western democracies have much to learn from Asian countries, just as Asia learned much from the West. Asian Values is a kind of modern-day Confucianism that is virtually the state ideology in Singapore, where Mahbubani has been its most prominent proponent through books, lectures and newspaper opinion pieces.

mai pen rai THAI "No problem". Or, as the Thais would say, feel free, try anything. Similar to CANTONESE *mo man tai*.

mainlanders A term for those persons, some 2 million in number, who fled China for Taiwan after the communist victory in 1949, in contrast to the native Taiwanese who had settled on the island from Fujian province over the decades. The term "mainlander" no longer denotes somebody who was literally born in China, as the followers of Chiang Kai-shek are dying out. Now it refers to somebody whose ancestral home was on the mainland. For example, President Ma Ying-jeou, born in Hong Kong but whose ancestors came from Hunan, would be considered a mainlander today. Up until 1996 Taiwan passports contained an entry for "native province," by which it meant not the actual birthplace of the passport holder but the province from which the holder's family hailed.

Makudonarudo Or, as Americans would say, McDonalds. One can also find numerous *kentakki furaido chikin* outlets and linger in a *staba* (Starbucks) for cup of *kohi* in Japan.

Malacanang Since 1825 it has been the home of 18 Spanish governor-generals, 14 American proconsuls and every president of the Philippines since 1946. It is located on the Pasig River in Manila. The origin of the name is disputed but is generally considered Tagalog due to the characteristic "ng" ending. An alternate official spelling is Malacanan Palace. The word "Malacanang" is used as shorthand for the Philippine president and administration much as "White House" is used in America.

Malay The word "Malay" can mean a language that is native to east Sumatra that became the *lingua franca* of trade in Southeast Asia and is now the official language of Malaysia and Indonesia – i.e. Bahasa Malaysia, Bahasa Indonesia, Bahasa Melayu (Brunei) and Malaynd. (Singapore). In Thailand it is called *Javi.* It is officially written in a Roman script (*Rumi* in Malaysian) and survives in Arabic script, *Jawi,* introduced by way of Java. Or, "Malay" can refer to the mostly Muslim ethnic group of some 300 million people encompassing Malaysia and Indonesia, southern Thailand plus other groups in Madagascar and minorities in Vietnam and Cambodia. Malay belongs to the broad western group of Austronesian languages (Malay Polynesian family). Other related languages are Javanese, Tagalog, Balinese and Madagascan.

The Malay Dilemma Title of a short but controversial and influential book by Mahathir Mohammad, who published it in 1970, a full decade before he became Malaysia's longest-serving prime minister (1981-2003). The "dilemma" of the title was the fact that while Malays made up the majority of the population, ethnic Chinese and Europeans owned most of the wealth. It called for, among other things, a program of affirmative action of favoring Malays that became the New Economic Policy.

Manchurian Candidate Novel by Richard Condon and a 1962 movie of that name starring Frank Sinatra. In it, a Korean War veteran returns to the US programmed to murder an American politician. The plot turned on the then-topical issue of brainwashing of American prisoners, some presumably held in camps in Manchuria, into "confessing" to germ warfare. The remake in 2005 kept the name, but being 50 years from the event, the allusions to brainwashing were probably lost on most viewers. Manchuria is a European name for that part of China that the Chinese call simply the Northeast. The name comes from the Manchu race, which dominated China during the Qing Dynasty but is all but extinct today. (See **Dongbei**)

mangosteen In spite of its name, this fruit has nothing to do with mangoes. It doesn't even look like one. It is a small round ball with curious looking lumps growing out of it. It is fairly easy to split the skin to reveal a white inner meat that breaks into six or eight slices like a tangerine. Soft and sweet, it goes well with **durians**.

Mangyongbong Name of an undistinguished North Korean passenger-cargo ship that from 1992-2006 regularly plied the waters between Niigata in Japan and Wonson in North Korea. It was the only direct link between the two countries, which do not maintain diplomatic relations. The 28-hour voyage across the Sea of Japan was one way for Japanese-Koreans to visit their ancestral homeland and bring presents and packages to relatives there. Tokyo long suspected the *Mangyongbong* was a conduit for smuggled goods. It had other beefs with North Korea, too, including the firing of the **Taepodong-2** ballistic missile over Japanese airspace and North Koreans abducting Japanese civilians in the 1970s. As part of bilateral sanctions, Japan banned visits to its ports. That meant the *Mangyongbong* had to find another line of work and re-invented itself as a cruise liner, traveling between **Rason** in the extreme northeast and the tourist spot Mount Kumgang.

Mangyongdae Prize Name of the prize given to the winner of the annual Pyongyang Marathon held each April to honor the birth of founding (and Eternal) President Kim Il-sung. It is named after Kim's birthplace near Pyongyang. The first race was run in 1981, and it was opened to foreign amateurs for the first time in 2014.

mansion JAPANESE from English for a type of ordinary condominium or apartment that bears little resemblance to the kind of abode the word implies in the West. It is considered one step up from a common *aparto* (apartment). Japanese have words for other styles of multi-family housing, including *ryou*, a kind of dormitory that large companies provide for their unmarried staff, and *danchi*, a block of public housing apartments usually considered decidedly downmarket.

matahari JAPANESE from English for "maternity harassment". Another of those borrowed and then compressed Japanese words from English. This vogue word describes a sexist attitude among Japanese men who taunt single women for not getting married and having children like they are supposed to.

... men, mon, mun Various ways of expressing "gate" in Chinese, Japanese and Korean. Most of the walls and fortifications that once surrounded Beijing, Tokyo or Seoul have been torn down, but the memories of old gates remain in various place names. The ghosts of the ancient Beijing wall live on in the number of place names in central Beijing which have the suffix *men* in their names. They include such places as Dongzhimen,

(the old Imperial East Straight Gate), Xizhimen, Qianmen and, of course, **Tiananmen** – the Gate of Heavenly Peace – at the far end of Tiananmen Square. Similarly in Tokyo the boundaries of the Shogun's palace extended farther out than the imperial palace grounds do today but the former gates are remembered in place names such as Toranomon, the Tiger Gate, or Otemon. The **Namdaemun,** or South Gate, recalls Seoul's ancient walls.

merdeka! MALAY for freedom. It is a particularly emotive word in Southeast Asia, meaning independence from European colonization, which most acquired soon after the end of World War II. Numerous squares, traffic circles and monuments throughout Indonesia and Malaysia have the word *merdeka* in their title, and politicians still use it as a battle cry. Indonesia celebrates independence on August 17, the day when Sukarno declared it in 1945, although the Dutch didn't recognize it until 1949. Malaysia observes independence day on August 31, when it received full freedom from Britain in 1957. Singapore's national day is August 9, the day it ended its brief union with Malaysia in 1965. Independence Day for the Philippines used to be July 4, the day in 1946 when the Americans withdrew. President Diosdado Macapagal changed it to June 16, the day **Emilio Aquinaldo** declared it in 1898. In 1998 the country celebrated 100 years of independence as if the American occupation had never happened. Thailand is proud that it was never a colony and has no independence day *per se*. But it does have several national holidays connected with the monarchy, including Chakri Day, April 6, commemorating the founding of the current dynasty; Coronation Day, May 5; the Queen's birthday, August 12; and the King's birthday, December 5.

Merlion A creature with the head of a lion and the body of a fish that has become perhaps the main symbol of Singapore. The head is said to represent Singapore's original name, *Singapura*, meaning lion city. The image is not really ancient. It was conceived in 1964 as the logo of the Singapore Tourism Board, which still maintains its trademark on the image even though it has changed its logo. The most famous of several statues of the Merlion is in Merlion Park in the financial district and was dedicated in 1972 by former prime minister Lee Kuan Yew. Another 37-meter Merlion statue can be found on the resort island of Sentosa.

Minamata disease Before Fukushima the greatest environmental disaster in Japan – indeed, one of the greatest in the entire world – was Minamata disease, a neurological affliction caused by severe mercury poisoning which can cause limb paralysis, difficulties in walking, mental confusion and death. It is named after Minamata Bay on the southern island of Kyushu. The Chisso chemical company had been dumping mercury-contaminated waste water in the bay for decades. In the 1950s and 1960s, many people living in the vicinity came down with strange illnesses tied to eating mercury-contaminated fish caught in the bay. Minamata disease was first suspected in 1956 and was officially pronounced a pollution-linked disease in 1968. Over the years, Chisso, which is still in business, has paid out about $8 billion to compensate victims. In 2004 the supreme court of Japan ruled that the national and prefectural governments bore some culpability for the pollution disaster.

mini constitution Journalistic shorthand for Hong Kong's post-1997 charter, formally known as the Basic Law of the Hong Kong Special Administrative Region of the People's Republic of China. Called "mini" even though it has about as many words as the US Constitution, though fewer than the Texas State Constitution. It was drafted by a committee of Hong Kongers and mainland Chinese and passed by the National People's Congress in April 1990. It spells out the intention of the **Joint Declaration** to grant Hong Kong a "high degree of autonomy" under Chinese sovereignty (see *gangren zhigang*).

minying MANDARIN for "run by the people." Despite thirty years of market reforms, the notion of private enterprise – *siying* – has a kind of negative connotation in a country still run in theory on communist principles. So most businessmen refer to their companies by the more politically correct term, *minying*, even if the company is purely a private venture.

Miyako Channel An increasingly sensitive body of water between the southern tip of Okinawa and the Japanese island of Miyako, part of the southern Sakishima group, southernmost of the Ryukyu chain. It is sensitive as it is wide enough to provide international space for warships to maneuver. Chinese see it as the principal gateway for its navy to the broad reaches of the Pacific Ocean (see **Blue Water Navy**). It is strategically sensitive as it is a place where the Chinese, Japanese and American navies grind together, sometimes literally. (See **First Island Chain**)

Modi, Narendra (1950-) Controversial yet charismatic Chief Minister of the state of Gujarat from 2001 to 2014, and Prime Minister of India since 2014. He is reviled by many for his unapologetic stance on the Gujarat communal riots of 2002, shortly after he became chief minister, yet grudgingly admired for his laser-like fixation on economic development. Indeed, in recent years his state led most of India in job creation. He began his political career as a ***pracharak*** or agitator for the right-wing Hindu nationalist organization the Rashtruya Swayamevak Sangh, better known as the RSS. He is a member of the Bharatiya Janata Party.

mogyoktang KOREAN for public bath houses. Koreans have a public bathhouse culture similar to the Japanese (see ***sento***). *Mogyoktang* are "monuments to equalitarian cleanliness, reducing all who enter to the basic entities of bone and muscle freed from all pretensions of riches and power", said Simon Winchester in *Korea: a Walk Through the Land of Miracles*. As in Japan, more and more homes have their own private baths, but the public facilities continue as they provide for "the pursuit of that most Confucian of ideals, the civilized pleasure of the purest kind." *Mogyoktang* are pretty basic; more elaborate establishments, featuring saunas, massage and exercise rooms, are known as *jjimjilbong*.

Momofuko, Ando (1910-2007) Inventor of instant ramen noodles, sometimes called Japan's greatest post-war invention, just behind the

Walkman but ahead of the karaoke machine. Ramen is, for all practical purposes, Japan's national dish, cheaper than sushi, available everywhere, perpetually fashionable. The basic (non-instant) ramen is a bowel of wheat noodles sitting in a hot broth, flavored with soy sauce, bamboo shoots, a slice of pork and garnished with a piece of dried seaweed. Originally from China, the dish took off with Japan's extraordinary economic expansion beginning in the 1950s, and became the **salaryman's** all-purpose fuel. Momofuku invented instant ramen noodles in 1958, which he called Chikin (chicken) Ramen. He founded the Nissin Food Products Corp to produce and sell his invention, and it is a going concern today. The little white styrofoam cups with the red lettering on them are as ubiquitous in the supermarkets of Asia as Coca-Cola. The largest market outside of Japan is China, including Taiwan and Hong Kong. Global consumption reached 98 billion servings in 2007, according to the Sixth World Instant Noodles Summit.

Montagnards Originally a FRENCH term for minority tribes (mountain people) in Vietnam, later adopted by Americans who valued their partnership in fighting the Viet Cong communists during the Vietnam War. They organized the tribals into defensive groups to guard against infiltration into what was then called the Central Highlands area of South Vietnam. In Vietnamese they are officially called *nguoi thuong* or "highland citizens" or more commonly by the derogatory term *moi*, meaning savage or slave. They generally live in the upland, more mountainous areas of Vietnam, hence the names, and are divided into several major tribes.

mooncake A traditional Chinese pastry eaten during the Mid-Autumn Festival, which is held on the night of the full moon of the eighth lunar month. They are about the size and shape of a hockey puck and are made with different fillings, ranging from red bean paste to egg yolks and cheesecake. They pack a lot of calories (between 800-1,200) into a small space because they are loaded with sugar and oil. Mooncakes have been a traditional part of Chinese celebrations for centuries, but as the country has prospered, the giving and receiving of the cakes has gotten almost out of hand. It is not uncommon for a business person to receive two or three dozen mooncake gifts, wrapped in fancy boxes, from clients, family and friends. The Chinese government, recognizing a good thing, recently decided to tax the mooncake gifts as income.

Moon Sung-myong (1920-) South Korean religious leader, businessman, political agitator, and founder of the Unification Church who has tentacles in numerous business activities, even having extensive holdings in sushi bars across the US. His Unification Church is known mainly for mass weddings rather than any particular theology other than loyalty to Moon and his large family. He began his self-proclaimed divine mission mainly as a crusade against communism (although he was fairly chummy with North Korea's leaders). His conviction in the US for tax evasion in 1984 was hardly a bump in the road. He used his year in prison to found the *Washington Times*, a money-losing but politically influential newspaper in the capital. Unlike other church-owned media organs, such as the *Christian Science Monitor*, it does not advance any religious ideas other than straight Republican conservatism. His followers are often ridiculed as "Moonies".

Mori, Minoru (1934-2012) Japanese property developer and chairman of Mori Building Company, best known for the pricey Roppongi Hills project and a patron of the arts through his Mori Art Museum. The development made Mori famous throughout Asia. His company's Shanghai World Financial Center is the tallest building in China. His father Taikichiro Mori was a university economics professor when, at age 50, he started the property company that eventually made him Japan's richest person. He patiently acquired parcels of land in the Toranomon area that were the foundation for numerous high-rise buildings that changed the face of Tokyo. At his death in 1994, his two sons, Minoru and Akira, split their inheritance into separate property companies.

moukari makka JAPANESE Literally "Are you making a profit?" but used as a greeting in Osaka, Japan's second city. People in Tokyo will say *ogenki desu-ka*, meaning "How are you?" People in Osaka greet each other with the phrase meaning something like "Are you making money?" The peculiar difference to standard Japanese goes back to the early days when Tokyo, then known as **Edo**, was an administrative center, while Osaka was mainly populated with merchants. It is one of the more interesting variations on standard Japanese known as *Kansai-ben*, or the dialect of the Kansai region, typified by Osaka speech.

mountain retreats In colonial days, well before the advent of air conditioning, Europeans escaped the summer or dry season heat by moving to towns at higher elevations. The archetypal mountain retreat was **Simla** in India, where the British viceroy had a summer home. Other Asian mountain retreats include Dalat in Vietnam, **Baguio** in the Philippines, **Karuizawa** in Japan and the Genting Highlands in Malaysia.

Muay Thai What most of the world calls Thai boxing, a sport with deep roots in Thailand. In addition to gloved fists, Thai boxers kick with their feet, and use elbows and knees – in all, about eight legal points of contact that are prohibited in regular boxing are fair game in Muay Thai. Thailand's most famous 19th-century monarch, **King Chulalongkorn**, took a personal interest in the sport and helped boost its popularity and establish its rules. Thai boxing is often portrayed in movies featuring various martial arts stars. It is a part of the Asian Games.

Murakami, Takashi (1962-) Prolific Japanese contemporary artist and sculptor known for blending low and high arts forms. Trained in the traditional *nihonga* art style but also heavily influenced by manga and anime, he advocates a kind of post-postmodern style called "super flat". He is probably Japan's best-known contemporary artist and has been exhibited all over the world. His work is also among the most valuable of living artists. One piece of sculpture called *My Lonesome Cowboy* netted more than $15 million at Sotheby's. In 2008 he was named one of the world's 200 most influential people, and the only artist on the list, by *Time* magazine.

N

Naadam Festival Mongolia's national festival usually held in mid-July. The biggest events are held in the capital Ulanbator and usually involve Mongolian wrestling, archery competitions and horse races, all traced back to the times when Mongolia was mostly a nomadic country. It is also celebrated in the neighboring Tuva Republic, which is a part of the Russian Federation although ethnically similar to Mongolia.

Nadeshiko The name of a hardy, pink-frilled carnation native to Japan that became the unofficial name for the country's women's national soccer team, which in July 2011 won the Women's World Cup. It was the first time that a Japanese team, male or female, had won an international soccer championship. The close victory over the US women's soccer team gave all of Japan a lift, coming four months after the disastrous Great East Japan Earthquake of March 11. The word was chosen as Japan's "top buzzword of the year" for 2011 by an organization that makes such pronouncements.

Naga serpent In front of almost every temple in Thailand one finds a representation of Naga serpents, mythical creatures from Hindu days. Usually these *naga* appear, their mouths wide open and fangs showing, at the entrance or stairway.

Nagata-cho A district in Tokyo's Chiyoda ward where the National **Diet** Building, political party headquarters and the prime minister's official residence (*Kantei*) are located. The phrase Nagata-cho is a Japanese version of "Capitol Hill" in Washington and is used that way by political journalists in speaking of political matters. The district is not entirely devoted to party politics as several corporations have their headquarters in the Nagata-cho. Nearby is the **Kasumigaseki** district, where most of the government ministries are housed.

Nahdlatul Ulama One of the world's largest independent Islamic organizations, with 30-50 million members, which funds charities and runs religious boarding schools in Indonesia. It is often abbreviated as simply NU. The organization was founded in 1926 out of concern at the spread of the austere brand of Islam practiced in Saudi Arabia (created the same year). It has a long tradition of promoting conservative and traditional beliefs which in a way insulates it from more radical jihadism. It most famous leader was Abdurrahman Wahid (popularly known as Gus Dur), who was Indonesia's fourth president in 1999, though he was removed from office two years later.

nakama hazure JAPANESE A feeling of being left out of the group, a serious emotion in group-oriented Japan. *Nakama* literally means a group that you do things with at work, or sometimes friends that you have known since primary school. The group at work would be more than just fellow colleagues but people with whom one can share thoughts and feelings. This attribute is sometimes used to explain why many Japanese **salarymen** are reluctant to blow the whistle on internal corporate corruption for fear of being excluded from the group.

Namdaemun Gate A 600-year-old edifice considered South Korea's greatest national treasure. Literally, it means the gate honoring courtesy, and it was the southern gate of the walls that once encircled Seoul during the Joseon Dynasty (1392-1910). Now it is isolated in a busy traffic roundabout in the center of Seoul, near the Namdaemun market. Construction of the gate began in 1395 and ended in 1398, when King Taejo, the founder of the Joseon Dynasty, ruled. It was opened to the public in 2006, and in February, 2008, a fire consumed the wooden superstructure, leaving only the stone gate below it intact. (See *... men, mon, mun*)

Na Nakorn A huge and powerful Thai family (of generals, top civil servants and politicians) which traces its roots to the traditional governors of the southern city of Nakhon Si Thammarat. They descend from King Taksin, the monarch who picked up the reins of state after the sacking of Ayutthaya in 1767, and who was in turn overthrown and murdered by the general who founded the present **Chakri Dynasty** in 1782. There were wholesale massacres of the family members that year and in 1809 and 1821.

Naneun Ggomsuda KOREAN Sometimes rendered Na Ggom-su, a highly popular podcast that regularly skewered South Korea's President Lee Myung-bak (aka "his highness") in particular and the conservative Grand National Party in general. Usually translated as "I'm a Petty Creep", which underscores its core cheekiness and the satirical nature of the content. It is highly popular with young people and gets about 2 million downloads a week. It provides a counterbalance to the mainstream media which is conservative and was supportive of Lee. Unlike in Thailand or China, which heavily censors the Internet, the government does not censor the site. However, some participants have run afoul of the law. One person was sentenced to a year in prison for "spreading false rumors" regarding the president's alleged stock market fraud. It is given some credit for the surprise victory of left-wing activist Park Woo-soon as mayor of Seoul in 2011. It is not certain how it will adjust to a post-Lee world, especially if someone like Park replaces him in the **Blue House**.

nanny state A common but in some ways misleading description of Singapore, especially from Western journalists. It may be true that the republic has a lot of nit-picking regulations such as the prohibition on chewing gum. But it is a nanny state that is tight with the dollar. The island state has no unemployment insurance, no minimum wage, no publicly funded old age pensions – only minimal health care through its Central Provident Fund that is the usual attribute of the welfare state (see **iron rice bowl**).

Naresuan, King Thailand's greatest warrior, King Naresuan the Great ruled Siam from 1590 to 1605, which makes him a contemporary of Britain's Queen Elizabeth I. He was taken as a hostage to Burma as a youth, where legend has it his bird defeated the crown prince of Burma's in a cockfight. He then expelled the Burmese from Siam. Whether the cockfight legend is true or not, most statues of King Naresuan in Thailand are surrounded by replicas of roosters. He was the subject of Thailand's longest and most expensive movie, *The Legend of King Naresuan,* which was screened in 2007, running nine hours in three separate three-hour episodes.

Narita Japan's most important international airport and a major entry point into Asia, now called Narita International Airport (formerly New Tokyo International Airport). It is pronounced *nah ri ta,* though habitually mispronounced as NaRITA by American airline pilots flying the transpacific route. Planning for Narita began in the 1960s when it became apparent that Tokyo's traditional portal, Haneda, was becoming overcrowded. Narita would handle international flights, Haneda domestic. Narita is located in the countryside, and efforts to obtain land were fiercely opposed by local farmers. Prime Minister Takeo Fukuda forced the opening in 1978, saying that Japan's prestige was at stake. The action resulted in a deadly confrontation with rioters who captured the control tower, forcing controllers seeking the safety of the roof to be evacuated by police helicopters. In 1991 the then minister of transport declared that the government would no longer force farmers to provide additional land for runway expansion. He also formally apologized to those who were displaced to build the first runway. This act of "sincerity" allowed the government to persuade landowners to sell enough land to build part of a second runway in time for the 2002 Soccer World Cup, which was jointly hosted by Japan and South Korea.

Narita divorce Two people get married in a lavish and expensive ceremony and leave Japan on a honeymoon to Europe, Hawaii or some other exotic destination. The new husband, having spent his life in school or work, is totally at sea, unable to make the simplest choice in a restaurant or negotiate the complexities of checking into a hotel. The new bride, steeped in magazine lore and having taken several trips abroad before, takes over. Arguments break out, the husband's ego is wounded, and the couple decides that maybe they aren't made for each other after all. On returning to Japan at Narita, they decide to go their separate ways.

National Security Law A strict but vaguely written law in South Korea, first enacted in 1948, two years before the Korean War (or "Civil War" as Koreans call it), that makes it a crime to praise, sympathize with or cooperate with North Korea. The main accusation of "aiding the enemy" can cover a multitude of sins, such as owning books on Karl Marx or drunkenly praising Kim Jong-il at a karaoke bar, or making anti-American comments on a blog. The law is often applied capriciously, depending on the convictions or prejudices of prosecutors and the state of relations with the North. 2010, a year noted for serious Northern provocations, also saw a spike in the number of prosecutions under the law. (See **113** in *Numbers*)

Naypyidaw The purpose-built capital of Myanmar, located in the interior of the country, about 320 km north of the former capital Yangon (Rangoon). The military junta that ruled Myanmar ordered civil servants to move to the new capital in November 2005 and officially proclaimed it the country's administrative center on Army Day the following year. The generals never deigned to explain exactly why they created this new capital or were willing to spend billions of hard currency building it except to say that Yangon was becoming crowded. Most outsiders presume that the generals wanted to insulate themselves from anti-government demonstrations that have broken out in Yangon. After all, hardly anyone but civil servants live in Naypyidaw. Some argue the junta fears invasion for "regime change" and wanted to move the capital to a more defensible position in the interior. The name means "royal city" in BURMESE, and the city is graced with statues of former warrior kings such as King Byinnaung. It is not easy to get to, having no international flights, but some journalists have entered and described a city that has much of the same sterile feeling of other purpose-built capital cities in their early years. The US maintains its embassy in Yangon, as do most other countries.

netto-uyo JAPANESE A combination of *netto* (Internet) and *uyoku* (ultra-right wing) to describe a group of mostly young people who spend a lot of time on the Internet saying rude things about China and South Korea and voicing other nationalist views. Their message used to be limited mainly to sound trucks whose loudspeakers emitted ear-splitting martial speeches. The *netto-uyo* made their weight felt in the 2014 Tokyo gubernatorial election where they helped extreme right-wing candidate Toshio Tamogami win more than 600,000 votes in his losing bid. Similar to Chinese netizens (see *fenqing*).

Nippon, Nihon JAPANESE Two names for Japan, both equally valid and both widely used. In 1934 the education ministry's now defunct *Kokugo Chosakai*, or committee on the national language, proposed making Nippon the official name, but it did not lead to legislation. Nippon has a more official connotation and is used on postage stamps, whereas Nihon seems to be used in everyday conversation. A Japanese person is a *Nihon-jin*. The English name, Japan, is derived from a Chinese word that more or less means "sun origin country", or land of the rising sun, *cipan*. The two *kanji* characters for Nippon or Nihon say mostly the same thing, one for sun and one for origin.

Nippon Chinbotsu In English, *Japan Sinks* – the title of a 1973 thriller by Sakyo Komatsu, later made into a television series and a movie. The novel postulates that Japan is dragged entirely underwater by a huge subduction zone. The novel played on the then-emerging scientific consensus about continental drift and movement of tectonic plates, of which Japan sits at the confluence of three and, of course, the Japanese obsession with earthquakes. Though the novel came out well before the Bubble Economy of the late 1980s and subsequent collapse, it often served as a kind of metaphor for Japan during the country's **Lost Decades**.

Nippon Kaigi JAPANESE for the Japan Conference, an innocuous-sounding name for the most powerful right-wing lobbying group in Japan, well represented among governing Liberal Democratic Party politicians. The group's aim is to turn back the clock on virtually all reforms, such as equality for women, introduced by the post-war American occupation; or, as they would put it, to "change the post-war national consensus based on the Tokyo Trials (which convicted Japanese leaders of promoting a war of aggression) and to revise the constitution." They want to renounce **Article 9** and generally change the emphasis from rights to duties. Prime Minister Shinzo Abe supports many of Nippon Kaigi's views and is honorary chairman of its parliamentary grouping. Chinese and Koreans often view Nippon Kaigi as proof that Japan once again wants to go down the path of war.

nisoku-sanmon JAPANESE Literally two pairs of shoes for three *mon*, but now an expression meaning something sold at a giveaway price. During the Edo Period (1603-1867), farmers used to make sandals called *kongo-zori* on the side. The footwear was sturdy but cheap, hence two pairs for three *mon*. Similar in English to selling something for a song.

Nissho Maru Incident In 1953 the Japanese petroleum company Idemitsu sent a tanker, the *Nissho Maru*, to Iran to import refined gasoline and diesel oil in defiance of an embargo organized by Britain to protest Iran's nationalization of its oil assets. British Petroleum sued Idemitsu in a case that lingered in the courts for years. It was, however, seen in Japan as a morale-building, heroic stand against Western interests coming soon after its defeat in World War II. Since then Japan, heavily dependent on Middle East oil, has always been a reluctant participant in trade embargoes with Iran and has sought exemptions in order to import some Iranian oil. The extreme nationalist writer Naoki Hyakuta wrote a best-selling novel, *The Man Who was Called a Pirate* (*Kaizoku to Yobareta Otoko*), based on this incident in 2012 and made a grand tour of Iran two years later.

Nixon Doctrine American foreign policy formulation announced by President Richard Nixon on Guam in 1969 of which the most important plank was the declaration that Washington expected that its friends and allies should take care of their own defense. The doctrine was closely associated with another buzzword of the era, "**Vietnamization**", which meant withdrawing US troops from Vietnam as they were replaced by properly trained South Vietnamese soldiers. Its main test came in 1972 when a communist offensive was defeated through a combination of Vietnamese soldiers and American airpower. However, it failed in 1975 in part because Congress had intervened to halt further bombing. In a larger sense it was aimed at accommodating a changing world in which there no longer was a monolithic communist threat. Ostensibly global, the Nixon Doctrine was aimed mainly at Asia.

NK08 Nato designation for a mysterious North Korean intermediate-range missile that was first unveiled at a military review in April, 2012, to honor the anniversary of the birth of Kim Il-sung. The missile was displayed on a wheeled launcher believed to have been supplied by the Chinese, giving the North Koreans, for the first time, a road-mobile long-range missile capability. It is different from the Taepodong-2 long-range missile which is launched from a known, fixed location and only after days of careful refueling and other preparations. When first displayed, some observers claimed it was a mockup, but Americans were reportedly concerned enough about this missile to deploy additional missile interceptors to Alaska.

Noli Me Tangere Probably the most famous Filipino novel, written by national hero Jose Rizal and said to be the *Uncle Tom's Cabin* of the Philippines. Indeed, Rizal said he was inspired to write *Noli* after reading the American anti-slavery book. Required reading for all Filipino school children.

Nomonhan Incident JAPANESE name for the 20th century's most important battle that nobody has ever heard of. It took place in August, 1939, on the remote border of Manchuria (then the Japanese puppet state of Manchukuo) and Mongolia, a client state of the Soviet Union. The main battle developed from a number of skirmishes between the Japanese Kwantung Army and the Soviet Union over their poorly defined border. The Russians call it the Battle of Khalkin Gol, after a river. The fighting turned decidedly in Russia's favor after the arrival of a new commander, Georgy Zhukov. He pinned the Japanese defenders down with artillery and air strikes, then used his tanks to encircle the Japanese army in a double envelopment. Zhukov would use much the same tactics in winning the much more famous Battle of Stalingrad in 1943-44. The overwhelming Japanese defeat had far-reaching consequences, as it persuaded the Japanese high command to choose the "Strike South" offensive against the Americans, British and Dutch in Southeast Asia rather than "Strike North" to occupy parts of Soviet Siberia. It hardly needs saying that the "incident" is totally ignored and forgotten in Japan, but not so in Russia. In 2009 Russian President Dmitry Medvedev and his Mongolian counterpart marked the 70th anniversary of the battle in a ceremony in Ulan Bator. Mongolia also has the Zaisan Memorial just outside the capital to commemorate this victory and other cooperative ventures with Russia.

Nordpolitik GERMAN for northern policy, which has come to describe a South Korean policy of reaching out to socialist countries, nominally supporters of its peninsular rival North Korea, such as China, Russia and the then-communist Eastern Europe. The term is a play on *Ostpolitik*, West Germany's diplomatic outreach to Eastern Europe. In KOREAN it is *Pukpang chonghaek*. Nordpolitik was initiated by President Roh Tae-woo in 1983 out of concern about South Korea's over-reliance, economically and militarily, on the United States and its allies. It got a big boost when Seoul held the 1988 Olympics and possibly culminated in 2010 when South Korea hosted the G-20 summit.

Normal Nation A Japanese code word for repealing or severely altering **Article 9** of Japan's American-written constitution that prohibits the use of force in settling international disputes. The term implies that Japan should become a "normal nation" able to use force of arms to advance its interests – just like every other nation.

Northern Limit Line A vaguely defined unofficial border between the western reaches of North and South Korea and a source of continuing trouble between Seoul and Pyongyang. A quick look at a map shows that the eastern maritime border of South Korea is cleanly demarcated, but on the other side of the country it meanders westward through numerous small islands. The line was drawn unilaterally by the United Nations following the end of the Korean War, but it is not recognized by Pyongyang, which says the line should have been drawn further south. Over the years, hundreds of fishermen from both sides have been seized by rival navies. The two navies fought skirmishes in 1999, 2002 and 2009. The most serious provocations came in 2010 with the sinking of the South Korean corvette *Cheonan* and the murderous North Korean artillery bombardment of the island of Yeonpyeong.

Nuclear village In JAPANESE *genshiryoku mura.* An expression for the tight circle of government bureaucracies, power utilities and manufacturers involved in promoting nuclear power in Japan. Here the word *mura* (village) implies a small, tight-knit community. The term came into wide use following the nuclear crisis at the Fukushima Daiichi nuclear power plant in 2011, but actually predates that event. It first appeared in a magazine article in 1997. The main pillars of the "village" are probably the Ministry of Economy, Trade and Industry (Meti); the Nuclear Power Division of the Tokyo Electric Power Co. (Tepco); and the Japan Atomic Industrial Forum, which represents, among others, many manufacturers, such as Toshiba, involved in making parts for nuclear power plants. (See *amakudari*)

nuoc mam VIETNAMESE for a fish paste condiment. Such condiments are common throughout Southeast Asia, but they are more closely associated with Vietnamese cuisine.

Nyepi BALINESE for a "day of silence" and fasting and meditation associated with the Hindu New Year, which begins the day after Nyepi. It is observed throughout Indonesia but is most closely associated with Bali. On the day of silence the normal revelry of Bali comes to a halt, the streets are deserted, the only sound the barking of dogs. Hindu security men called *pecalang* enforce the silence, ordering cars off the road or people to turn down, or turn off, their televisions and radios. Even foreign tourists are expected to stay in their hotels. If Nyepi falls on a Friday, Muslims are permitted to attend Friday prayers so long as they walk to the mosque.

O

O-N Cannon A term Japanese sports writers adopted in the 1960s and 70s to describe the batting powerhouse of Sadaharu Oh and Shigeo Nagashima, two star players for the Yomiuri Giants baseball team. Oh usually batted third followed by Nagashima in the "cleanup position", a pairing reminiscent of Babe Ruth and Lou Gehrig in the heyday of the New York Yankees. Oh hit 868 homeruns during his career with the Giants, eclipsing the American homerun king, Barry Bonds, by 106. Japanese baseball teams are named after their corporate sponsors. The Giants are owned by the Yomiuri news group, and their location in Tokyo, Japan's largest city, and long record of championships makes them the New York Yankees of Japan. Nagashima had a long career as manager of the Giants before retiring in 2001; Oh managed several other Japanese teams before retiring in 2008.

o-wabi kaiken JAPANESE for formal public apology. It is a familiar tableau: Middle-aged men, dark suits, packed press conference, grave expressions, heads bowed deeply, as the company president and chairman offer their sincere regrets for some major foul-up. Usually they speak in generalities, expressing deep regret for causing "concerns" or making trouble, rather than directly addressing the issue at hand. In 2010 Toyota president Akio Toyoda apologized for a major recall of its cars for problems of acceleration that allegedly led to some deaths in this manner: "I deeply regret that I caused concern among many people." The term relates mainly to business practices, and should not be confused with situations that arise over governmental apologies, or lack of apology, for Japan's wartime activities.

Oecusse Tiny, isolated enclave of independent Timor Leste, located on the northern coast of the Indonesian province of West Timor. It is only about 800 square km in size with 67,000 people. The only link with Timor Leste proper is a twice-weekly ferry. The connection with the former Portuguese colony of East Timor goes back hundreds of years. The first European settlement on Timor, dating back to the early 16th century, was here, and it was also the location of the first contacts with Roman Catholic Christianity. Colonization gave rise to a small settlement at Lifau, which was the capital of Portuguese East Timor until 1769 when it was moved to Dili. Now Lifau is part of the enclave's largest settlement, Pante Makasar, which boasts only about 5,000 inhabitants. The territory's existence stems from a treaty signed by the Portuguese and Dutch in 1916 effectively partitioning Timor between them.

Ogasawara Group A string of islands extending due south of Tokyo for about 1,000 km, known in the West as the Bonin Islands. The most famous of the group is, of course, Iwo Jima, site of a bloody battle during World War II. Another island in the chain, Chichi Jima, was the site of an important radio relay station for Japanese Imperial troops in Southeast Asia. Considered impregnable to invasion, the island was constantly bombed by US Navy planes. On one such raid, the future President George H.W. Bush was shot down but rescued by a submarine. He was lucky as other downed pilots were killed and, it is alleged, eaten. The island's Japanese commander was convicted of war crimes and hanged. The chain was returned to Japan in 1968. Chichi Jima currently has the island group's only sizeable population of about 2,000. Administratively, it is part of Tokyo prefecture. The group has interesting flora and fauna and is popular with eco-tourists. In 2011 the chain was designated a World Heritage Site.

ojingoa A concoction made of cold water arrow squid and peanut paste highly valued by Koreans, who are said to consume about half a million metric tons of the stuff every year. It is a common sight hanging in plastic bags in foodstuff stores. Korean fishing boats scour waters of the world far and wide to keep Koreans supplied with squid.

Okinotorishima A tiny atoll at the extreme southern end of the **Ogasawara Group** of islands, also known as the Bonin islands. At low tide only two islets about the size of a bedroom rise a few centimeters above water level. There is a dispute whether this is enough to declare Okinotorishima a real island and claim exclusive rights to resources within the island's 200-mile **Exclusive Economic Zone** (EEZ). Japan claims that it does; while not denying Japan's territorial claim, China disputes this. The tiny sea feature also has some strategic importance, as it lies midway between Guam and Taiwan. Chinese "research" ships have been known to take measurements of the undersea contours around the atoll. In 2005 Tokyo's nationalistic governor, Shintaro Ishihara, actually set foot on the island to buttress Japan's claims. The atoll is part of the Ogasawara chain, which is part of Tokyo prefecture; so Ishihara is sort of the mayor of Okinotorishima.

okkake JAPANESE for a person who chases after an entertainment idol. In Japan *okkake* refers mainly to a large throng of women who follow after a particular performer in the all-women revue known as Takarazuka. It is similar to the English word groupie, but does not have the same sexual connotations. *Okkake* congregate around the main Takarazuka theater in Tokyo and other places in Japan and often follow after their idol when the revue moves to another city. The Takarazuka revue is named after a suburb of Osaka, which remains its operating base. It is owned by the Hankyu Railway Company.

OLs See **lifetime employment**

omiai JAPANESE In Japan's tradition of arranged marriage, *omiai* is the first meeting between prospective bride and groom chaperoned by parents or marriage broker. Even in this day and time, arranged marriages are a common feature in Japan and other Asian cultures. Parents usually do the arranging or they turn to professional or amateur matchmakers. No

couple in Japan, however, is forced into a marriage. Forced marriages were abolished in China soon after the communist victory in 1949, as were such traditional Confucian practices as wife purchase and concubinage.

omoi yari yosan JAPANESE Literally a gift or budget out of consideration for somebody, usually translated as the "sympathy budget". This is a large sum of money, above strictly treaty obligations, that Japan pays to the US government to help defray the cost of maintaining military bases in Japan. Under the 1960 security treaty Japan is only obliged to provide "facilities and areas" for the US. But over time, especially with the rise of the yen, the **Diet** has appropriated additional monies to "smooth the operations" and help to cover the costs of, for example, the large numbers of Japanese nationals who work on the various bases. The budget varies year-to-year but now comes to about 200 billion yen annually. Controversial in Japan, each annual negotiation prompts criticism in various media as to why so much money needs to be spent to support foreign forces on Japanese soil.

Operation Chromite The code word for Gen. Douglas MacArthur's daring flanking invasion at Inchon on September 15, 1950. Within two weeks the US forces had recaptured Seoul and forced the North Korean army to retreat back beyond the 38th parallel. If MacArthur had been content with that swift victory, the history of Asia would have been different. Instead, he plunged across the line into North Korea, only to be forced into a humiliating retreat when the Chinese entered the war.

Operation Spectrum The code name for a crackdown by the Singapore government in 1987 against a group of social workers and other activists accused of being involved in a Marxist conspiracy. Over the next year between 16 and 22 people were detained without trial under the **Internal Security Act.** In addition to its impact on the activists and on the island republic, it led to serious conflicts with the Western news media which looked with skepticism on the supposed threat, saying that the social and religious workers arrested were naïve idealists, not dangerous communist agitators. Several publications, including *Asiaweek* and the *Far Eastern Economic Review,* were "**gazetted**", meaning that their circulations were severely constrained. The term came from the publication of the Home Ministry order in the National Gazette.

OPLAN 5027 The joint South Korean and American operations plan for full-scale war on the Korean Peninsula, first produced after the Korean War and regularly updated to consider new conditions, including biological and chemical attacks and presumably nuclear attacks as well. Early versions anticipated troops falling back to a defensive position near Seoul and holding on until the arrival of large reinforcements from the US. These versions anticipated needing more than 600,000 American troops. As this is more than the ground forces of the US Army have today, it is assumed that it now depends more heavily on precision air strikes, possibly even drones.

Orascom An Egyptian business conglomerate and major mobile phone purveyor with growing connections to North Korea. Its telecom subsidiary Orascom Telecom Holdings in late 1998 founded Koryolink to provide 3G mobile phone services to North Korea. It reported having signed up 660,000 subscribers in the first half of 2011. As part of its deal, Orascom is supposed to complete the 105-story white elephant known as the **Ryugyong Hotel** in Pyongyang.

otaku JAPANESE term for a person who is obsessively devoted to something or someone, sometimes translated as "geek". The object of interest can be almost anything from an anime character to an Idol star to a railroad to a particular bag of rice. Fans know everything about their object of affection, not just birthday but clothing size and other personal information. Some businesses try to cash in on the phenomenon by selling things to aficionados. The local agricultural association in northern Akita prefecture makes money on Akita Komachi rice in bags featuring illustrations from Aoi Nishimata. It sells at a premium over rice in plain bags.

Ozawa, Ichiro (1942-) Although he never became prime minister (at least not yet, though he hasn't stopped trying), Ichiro Ozawa was perhaps the most influential Japanese politician of the past 20 years. He engineered the vote of no confidence in 1993 that brought down the government of Prime Minister Kiichi Miyazawa, installing for a brief time the first opposition government in decades and starting the slow political movement that saw the formation of a genuinely viable opposition. He joined the Democratic Party of Japan and would have been its first prime minister had he not resigned as party president because of allegations of misusing political funds only three months before the DPJ's electoral triumph in 2009. In 2011, he nearly ousted Naoto Kan as party chief, and thus premier, in a party primary. He was acquitted of the political funds irregularities in 2012. That year too he bolted the DPJ to form a new party called People's Life.

P

Pabst Blue Ribbon The working class beer has moved upmarket in communist China, where it is sold as an upscale beverage, sort of like Napoleon Brandy. What sells for a couple of dollars a can in the US has been repackaged in an elegant bottle and sold for the equivalent of $45. The figure "1844" tacked onto the label is the year the beer was first brewed in Milwaukee. It is one of several famous American brand names that have lost much of their luster at home but have got a new lease on life in Asia. They include the venerable Buick automobile, which has become one of China's leading luxury car brands since it was first introduced in 1998, and Krispy Kreme donuts. For years the donut shop in Shinjuku, Japan, has had a winding rope line to keep orderly the crowds of people waiting to get into the store.

Pacific War What the Japanese call World War II. Three days after the Pearl Harbor attack the Japanese cabinet formally named the new and larger conflict the Great East Asia War, linking the ongoing conflict with China – the Sino-Japan Incident – with the newer one with the Americans, British and Dutch. It proclaimed the new conflict with the explanation that it involved Asian nations achieving their independence from the Western powers in a Greater East Asia Co-Prosperity Sphere, a rationale advanced by many Japanese nationalists even today. The American occupation banned both terms, and after the Occupation the more neutral term took its place. Also known as the Fifteen Year War, tracing its origin to the Mukden Incident of 1931.

Pacquiao, Manny (1978-) A world-class welterweight boxer and probably the most famous Filipino in the world, known throughout his country by the nickname "Pacman". He holds ten world titles and was named "Boxer of the Decade" by the Boxing Writers' Association of America. He is so popular in his own country that his face graces a postage stamp. In 2010 he easily defeated a scion of a long-established political clan to win a seat in the Philippine Congress. Next stop, **Malacanang Palace**? There have been stranger occupants.

Pak Se Ri [pahk-say-ree] (1977-) A popular South Korean female golfer who became, at 20, the youngest golfer to win the US Women's Open (the playoff took 20 holes to finish, making it also the longest Women's Open on record). She went on to set other records and in 2007 was inducted as the youngest living member of the World Golf Hall of Fame. Her popularity boosted revenues for the Ladies Professional Golf Association from the sale of television rights in Korea and helped encourage other Korean golfers, men and women, to play on the international circuit.

Pali A "dead" language native to the subcontinent similar to **Sanskrit**, which is the liturgical language of Theravada Buddhism. It is studied throughout Southeast Asia to help readers gain access to early Buddhist scriptures.

Pal, Radhabinod (1886-1967) An Indian judge who served on the 11-member International Military Tribunal for the Far East, better known as the Tokyo Trials. He was the only judge to issue a blanket verdict of not guilty on all 25 **"Class A"** war criminals and thus is a hero to Japanese nationalists. Pal essentially parroted the Japanese rationale for going to war as being motivated by self-defense and a desire to liberate Asia from European colonialism. Pal considered Japan's move into China as aggression but no different from what Europeans and Americans had done. His 1,235-page dissent was suppressed by the Occupation and became public only after a peace treaty was signed in 1952. He is remembered by several memorials in Japan, including one at the museum attached to the Yasukuni Shrine where the spirits of 14 Class A defendants are enshrined. (See **Yasukan Museum**)

Pancasila The official philosophy of Indonesia, conceived in 1945 by the country's founder Sukarno and embodied in the preamble of the constitution. The word comes from two SANSKRIT words meaning five (*panca*) and principles (*sila*). The five principles are belief in one God, justice and civilization, unity of the nation, democracy and social justice. As a philosophy, *Pancasila* is not much more than a collection of platitudes, but they are useful platitudes. When Indonesia gained independence in 1949, the founders insisted on a culturally neutral identity rather than defining Indonesia by any one religion as in an Islamic state. In this way the practitioners of minority religions are on an official equal plane with the majority Muslims, not second-class, barely tolerated citizens as in other Muslim-majority countries. Over the years, some Muslims have tried to turn Indonesia into an official Islamic state but without success.

Panda More specifically the Giant Panda, it is probably the most instantly recognizable symbol of China, now used as a kind of ambassador of goodwill. Beijing loans out the cuddly-looking bears, usually in pairs, to countries with which it wants to cultivate goodwill. As of 2012, Beijing had loaned pandas to zoos in nine countries: Japan, South Korea, Thailand, Austria, Spain, Australia, the United Kingdom (Scotland) and France. Pandas feed on bamboo, and all zoos that receive pandas from China have to find their own supply. At the National Zoo in Washington, each panda eats 23 kg a day.

Panglong Agreement An accord reached in the small Shan town of Panglong in 1947 setting out the principle of a federal state. It was based on three main planks: decentralization within a federal union of Burma, formal recognition of the ethnic fiefdoms in the hills and the right to secession after a number of years. The pact was negotiated by Burmese independence hero Aung San (father of Aung San Suu Kyi) who was assassinated only a few months later. The agreement was ignored in the newly independent Burma, whose leaders preferred a more unitary state which led to the endless rebellions that have dogged Myanmar for decades. Yet the agreement still resonates and is seen as one possible basis for an overall settlement. The date of the agreement, February 12, is still marked as "Union Day" in Myanmar. There is a pillar in Panglong that celebrates the agreement but has been mostly ignored by recent governments.

pantun MALAY A form of Malay poetry utilizing short, four-line verses. Originally in Arabic, it is now written in the Malay language. Its strict construction is reminiscent of the Japanese *haiku*.

Park Tae-joon (1927-2011) South Korean businessman who founded one of the world's largest steel companies and thus played an important role in his country's rise from a poor agrarian state to an industrial powerhouse. Korea's strong-man president, Park Chung-hee, hand-picked Park (a former army comrade but not related) to jump-start Korea's steel industry, directing state funds, including $500 million in Japanese reparations, to finance the company. It was part of a successful industrial policy of selecting critical industries and directing state funds to them, creating what came to be known as *chaebol.* Park Tae-joon selected the east-coast seaport of Pohang to build its first complex of fully integrated steel mills. (The company was originally named Pohang Iron and Steel, now Posco). Park entered politics and served as prime minister under President Kim Dae-jung.

Pattani Insurgency A festering rebellion in Thailand's three southern-most provinces, Narathiwat, Pattani and Yala, that has taken the lives of about 5,000 people since it flared up anew in 2004. The three provinces were annexed to Thailand in 1909 but have relatively little in common with Thais. They are Muslim, Thais are Buddhists. They even speak a different language. Though somewhat inchoate, the insurgency is mainly an independence movement aimed at reviving a Pattani Sultanate. International influence seems weak, compared with jihadist attacks on western tourist watering holes such as Bali. There haven't been any attacks on Phuket, even though it is fairly close. The insurgents seem to particularly target teachers, claiming they indoctrinate children to assimilate with Thailand. By rights, the provinces probably belong in neighboring Malaysia, but that country makes no such claim and the insurgents don't seem to want to unite with Malaysia.

Pearl River Piano China is more than just an assembler of iPads and television sets. It also has a thriving industry making musical instruments, particularly pianos, violins and guitars. One of the most important is Pearl River Piano. It has been steadily increasing its reputation and sales since 1985 when it made its international debut. In 1999 it purchased one of Europe's oldest brands, Ritmüller, to help it enter the European market. Since 2002 Pearl River has been the world's largest maker of pianos with an approximate 20 per cent market share. It still lags the world's top brands, Steinway of the US and Blüthner of Germany, in quality. Guangzhou is the center for making musical instruments in China.

Pepero The brand name for a candy stick dipped in chocolate and made by the Lotte Confectionery Company. It is similar to Pocky, a Japanese chocolate candy snack devised in the 1960s. This candy gave rise to Pepero Day, which is South Korea's version of Valentine's Day. That day is now November 11, supposedly because the numerals 11.11 resemble four sticks of Pepero (Nov. 11, 2011 was a specially propitious date – 11.11.11 – and requests for Caesarean section deliveries surged as expectant mothers wanted their child to be born on the auspicious day). Convenience stores pile up boxes of Pepero as the great day nears. Lotte denies trying to contrive a holiday to sell candy, but nevertheless gets nearly half of its Pepero sales in November. There is no equivalent Pocky Day in Japan, which has its own peculiar Valentine's Day traditions.

Petanque FRENCH Petanque is a variation on bowls in which players stand in a circle and throw a metal ball towards a small wooden ball. It is mainly a French game but it is played in many parts of Southeast Asia, including Laos and Vietnam, because of past French influence. The 2007 World Petanque Championship was held in Pattaya, Thailand. It is played in the Asian Games.

Peranakan A term for overseas ethnic Chinese living in Southeast Asia, also known as the Straits Chinese. They trace their ancestry to Chinese traders who began visiting what is now Malaysia, Indonesia and Singapore in the late 15th century. In the 19th century the Peranakan were given a distinct identity by the Dutch and British colonial rulers. They often learned Dutch or English and played a role as intermediaries. Their life was described in a popular Singaporean television series, *The Little Nyonya,* which aired in 2008 and became one of the most popular Singaporean television programs. (*Nyonya* is the word for a female Peranakan). It covered 70 years in the life of an extended Peranakan family living in Malacca. The series was popular outside of Singapore and was the first Chinese-Singaporean television drama dubbed into the Malay language.

Philippine Independent Church A break-off sect of the Roman Catholic church that severed ties with the Vatican soon after the end of the Spanish era, partly because the Pope of that time supported the Spaniards in 1898. It is also known as the Aglipaysan Church after its first supreme bishop, Gregario Aglipay. Since 1960 it has affiliated with the Episcopal Church. It is said to be the second largest faith in the Philippines with about six million members, mostly concentrated in northern Luzon. It is rumored that former President Ferdinand Marcos, who hails from that region, was baptized into the sect.

Philippine languages The archipelago has between 120 and 170 languages and dialects, of which 20 are spoken by more than one million people. The most popular languages are Tagalog, spoken in metro Manila and environs, Cebuano, the language of the Visayas and Mindanao, and Illocano, spoken throughout the northern half of Luzon. Government policy is to turn Tagalog into a national language called Filipino, but many other languages persist. Any country with such diverse languages needs a *lingua franc*a, and that role is played by English, which is taught throughout most schools, making Filipinos virtually native speakers. The humblest Filipino domestic helper in Hong Kong is probably trilingual, speaking Filipino, English and her native language, unless she happens to come from Manila where Filipino is the native tongue.

Phuket World-famous international resort in southern Thailand. Both a city and province. Most tourists, about four million of them a year, head for Patong or several of the other beaches for which the province is famous. But before the tourists arrived, Phuket was mainly a tin-mining town, populated by Hokkien Chinese from Fujian province. Many followed the tin route from Penang to Phuket. They brought with them, from Penang's Georgetown, the colonial Sino-Portuguese architecture which is a fine blend of Chinese shophouses and European mansions. The old town still boasts many fine examples. Phuket hosts its own distinct annual Vegetarian Festival, or *Ngan Kin Jeh*, when Phuket town becomes a sea of yellow and white – the yellow color is used on banners placed in front of restaurants that only sell vegetarian food.

pinisi INDONESIAN A beautiful Indonesian vessel based on a traditional design which dates back more than 150 years. They were originally designed and built by the **Bugis**, a seafaring people originating from the island of Sulawesi, and used to carry cargoes between the many islands of the archipelago. In recent years they have been adapted to the yacht-based tourism industry, offering cultural or diving trips to exotic locations such as the Komodo archipelago. The name originally referred to the rig and sail configuration, usually consisting of seven to eight sails with three foresails set on the main bowsprint. (See **junk**)

Ping-pong diplomacy General term for events surrounding the 1971 World Table Tennis Championship held in Nagoya, Japan. A Chinese ping-pong team participated in the tournament, thus becoming the first Chinese sports team to compete outside of China since the beginning of the Cultural Revolution. That led to informal contacts with American players. Impulsively Mao Zedong ordered the government to invite the American team to China and on April 10, 1971, nine American players crossed into China via Hong Kong to play in the Great Hall of the People, witnessed by no less than Zhou Enlai. It is considered a kind of curtain-raiser for President Richard Nixon's visit to Beijing the following year.

Pinyin One of two systems, and now the most widely used, for rendering Chinese characters into the Roman alphabet. It has largely replaced the old **Wade-Giles** system of Romanization which was standard for much of the 20th century and which is still found in many books on China published in the West. Thus it is Deng Xiaoping in Pinyin and Teng Hsiao-ping in Wade-Giles; similarly Mao Zedong was Mao Tse-tung in Wade-Giles. Pinyin was officially adopted in 1958 and is now standard throughout the Chinese world, except on Taiwan, where people still spell names in the Wade-Giles system. Thus its first democratically elected president was Lee Teng-hui in Taipei and Li Donghui in Beijing.

Plain of Jars An area of central Laos (in Xieng Khouang province) that is covered with hundreds of large earthenware jars whose function has been lost in history – although they are thought to be associated with prehistoric burial practices. It is a sort of Asian equivalent to the megaliths on Easter Island. They were first investigated scientifically in the 1930s by French archaeologists. The Vietnam War delayed further investigations, which are still hampered by the presence of large numbers of unexploded bombs left over from the Secret War waged against the communist Pathet Lao, who now rule Laos.

Plaza Accord An agreement reached in 1984 by what was then the Group of 5 – Britain, France, Japan, West Germany and the United States – to bring down the value of the yen, which at that time was trading at about 250 yen to the dollar, a great boon to Japanese exporters and a source of worry for Americans and others concerned about expanding trade deficits. By the end of 1984 the yen was down to 200, by 1987 it was about 120 and by 2012 about 80. The accord helped to ignite the Bubble Economy, which sent stock and real estate prices into the stratosphere (*baburu keizai*). It is so named because the finance ministers met in the Plaza Hotel in New York. (See *endaka*)

poco-poco dance A line dance popular throughout Southeast Asia. The origin is unclear but is thought to have originated in Indonesia some 20 years ago to accompany a song by the same name. It is also a Jamaican word that relates to a wild dance under the possession of spirits. In Malaysia, where many people practice the dance as a form of fitness or recreation, Muslim leaders seek to ban it, saying that its origin reflects Christian rituals and is un-Islamic.

Polo Not the game played on horses, but the code word for Henry Kissinger's two secret trips to China in 1971 (Polo I and Polo II) to lay the groundwork for President Richard Nixon's landmark trip to Beijing the following year. Presumably the name was taken from that earlier adventurer, Marco Polo. (See **Shanghai Communiqué**)

pomelo A round, green fruit about the size of a cantaloupe grown in Thailand and other parts of Southeast Asia. It is often seen piled to overflowing on carts, looking like so many green cannonballs. The meat is pulpy like a grapefruit, but with a sweeter and more pungent taste.

Port Arthur Massacre A small tourist town in Tasmania, Port Arthur was the site of the biggest mass murder in Australia's history. One Martin Bryant walked into a restaurant on April 28, 1996, finished his meal and then pulled out an AR15 assault rifle and began shooting. In all, he killed 35 and wounded two before surrendering. Unusually for such cases, he survived to tell his story – or sort of, as he never actually confessed, and there are conspiracy theorists who still maintain he was a patsy for other shooters. He was judged legally sane, convicted of 35 counts of murder and sentenced to life in prison without possibility of parole, Australia's stiffest sentence. The government's response was swift. It strong-armed states and territories into enacting uniform gun control laws, even threatening to cut off federal funding if they did not comply. The upshot: mandatory gun licensing and an almost complete ban on all semi-automatic weapons. (See **Uiryeong Massacre**)

posting A system that regularizes the transfer of Japanese baseball stars to the American Major Leagues and compensates the Japanese clubs for the loss of their services. The system was created in the late 1990s after pitcher Hideo Nomo exploited a loophole in his contract to play for the Los Angeles Dodgers. This system works this way: The Japanese league has an auction to sell off the rights to one of its players. The winner "posts" the fee with the club. It then has 30 days to reach a separate agreement with the player. If they succeed, the losing Japanese club keeps the posting fee. If they can't reach an agreement, the fee is returned. In 2012 the Texas Rangers acquired star pitcher Yu Darvish of the Nippon Ham Fighters by first posting $51 million with the Fighters and then negotiating a six-year, $60 million contract with Darvish for a total payout of more than $100 million. Other major Japanese players acquired under the posting system are **Ichiro** and Daisuke Matsuzaka (see **Dice-K**).

Pramoj, Mom Rajawongse Kukrit (1911-1995) A kind of Thai Renaissance man: soldier, politician, journalist, novelist, aristocrat and patron of traditional Thai arts. He was related both to the Thai royal family and to the Bannags, an extended Chinese-Thai family that was the real power in 19th-century Siam. His brother Seni Pramoj served briefly as prime minister after the end of World War II; he was Thai ambassador to the US when the dictator Phibun declared war. Seni refused to deliver the declaration to the State Department and locked it away in his desk drawer for the duration.

Preah Vihear This magnificent ancient Hindu temple dating back to the 11th century and beyond has the misfortune to be located exactly on the border of Thailand and Cambodia and thus has become a pawn of nationalist extremists on both sides, but especially in Thailand. The Thai army occupied the temple site and surrounding territory in the early 1950s but withdrew after the World Court determined in 1962 that the temple was in Cambodia. Many nationalists in Thailand never accepted this decision, but no serious challenge was made until in 2008 when Phnom Penh successfully secured its designation as a World Heritage site.

At the same time it became an issue in the "**yellow shirt** versus red shirt" political turmoil that engulfed Thailand, with the red shirts accusing the government of not upholding Thai sovereignty over the temple. This led to short but sometimes deadly armed clashes between the Thai and Cambodian armies. The Cambodian people seemed to rally behind their government in support of its strong stance against the historical enemy.

Premji, Azim (1945-) Indian entrepreneur who built Wipro, famous for offshore services, from the small cooking oil company he inherited at age 21 into a global technical-services giant. In doing so, he made himself one of India's wealthiest businessmen. Premji is the vanguard of a growing number of philanthropists among India's newly rich, making him sort of the Bill Gates of India. In late 2010 he founded a rural education foundation with an initial gift of the equivalent of $1.9 billion to help train teachers for 2.5 million Indian schoolchildren and allow the opening of 1,300 free schools across the country. Several other among India's rich Silicon Valley entrepreneurs, such as Shiv Nadar, the founder of the technology company HCL, are also giving much of their fortunes to good works.

princelings A term applied to the sons of prominent Chinese Communist Party cadres but more specifically to the children of revolutionaries who played a major role in the communist victory in 1949. Among the most important princelings are **Xi Jinping**, son of politburo member Xi Zhongxun, who succeeded Hu Jintao as president and party leader. Another was Bo Xilai, son of Bo Yibo, the former party leader of Chongqing. The sons of Hu and Premier Wen Jiabao have pursued successful careers in business, but are not strictly speaking princelings as their fathers were not revolutionary leaders. Being a princeling is not always an advantage in that it can stir jealousy and accusations of nepotism. Deng Pufang, the son of Deng Xiaoping, never got higher than an alternate member of the Central Committee, much less the all-powerful Politburo. The Chinese have another new phrase, *fu er dai*, to describe the sons and daughters of ordinary rich people, translated as "second rich generation" or simply "rich kids." Some *fu er dai* live dissolute lives of conspicuous consumption; others labor faithfully to maintain and expand the family enterprises that made them rich in the first place.

princely states During the British Raj, India consisted of large territories ruled directly by Britain and dozens of nominally independent states and statelets governed by maharajas, known as the princely states. Most were tiny, but a few, such as Kashmir and Hyderabad, were fairly large and powerful. At the time of independence their rulers were ostensibly given the choice to join the new Indian Union or remain independent. Hyderabad opted to remain independent, but in 1948 the new Indian government sent in troops and forcefully annexed the country. The former princely state was dismembered, with parts given to other states. Kashmir being majority Muslim would have opted to join Pakistan (Kashmir is the K in the country's name), except that its ruler, Maharaja Hari Singh, a Hindu, chose to join India. That has been the root of the conflict that lives to this day (see **Line of Control**).

Prius Name of the world's first mass-produced hybrid car, built by Toyota Motor Corp at its Toyota City factory. The vehicle was introduced at the 1995 Tokyo Motor Show and sold commercially beginning in 1997, initially in Japan, and later in more than 70 countries. As of 2010, Toyota had sold about two million Prius cars. The term Prius comes from LATIN for "before", apparently meaning that Toyota is in the vanguard of hybrid cars. In 2004 Toyota conducted an online contest to pick the plural for Prius. More than 18 million people voted and the winner, with about 25 per cent of the total, was Prii. Other choices: Priuses, Preien, Priunas. (See **One Lakh Car**)

Proton Saga Malaysia's national car project and running sore for three decades. Since it was initiated under former Prime Minister Mahathir Mohammad in 1985, it has undergone endless troubles and several near-death experiences before being resuscitated by the government. It never achieved the economies of scale needed to flourish, despite high tariffs on imports. The original design was based on the Mitsubishi Lancer, and for a while the Japanese company owned a stake in Proton, giving rise to the slogan "Japanese engineering and Malaysian style". It has undergone several permutations over the years. The project was part of Mahathir's vision to turn Malaysia into an industrial powerhouse, instead of being just a plantation for rubber trees and palm oil.

Psy See **Gangnam Style**

Pueblo Incident The *USS Pueblo* was a navy intelligence surveillance ship that was captured on January 23, 1968, by North Korean ships and aircraft off the coast near Wonsan (in international waters, Washington has always maintained). The 82 surviving members of the crew (one was killed) were taken from the ship and held captive for 11 months, then released after Washington "apologized" for the intrusion, an apology it repudiated just as soon as the last captive set foot in South Korea. The ship was kept in Wonsan harbor until 1999 when it was towed around the Korean peninsula and ended up as a floating museum in Pyongyang. Washington officially considers the *Pueblo* a captive. The Pueblo Incident came at a dark time in the Cold War, just two days after North Korean commandos attempted to assassinate South Korean President Park Chung-hee at the Blue House and two weeks before the massive Tet Offensive in Vietnam.

Pudong Literally the east bank of the Huangpu River in Shanghai. As recently as 25 years ago, this was mostly farmland with access only by ferries. Since 1990 it has blossomed into a financial hub. It is the location of the Shanghai Stock Exchange, one of two in the country (the other is in Shenzhen), and Shanghai's new international airport. The remarkable modern skyline, punctuated by such amazing buildings such as the Oriental Pearl Tower, makes for a dramatic contrast with the art deco style of 1930s buildings on the opposite site of the river. (See **bund**)

Pu'er A large-leafed tea grown in China's Yunnan province, famous for its aromatic flavor and medicinal properties such as lowering cholesterol and curing hangovers. It is as old as the Tang Dynasty, when it was popular with noblemen. The name derives from the market town of Pu-er where it was originally processed and sold. It is said that the tea's unique taste was developed because it took weeks to transport the tea leaves from the farms over mountains to the processing centers. The method of making Pu'er tea is said to be a secret, closely guarded for centuries. It requires ten years to mature and gets better with age. Pu'er tea was often treated as a kind of money and was the object of a famous speculative bubble in the early 2000s, as thousands of farmers and other ordinary Chinese poured their savings into the bricks of compressed tea leaves. By the market's peak, the tea sold for as much as $150 a pound before the bubble burst and investors lost their money in what became known as the Pu'er Tea Debacle of Menghai County.

puputan BALINESE If you happen to be near the governor's mansion in Denpasar, you might notice a monument with three Balinese soldiers brandishing their spears. It commemorates a famous *puputan* or "fight to the death" against Dutch invaders in 1906. The defending Balinese and their kin made suicidal charges brandishing swords and spears against Dutch bullets, an Asian example of pitting European modern weapons against the swords and spears of indigenous populations. About 1,000 Balinese died in the uneven battle. It is not forgotten in Bali, which in 2006 marked the 100th anniversary of the massacre with appropriate ceremony.

Putonghua Chinese "common speech" or what is known to the West as MANDARIN. It is basically the native language of Beijing and other parts of northern China and is the country's official language. But hundreds of millions of Chinese people grow up speaking other languages which the Chinese call *fangyan*, or "dialects'. This is a politically charged word, as it implies that these other languages are subordinate to Putonghua, even though most linguists would say they are separate languages, as different from each other as Italian is to French. Probably the most widely spoken *fangyan* are Cantonese, used in the south, and Shanghainese. There are also the languages of minority groups, such as Korean, Tibetan and Mongolian. While Chinese may not always understand each other through the spoken word, the written word is common to all Chinese languages.

Puyi or Pu-Yi (1906-1967) The last ruler of the Qing dynasty and a tragic figure in Chinese history. He was named emperor in 1908 when only two years old, just before the death of the "dowager empress" Cixi. He in turn abdicated in 1912 following the **Xinhai Revolution** that established republican China. In 1934 the Japanese installed Puyi as the "emperor" of its puppet state in northeast China called Manchukuo. In 1945 the Russians caught him trying to flee to Japan and held him captive for several years until, with the success of the communist side in the Civil War, they turned him over to do with as they liked. After a decade in "re-education" camps, Puyi was allowed to live modestly and quietly in Beijing. When the Cultural Revolution broke out, Puyi drew the unwanted attention of Red Guards anxious to eliminate any trace of traditional China. But he died before they could do him serious harm. Puyi was the subject of a lavish Hollywood movie titled *The Last Emperor* in 1987 starring John Lone. The Chinese produced their own version with the same name about that time too.

Puyo (Buyeo) Small, nondescript market town south of Seoul which was once the capital of the Baekje Kingdom, one of three ancient Korean kingdoms. It was to Korea what Ayutthaya was to Thailand, except that it was sacked by a native and Chinese army in 660 AD, more than a thousand years before the Siamese capital fell in 1767 to the Burmese. As with the Siamese capital, the royal palace was demolished. The town today has far fewer monuments and ruins than its Thai counterpart. Perhaps the most famous is Nakhwa-an, a rocky cliff rising 40 meters above the Baengma River. Here, according to legend, was the site of one of history's largest mass suicides when some 3,000 palace maids and royal female retainers leaped to their deaths rather than surrender to the victorious Shilla-Tang Dynasty army. Nakhwa-an means "rock of the falling flowers," an allusion to how the maids' fluttering robes looked like flower petals falling from a tree. A memorial pavilion was erected atop the cliff in 1929. The Baekje Kingdom was sophisticated. Emissaries from Puyo introduced Buddhism to Japan and helped build some of its earliest and most famous temples.

Q

Qantas The flag carrier of Australia, known throughout Asia as one of the world's premier airlines. Founded in 1920, it is also the oldest continuously flying airline in the world. The name comes from the initials of its original name: Queensland and Northern Territory Aerial Services. That denotes that fact that it was born in the tiny outback town of **Winton**, Queensland (population about 1,000) and originally served the nearly empty northeast quadrant of Australia. It was instrumental in founding the Royal Flying Doctors Service created to provide medical service to remote towns and ranches. It has been known by its current name since 1934.

qigong [chee-gung] MANDARIN term for a broad range of slow, stylized body movements, rhythmic breathing and mental exercises, which has deep roots in Chinese culture. It is common in China and Hong Kong (and even in Japan) to see large groups of middle-aged men and women performing *qigong* or *tai chi* exercises in public parks. *Tai chi* is similar to *qigong* but closer to their common martial arts roots in that practitioners sometimes incorporate weapons (such as wooden swords) into their exercise routines. Some elements, such as *qi* or bodily energy, figure in Traditional Chinese Medicine (TCM) which defines good health as harmonious bodily function and disease as disharmony, coupled with a broad range of medical practices and herbal medicines developed over centuries. TCM has some grudging recognition in the West as an alternative form of medicine. (See **Falungong**)

qipao [chee-pao] MANDARIN for a one-piece, full-length Chinese women's garment with a high collar and long slits on either side. It traces its origin back to the beginning of the Qing (Manchu) dynasty in the 17th century, but the present style is modeled after dresses worn by socialites and upper-class women in 1920s Shanghai. Not in good favor with the newly victorious communists, the *qipao* migrated to Hong Kong, where it is more popularly known from CANTONESE as the ***cheongsam***. It is now worn mostly at weddings and other formal occasions or by hotel workers and airline attendants. It is also seen commonly in retro advertising posters from the 1930s.

Qufu A middle-sized city in China's Shandong province that is famous as the birthplace and home of Confucius (Kong Fu-zu). It was also capital of the ancient Kingdom of Lu. The town abounds in temples, not all of them directly connected with the Master. Three places are directly associated: the Temple of Confucius, the Confucius Cemetery and the Kong Family Mansion. All have been officially designated as World Heritage Sites since 1994. Actual descendants of Confucius are said to live in the mansion. Hundreds of artifacts associated with the sage were destroyed by Red Guards during the Cultural Revolution, which had declared Confucius an enemy of modernity. A part of the old town is still surrounded by walls originally erected during the Ming Dynasty.

Quoc ngu VIETNAMESE term for their Romanized script. The script was introduced by early Christian missionaries who made Vietnam a major Roman Catholic nation in Asia. This process culminated in 1651 in the publication (by a Jesuit priest) of a dictionary in Latin, Portuguese and Vietnamese, using the *Quoc ngu* script. Until that time, Vietnam had used only Chinese characters in their writing. The introduction of *Quoc ngu* eased the spread of education while serving the cause of Catholicism by facilitating the dissemination of easier-to-read holy books and catechisms.

Quotations from Chairman Mao See ***Hongbaoshu***

R

Raffles, Sir Stamford (1781-1826) British civil servant and empire builder of the early 19th century. Raffles, of course, is most famous as the founder of Singapore, but he also made significant contributions to understanding the history of Indonesia while serving as governor of Java. Raffles believed that Java was the site of many impressive civilizations, especially in the Hindu-Buddhist period. He learned Malay and in 1817 published *The History of Java*. He is credited with rediscovering the magnificent Borobudur monument and the capital of the Majapahit empire. (See **Trowlan**). Many objects he collected are in the Raffles Collection of the British Museum.

Rashomon 1950 Japanese film by director **Akira Kurosawa**. Its enduring appeal comes from Kurosawa's superb treatment of an ancient and universal theme: What is truth? A samurai and his bride come upon a bandit in a forest grove, where the traveler dies and the wife is ravished. The only witness is a woodcutter. The story turns on the magistrate's efforts to extract the facts from completely different yet equally plausible perceptions of what occurred.

Rason A port city in the extreme northeast corner of North Korea which the government wants to turn into a genuine special economic zone. Actually, Rason was first designated a special economic zone in 1991 (when Rason was two separate cities, Rajin and Songbon). The zone was supposedly modeled after the successful Chinese zones, but for two decades it was generally ignored. It was located about as far away from Pyongyang as could be and still be inside the country, as if the Kims were afraid that their Stalinist rule might be contaminated by any hint

of foreign investment. For years the only foreign enterprise it attracted was what must be the world's most forlorn casino, built by a Hong Kong businessman. Infrastructure, such as roads, electricity, and Internet connections, are said to be minimal. However, there are signs that Pyongyang wants to breathe life into the zone leveraged by new investor interest from China. Once, only a gravel road linked Rason with China; it has been paved, and rail connections with Russia expanded. Simply from its location, the zone could be a success, being close to both China and Russia. The port at Rason offers China's landlocked Jilin province closer access to the sea. Also, one of the world's largest iron ore mines is nearby at Masan.

reformasi MALAY A political movement in Malaysia associated with former deputy prime minister Anwar Ibrahim. It was formed shortly after Anwar was removed from his post of deputy premier, and scored its greatest success in the 2008 general election when Anwar's new People's Justice Party won 31 seats in parliament, the best opposition showing since independence in 1957. Usually it is in a loose alliance with the two other opposition parties, the Islamist Parti Islam si Malaysia and the mainly ethnic Chinese-backed Democratic Action Party. Anwar has been in and out of court on sodomy charges for more than a decade. (See **UMNO)**

renminbi MANDARIN for people's money, the official currency of China, also known as *yuan*. Renminbi is basically the currency, *yuan* are the units; analogous to pounds (*yuan*) and Sterling (*renminbi*). For most of its history, the *renminbi* has been pegged to the US dollar, but in 1995, under severe international pressure, especially from Washington, it was allowed to float within a very narrow range. It is occasionally raised when needed to pacify trading partners. Washington still maintains that the currency is kept artificially low in relation to the dollar (*meiyuan* in MANDARIN) to accommodate export industries, and the subject is high on the agenda of virtually every high-level meeting between China and the US. Hong Kong and Macau have their own currencies, and the *renminbi*, though widely used in the two territories, is not actually legal tender. (See **Hong Kong dollar peg**)

Renren China's most important social-networking company (the word means "everyone" in MANDARIN). China is the world's largest Internet market, and Renren reportedly had some 125 million users in 2011. In its initial public offering on the New York Stock Exchange in May 2011 the company raised more than $700 million and saw its stock rise 30 per cent in the first day of trading. That valued the company at more than $7 billion, even though it had yet to make a profit. Along with other Internet companies in China, investors run the risk that the site might be shut down or heavily censored by the government.

"responsible stakeholder" An American term to describe what it views as the proper role for a rising China to take in world affairs, abiding by accepted international norms and shouldering additional responsibilities commensurate with its increasing capabilities. It was first enunciated by former Deputy Secretary of State Robert Zoellick in 2005. In effect, it was an invitation for China to become a privileged member and shaper of the international order.

rice It is often said that Eskimos have a dozen words for snow. Asians have numerous ways of describing their staple, rice. In Indonesia, rice growing in the field is *padi*; threshed rice is *beras*, and cooked rice is *nasi* (as in **goreng**).There are an estimated 120,000 varieties of rice. Nowadays, farmers are likely to plant one of the modern varieties for their high yields. Rice seeds are first planted in nurseries and after having a month to mature are transplanted to paddy fields and planted, clump by clump, in the mud. The key to high yields is a constant flow of water. In traditional cultures, elaborate ceremonies are taken to appease the rice spirits to ensure bountiful rainfall. In Japan the emperor himself plants a token rice field, emphasizing the importance of a good crop. Once the rice is safely stored or sold can the harvest festivals begin.

ring roads Beijing is defined by the ring roads that encircle the city in ever widening concentric circles, ranging from the Second Ring Road to the Sixth at about one-mile intervals. (There is no First Ring Road, for reasons lost in the mists of time.) The Second Ring Road generally follows the pre-revolutionary path of the walls that once enclosed Beijing. The Communists, in their zeal to overturn the old order, demolished the city walls in the 1950s and 1960s and built a road. In a way, the Second Ring Road defines central Beijing much as the **Yamanote** train loop line defines downtown Tokyo.

Rohingyas A Muslim minority people living in Rakhine State (also known as Arakan) in northern Myanmar, bordering Bangladesh. They are said to be similar to Bengalis as well as other dark-skinned peoples of South Asia. They were converted to Islam by Arab traders and form the only significant Muslim population in predominantly Buddhist Myanmar. They are discriminated partly on account of their religion and their dark skin (called *kula* – a **Pali** word meaning black.) Though considered one of Myanmar's indigenous peoples at independence, the Rohingyas were stripped of citizenship in 1982. They are also subject to other discrimination, such as travel restrictions and limits on education. The Rohingya population in Myanmar is estimated at about 750,000. Many thousands more live as refugees in Bangladesh or elsewhere in South Asia and in the Middle East.

Rose of Sharon Blooms Again The title of a pan-Korean, ultra-nationalist thriller by Kim Jin-myung, published in 1993. In it a South Korean scientist collaborates secretly with North Korea to build an atomic bomb, which is dropped on Tokyo. It was very popular in Korea; not so popular in Japan. The book was published before North Korea exploded the first of two atom bomb tests. The Rose of Sharon is the national flower of South Korea. Despite its name, it is a hibiscus.

Royal Selangor Pewter The world's most famous maker of pewter objects and one of the oldest and best-known Malaysian business enterprises, founded in 1885. The "Royal" in its name was not bestowed by the British monarch, even though Malaysia was once a British possession. It was given by the Sultan of Selangor. Its main pewter factory in Kuala Lumpur is a tourist attraction. Pewter is mostly tin with a smidgeon of copper or other alloys. It has been cast since the end of the Bronze Age.

Rugby Sevens A variant of rugby played with only seven players instead of the usual 15. It traces its ancestry to the late 19th century but really got its boost as a global sport in Hong Kong where the annual Rugby Sevens tournament is a major event – at least for expats. The tournament was cooked up in that bastion of British colonialism, the Hong Kong Club, in 1975. The sponsors wanted to host a major international rugby tournament, but realized if it were composed of the regulation number of players over 80-minute games the tournament would spread over two weeks or more. The Rugby Sevens is played in 15-minute intervals and thus everything can be packed into one festive weekend. Some anxiety surrounded the 1997 handover of Hong Kong to China, especially when two high-profile sponsors, Cathay Pacific and the Hongkong and Shanghai Banking Corp, both pillars of the British establishment, pulled out. However the Sevens easily weathered the handover and is firmly entrenched in Hong Kong's social psyche. Teams from New Zealand, Fiji and Australia dominate.

Ryugyong Hotel The Ryugyong Hotel in central Pyongyang must be one of the world's strangest buildings – and one of the ugliest. The 330-meter, 105-story white elephant towers over the nondescript Pyongyang skyline. Construction began in 1987, it is said, as a reaction to the Stamford Hotel in Singapore which was built by a South Korean company, though it is only 226 meters high. Work on the Ryugyong was halted in 1992, shortly after the Soviet Union collapsed and cut off aid, and it remained derelict for 16 years until in 2008 work resumed under an arrangement with the Egyptian conglomerate **Orascom**. However, it is the telecom subsidiary, not the construction arm, that is said to be guiding the work, raising suspicions, denied by Cairo, that it was necessary to win a contract to provide mobile phone service for North Korea. Some sources maintain that the hotel is not repairable because of past engineering mistakes and use of poor building materials. And if completed, who would occupy the 3,000+ rooms? Pyongyang is not exactly a tourist destination. If it is more for prestige, then the North is about to be overtaken by the construction of two even taller projects in South Korea. The Busan Lotte Tower will be 510 meters tall with 110 floors and the Lotte Super Tower in Seoul is 556 meters tall with 123 floors.

S

Sangokujin JAPANESE The literal meaning is something like third-world person. It was actually coined by American occupiers to describe the large numbers of Koreans and Taiwanese, from former Japanese colonies, living in Japan after the surrender. In those chaotic times, many turned to gangs and the black market to make ends meet, which in today's Japan gives the term a derogatory tone. Probably the only important person to regularly use the word *Sangokujin* is the controversial four-term former governor of Tokyo, Shintaro Ishihara. He also uses another obsolete and faintly derogatory word, *Shina*, for China. It was often used during Japan's occupation of parts of China during World War II. The current Japanese word for China is *Chugoku*, which means central country or middle kingdom. It is also the term for the far western tip of Honshu. The word now used for ethnic Koreans in Japan is **Zainichi**.

Sao Kay Sang (1928-1962?) The Shan States of Myanmar were made up of many small princely states, sort of like India, called *saopha*. Sao Kay Sang was the last of a long line of princes that ruled Hsipaw in the northern part of the country. What became of him is a mystery, as he disappeared in 1962, the year that General Ne Win seized power, creating a military dictatorship. He was arrested in his capital, Taunggyi, while visiting an ailing aunt, and was not seen again. It is presumed he died in captivity or possibly under torture by Ne Win's soldiers. (See **8888 Uprising**)

Saemaul Undong A rural self-help organization in South Korea created in 1971 by the late dictator Park Chung-hee to try to close the gap between the cities and impoverished countryside. *Saemaul Undong* (New

Community Movement) is one reason why most South Korean villages have electricity, clean running water, decent schools and other amenities. Although the movement has undoubtedly contributed to the betterment of rural Korea, some see it as a way for the central government and politicians to get their tentacles into the regions.

saiban-in JAPANESE for a relatively new system of lay judges. In a major reform of its judicial system, Japan in 2009 introduced the *saiban-in* system, in which ordinary people taken from the voter rolls are obliged to serve on judicial panels as lay judges, side-by-side with professional judges. Normally, the judicial panel is composed of six *saiban-in* judges and three professional judges. They can hear witnesses and evaluate evidence. They then vote on the guilt or innocence of the accused. At least one of the professional judges must agree with the lay judges for the verdict to stand. It is thus similar to, but also very different from, the common-law jury system. Ironically, Japan had a fully fledged jury system in the 1920s and 1930s, but it was abandoned during the war for manpower concerns (no women were allowed to serve on juries).

Sakamoto, Ryoma (1836-1867) Rebel samurai and one of the driving forces of the 19th-century Meiji Restoration. He remains to this day one of the most popular historical figures of that era. His life has been an inspiration for no fewer than seven television "samurai dramas", most recently NHK's *The Legend of Ryoma Sakamoto*. His life and ideas continue to inspire Japanese leaders who want to break out of Japan's apparent stagnating economy and political gridlock with fresh ideas. Rising Osaka mayor Toru Hashimoto likens his eight-point reform platform to Sakamoto's *Senchu Hassaku* (Eight Point Program composed aboard a ship). It encompassed revolutionary Restoration principles such as a national army and bureaucracy, an end to feudalism and a constitution. (See ***Ishin***)

sakura JAPANESE for cherry blossom, the national flower of Japan. It has been popular since ancient times, and featured in poetry and art. The first printed reference dates to 712. The custom of viewing cherry blossoms –

hanami – dates back at least to the Heian Period. Today Japanese typically lay out tarpaulins beneath cherry trees in parks, set up picnics, meet friends and consume a lot of alcohol. Every spring the nation patiently awaits the first pink buds to appear on bare branches. Cherry trees bloom at different times during the spring depending on location. Newspapers print charts of the "cherry blossom front", or *sakura zensen,* as it spreads northward from Okinawa. Some famous cherry trees have been living and blooming for hundreds of years. *Sakura* is also the name of probably the most instantly recognizable Japanese tune, especially when played with the plunk, plunk, plunk of the Japanese harp known as a *koto.*

Samdech CAMBODIAN for "great nobility". Cambodia's rulers' full names and titles all begin with Samdech, as in Samdech Akka Moha Padei Techno Prime Minister Hun Sen (The Noble and Supreme Great All-Powerful Commander in Chief Prime Minister Hun Sen.) He is so-called even though he was born into a peasant family and dropped out of school, yet he carries himself, and increasingly governs, in the style of Cambodia's past great kings. (See **Jayavarman II**)

sandwich class A term popular in Hong Kong to denote people in the middle class who feel squeezed – "sandwiched" – between the truly poor, who get public housing assistance, and the rich, who can easily afford Hong Kong's extraordinarily high property prices.

salaryman In JAPANESE, *sarariman.* The beneficiary of a system in Japan in which a large corporation looks out for an employee for his entire career in exchange for the employee's total loyalty over that period. Corporations reward this loyalty with other benefits such as dormitories for younger staff, help in arranging marriages and so on. Lifetime employment had its glory years in the days of rapid growth but never covered more than a portion of the male workforce, and never applied to women, who were expected to spend a couple years as "office ladies" (**OLs**), making tea and photocopying documents until they married and quit their jobs. The system began to break down in the **lost decades** of the late 20th and early 21st century. Japanese employers have been moving toward more use of temporary workers, who do not have guaranteed employment, to give them flexibility to weather the winds of globalization. They are called *freeters*, a word combining the word for freelance with the German word for worker (*arbeiter*). (See **lifetime employment**)

Samtow Sucharitkul (1954-) Thai composer, writer and all-around Renaissance man who has been working on what may be the longest integrated work in classical music in history. His compositions often reflect Thai history, sometimes turning a foreign scene into an Asian one. Hence the Egyptian setting for Aida becomes the ancient Thai kingdom of Ayutthaya. His latest work, *Jataka*, based on traditional stories, will eventually replace Wagner's *Der Ring des Nibelungen*, which takes 16 hours to stage, as the world's longest classical opera. Samtow is also a notable writer of science fiction and horror books including *Vampire Junction*, a cult classic.

sanlunche [san loon che] MANDARIN for three (*san*) wheeled vehicles. The term covers a whole family of conveyances. Some, especially in tourist-rich parts of Beijing and other cities, are the familiar pedal-powered rickshaws. There are three-wheeled motorcycles with an enclosed cab for the passenger and street-sweepers' vehicles with garbage bins mounted on the back. There are tricycles with lunches for day workers, toolboxes to repair bicycles and other *sanlunche*, but probably the most common are general delivery carts. (See *tuk tuk*)

San Ma Lo CANTONESE name for Macau's main cross avenue, officially Avenida de Almeida Ribeiro. The main street linking Macau's inner and outer harbors was constructed in 1913. Earlier efforts had been hampered by the presence of a big bazaar at the Inner Harbor and *feng shui* concerns. The street was named after an obscure Portuguese Minister for Colonies who signed off on the project and was soon forgotten. Everyone in Macau, Chinese and Portuguese alike, calls it *San Ma Lo*, which translates into something like "New Street" or "Street of Horses," presumably because it was straight enough to accommodate parades of mounted cavalry.

Santo Nino de Cebu The "Holy Child of Cebu" is a wooden statue to the Christ child and probably the oldest Christian icon in the Philippines, perhaps in all of East Asia. It was presented as a gift in 1521 by Ferdinand Magellan, during his famous world-circling voyage, to the local rulers whom he persuaded to convert to Christianity. The statue is only about 30 centimeters tall and enclosed in a velvet vestment and a gold crown. The statue is permanently housed under bullet-proof glass at the Basilica del Santo in Cebu. A feast of the Christ child is celebrated in January.

santris INDONESIAN for devout Muslims. In Indonesia, especially in Java, the word has come to refer to orthodox Muslims, as opposed to nominal Muslims who incorporate many native animist, Hindu or Buddhist beliefs into their religious practices. Nominal Muslims are known as *abangan*, and they vastly outnumber *santris* among the country's 90 per cent Muslim population. The word *pesantren*, meaning an Indonesian village religious school, comes from *santri*.

sari-sari store FILIPINO Small grocery store found on virtually every street corner in the Philippines. *Sari sari* means something like "odds and ends", which generally describes the merchandise for sale. It includes such day-to-day items as candy, mosquito coils, soft drinks, beer, cooking oil and some over-the-counter drugs among many other things. They are mom and pop enterprises, not franchises, and fulfill a need where more modern, international brand-name convenience stores are unavailable. (See **100 yen shops** and **combini**)

SARS Acronym for Severe Acute Respiratory Syndrome, a mysterious bronchial disease that gripped Hong Kong and China for several months in 2003. It is believed to have originated with an infected Chinese doctor from Guangdong who checked into a Kowloon hotel. Near-panic ensued after some 300 people came down with the illness in one Kowloon Bay apartment block. It threw Hong Kong into a frenzy of hygiene. Hotel occupancy plunged into single digits; the airport was deserted. Chinese authorities first denied the presence of the disease, then flip-flopped and went on a national crusade of public health. SARS burned itself out after a few months – nobody really knows why. Was it all that temperature-taking in Beijing, the culling of tens of thousands of civet cats in Shenzhen, a change in climate, or luck?

Sato The most common Japanese family name, followed by Suzuki, Takahashi, Tanaka and Watanabe. The striking fact about Japanese surnames is their sheer number, compared with China and Korea. There is no precise count but the consensus is that there are about 100,000 names or roughly one name per each 1,000 people. Chinese surnames are the most ancient in the world, going back 3,000 years. Even so, despite a population of 1.3 billion, China has only a few thousand surnames. Korea has only a few hundred, and the top five – Kim, Lee, Park, Choi and Jung – cover more than half of the population.

satyagraha SANSKRIT *Satya* means truth, and truth comes from *graha* or soul, thus the word means basically "soul power". It is a form of non-violent resistance to oppression associated with Mohandas Gandhi. One can date the birth of *satyagraha* very precisely to September 11, 1906, when Gandhi, then a proper British barrister in South Africa, organized a meeting to protest a new law requiring that "Asiatics" carry internal passports at all times. It shows that *satyagraha* was not exclusively a tactic to overcome colonial rule, nor was born in India. Prime Minister Manmohan Singh used the occasion of the 100th anniversary of *satyagraha* in 2006 to make a state visit to South Africa, where he visited sites associated with Gandhi's early years there. Ironically, he was on the receiving end several years later when an activist named Anna Hazare, assuming the mantle of Gandhi, undertook several fasts to protest endemic corruption in Indian politics. Fasting can be a tactic of *satyagraha* (Gandhi fasted on occasion), but it is only one of many tactics. A person performing soul power is known as a *Satyagrahi*.

sawatdee (**also** *sawaddi* **or** *sawasdee*) THAI greeting. The term is not ancient. It was coined in the 1930s and it came into use as a general greeting only during World War II. The nationalist dictator Phibulsongkram promoted its use as a part of a campaign to unify and modernize Thailand, which also saw the country's name changed from Siam. The word is derived from SANSKRIT *svasti* meaning well-being. It has the same root as swastika. (See **Siam**)

sayang! What a Filipino might say after he spills something or misses winning the lottery by just one number. In MALAY it has a different meaning related to love or longing. A type of love ballad borrowed from the Portuguese is called a *Dongdang Sayang*. In Macau's PATUA the word *saiang*, derived from Malay, means a kind of longing similar to the Portuguese *saudade*.

sayonara JAPANESE for goodbye or farewell. But it packs a lot more emotion than a simple goodbye. The implication is that the person is going away on a long journey and will be separated for a long period of time, perhaps forever. School children going their separate way for a day would more likely say *ja ahtode* – see you later. Title of James Michener's tragic love story between an American pilot and Japanese dancer.

"sea of fire" What North Korea, through the voice of the Korean Central News Agency, regularly threatens will be the fate of South Korea's capital Seoul or US military bases if they don't behave. When the threat was first issued against the capital in 1994 it caused deep fear and outrage among the city region's 10 million inhabitants, although now they are used to it. Although the threat is made frequently whenever Pyongyang is irritated about something, such as joint US-South Korean military exercises, it is not entirely empty. Seoul is close to the border with North Korea, and the mountains behind the boundary in North Korea are said to be stocked with long-range artillery within range of the city. The North also possesses missiles and possibly functioning nuclear warheads to place on them.

Senkaku Japanese name for a small chain of uninhabited and essentially useless islands off by themselves in the East China Sea. They are claimed by both Japan and China, which calls them the **Diaoyu**. Both sides have their own narrative to support their claims. Japan annexed them in the late 19th century, claiming that nobody else in the neighborhood seemed to want them. Chinese base their claims on the fact that fishermen from Fujian province and Taiwan regularly fished in the waters going back to ancient times. For a few years some Japanese actually lived on the islands, which are privately owned but are no longer inhabited. Occasionally, nationalists from either side land on the islands and plant flags or even set up a lighthouse to assert sovereignty. The Japanese coastguard regularly patrols the nearby waters. A major dispute flared in the summer of 2010 when Japanese authorities detained the skipper of a Chinese fishing boat which it said had rammed one of their cutters. Tokyo released the captain after Beijing made certain veiled threats to restrict exports of rare earths to Japanese industry.

senpai/sensei JAPANESE Two words that help describe relationships in Japan based in part on age or responsibilities. *Senpai* refers to someone older or of higher rank in some context, such as school or the workplace. More than just seniority, it implies a relationship with reciprocal obligations.

It is tacitly understood that the *senpai* looks after the well-being of their *kohai,* or junior. It is especially true if they belong to the same school or athletics team. *Sensei* is a term of respect that is usually translated as teacher but can apply to other professions such as doctors, dentists, religious leaders, lawyers or others with some authority or learning.

sento JAPANESE for public baths. Over the centuries, public baths have served as centers for community life, sort of like pubs in England or general stores in old New England, a place where neighbors came not just to get clean but to pass the time. The first *sento* in Edo opened in 1591, only a year after Ieyasu Tokugawa moved his capital there. Until recently it was considered obligatory to visit a *sento* on New Year for a ritual of purification. With the advent of private baths, *sento* are slowly dying in Japan, but aficionados work hard to keep them from dying off entirely. Meanwhile some *sento* owners strive to stay current by turning their establishments into health spas, complete with saunas, massage, karaoke and other techno-health instruments. In urban *sento*, the bath water is heated, and the buildings can be instantly recognized by the tell-tale chimney. Not to be confused with *onsen*, or hot springs using naturally heated water. *Onsen* are often located in mountain retreats.

seowon KOREAN Private academies that teach Confucian values. They trace their ancestry back hundreds of years to a time, before mass education, when they provided virtually the only kind of instruction for those wanting to pass exams necessary to enter the Korean mandarinate. They went into decline as Confucianism fell out of favor as a drag on modernization and source of other social ills. They are enjoying a modest comeback as a kind of reaction to the brutal Korean education system with its emphasis on rote memorization, foreign languages and mathematics. The *seowon* emphasize the Confucian values of harmony as well as more traditional activities such as how to address a parent and the tea ceremony.

sepak MALAY and **takraw** THAI A sport popular in Thailand and throughout Southeast Asia. The terms come from the Malay for "kick" and the Thai for "ball", hence *sepak takraw* means kickball. *Takraw* is similar to volleyball as it is played with a net, but it also simulates soccer in that a player (save for the server) cannot use his or her hands. The sport requires great agility, with players sometimes doing a full flip after spiking the ball. Origins of the sport go back centuries. It is played throughout Southeast Asia, although it is most popular in Thailand (the home of kick boxing), which hosts the annual championship. It is also played in the Asian Games, but so far has not attracted interest from Olympics organizers.

setsuden JAPANESE for conserving electricity, which became the buzzword of the year after the 2011 Great East Japan Earthquake and tsunami destroyed four nuclear power reactors at Fukushima and resulted in many more plant closures across Japan, sparking fears of rolling blackouts in the capital, Tokyo, and a plea to conserve electricity. The two kanji characters for *setsuden* were seen on notices everywhere explaining that this elevator or that escalator was out of service, this building had dimmed its lights or curtailed operating hours to save on electricity.

Shanghai Communique A joint statement of guiding principles issued in February, 1972, following the end of President Richard Nixon's historic trip to China. The general provisions have guided Sino-US relations ever since. The key provision: "The United States acknowledges that all Chinese on either side of the Taiwan Strait maintain there is but one China and that Taiwan is a part of China. The United States government does not challenge that position. It affirms its interest in a peaceful settlement of the Taiwan question by the Chinese themselves." Under the communiqué Washington promised to withdraw troops from Taiwan. Later, President Jimmy Carter broke off diplomatic relations with Taipei and established them with Beijing. The other important document guiding relations is the 1979 **Taiwan Relations Act**, which requires assurances that Taiwan can defend itself from a Chinese attack, although it does not specifically promise to come to its defense. (See **One China Policy**)

Shenzhou The name for a series of manned and unmanned spacecraft that are the workhorses of China's space program. The name is translated various ways, including "Divine Craft", and reportedly was personally selected by former President Jiang Zemin. The Shenzhou's design is based on the Russian Soyuz but is said to be larger. The first Shenzhou was launched in 1999, and the first Chinese craft to carry a man – Yang Liwei – into space was the Shenzhou-5 launched on October 15, 2003. Thus China became the third country in the world to have an independent spaceflight capability. Five more manned flights have taken place with crews of two and three astronauts. The latest in the series, Shenzhou-11, docked in 2016 with the Tiangong-2 space station. (See *taikongnaut*)

shengnu MANDARIN for "leftover women" who are 30 years old but still unmarried. This relatively new word, taken from *shengcai*, or leftover food, describes a phenomenon of successful women having a hard time finding husbands because men are reluctant to "marry up," that is, to link with women who are more successful than they are. The phenomenon is an old story in other prosperous parts of Asia. As far back as 1980 Singapore's prime minister Lee Kuan Yew was worrying about the falling birthrate, especially among the well educated, and the difficulty that highly educated women had in finding mates. Singapore being Singapore, the solution was the Social Development Unit, a government-run dating service. The birthrate is still falling.

shijin JAPANESE for "private person". How some Japanese public officials sign their name in the guest book of the **Yasukuni Shrine** in Tokyo can have international implications. Japanese prime ministers find it politic to pay their respects to Japan's war dead in August, the month that Japan's surrender ended the **Pacific War**. Chinese object to such visits because of the 1978 enshrinement of 14 Class A War criminals. So to appease the Chinese, Japanese premiers try to stress they are paying their respects as private individuals and not in their official capacity. Former premier Junichiro Koizumi's insistence on visiting the shrine each year during his tenure and signing as prime minister sent Sino-Japanese relations into a tailspin. Since then most Japanese leaders have avoided the shrine altogether. (See **Yasukan Museum**)

Shinjuku Station The world's biggest and busiest railroad station serves six railroad companies, a dozen subway lines with 14 major platforms and boasts more than 60 entrances. About 3 million commuters pass through Shinjuku station's automated ticket gates and stairways each day.

Shimantan dam break The world's deadliest dam break occurred in China's Henan province in 1975, drowning about 26,000 people. In all, some 170,000 people died from drowning or later from disease and malnutrition. The Shimantan reservoir dam was part of an extensive hydroelectric project. It was designed to handle a projected 1,000-year flood. Unfortunately, that year the rains equaled a 2,000-year flood.

Shin Kyuk-ho (1922-) Korean-Japanese businessman who founded the mammoth Lotte confectionery conglomerate in 1948 by making and selling chewing gum on the streets of Tokyo. It is difficult to describe Lotte as either a Korean or a Japanese corporation, as Shin (Japanese name Takeo Shigamitsu) divides his time equally between Japan and Korea. The name Lotte is neither Japanese nor Korean. It comes from the character of Charlotte in the great German novel *The Sorrows of Werther* which Shin admired. Lotte owns professional baseball teams in Japan (the Chiba Lotte Marines) and in Busan, South Korea.

sho ga nai JAPANESE World-weary expression usually translated as "it can't be helped".

shokku JAPANESE from English for shock! A phrase that has entered the language for any sudden political blow. The original *shokku* was the Nixon *shokku* of 1972, when he announced his planned trip to China to restore relations, informing the Japanese only minutes before the announcement. Soon after came another Nixon *shokku* when he delinked the dollar from gold. More blows came with the oil *shokku* of 1974 when OPEC cut oil production. Now used for almost any unwelcome news involving Japan.

shophouses Distinctive two- and three-story edifices, shophouses are the quintessential Southeast Asian building. Influenced by Chinese courtyard houses (see *siheyuan*), melded with Portuguese or other colonial architecture but unique to the region, shophouses were designed in the 19th century to accommodate businesses on the ground floor and living quarters upstairs. These buildings sprouted across Southeast Asia as Chinese traders took root in the *Nanyang*. They typically have a narrow frontage, sometimes as little as four meters wide, but are quite deep, extending all the way to the alleys between blocks. Singapore demolished many of its shophouses in the 1960s and 70s to make way for modern buildings. Since the 1990s, cities like Singapore and Penang have restored their shophouses, turning them into boutique hotels, hip clothing stores, art galleries and cafes. They are valued as private apartments too, and often sell for $2 to $3 million.

Shuangbai fengzhen MANDARIN, literally "Double Hundred Policy", but usually translated as the "Hundred Flowers Campaign". It was launched in 1956 by Mao Zedong with the poetic words "let a hundred flowers bloom, let a hundred schools of thought contend." It was ostensibly meant to encourage intellectuals to debate and criticize freely. It appears that Mao thought it would bring forth paeans of praise to the communist regime. Rather, it let loose an avalanche of opinions critical of the party and its doctrines, including the heresy of advocating multiparty democracy. Taken aback, the government quickly cut off the policy. That led to the Anti-Rightist Campaign of 1957-58 to arrest those who had been foolish enough to take the purported opening to liberal thought literally.

Shwe gas fields One of the world's largest confirmed deposits of natural gas, located off the coast of Arakan state near Sittwe in northwest Myanmar. The country's largest gas project is destined mainly to carry gas to China through a large pipeline that crosses northern Myanmar and ends at Kunming. (The pipeline will also carry petroleum.) It is controversial among human rights activists because of the government's habits of using unpaid labor and confiscating land for pipeline projects. The word *shwe* means "golden" in Burmese, and is the same word found in the world-famous *Shwedagon* or Golden Pagoda in Yangon.

Siam Former name for Thailand. The name was dropped in June, 1939, by Field Marshal Phibulsongkram (usually referred to as Phibun for short) who set out to reunite all the Thai-speaking parts of Indochina and Burma that had been "stolen" by the French and British in the heyday of European imperialism. This included all of Laos, the western provinces of Cambodia and the Shan states of Burma. The people of these regions call themselves "Tai", so the new enlarged country was to be called the "Land of the Tai", *Muang Thai*, or simply Thailand. The **Victory Monument** in Bangkok celebrates these conquests. They didn't last long, however. Phibun allied Thailand with Japan during World War II and paid a price when Japan surrendered. Thailand had to give all of the conquests back. Phibun and other generals were arrested and tried as war criminals by the new democratic government installed by Washington. The country's name reverted to Siam. In 1948 the generals staged a coup, reinstalled Phibun as dictator and changed the name back to Thailand. There was some sentiment in the 1970s to revert to Siam again but that was scotched by another military coup.

Siberian tiger The largest of the tiger species, native to northeast Asia. The beasts used to range throughout China's northeast, the Korean peninsula and as far west as Mongolia but now are limited mainly to the southeast corner of Russia east of the Amur River. An endangered species, only 350-400 Siberian tigers are believed to exist in the wild. For thousands of years, tiger bones have been used in Chinese traditional medicine, but since 1993 the use of tiger bone for medicinal purposes has been banned.

siheyuan MANDARIN for "courtyard residence" and the word for the classic residential architecture of old Beijing. The *siheyuan* is constructed on a north-south axis and consists of four buildings enclosing the interior courtyard. Access is through a single gate, usually painted a bright red. In older times the residence would serve as the home of a single important family, with well-defined spaces for the head of the family, grandparents, servants, even concubines. Now often subdivided for multiple families if not torn down to make room for a large apartment complex or other structure. The basic design served as the template for most Chinese architecture from temples to palaces. Often confused with *hutong*, which strictly speaking are the alleys or lanes between *siheyuan*. Many of the remaining structures in Beijing are concentrated in the Dongcheng district north of the Forbidden City.

silat MALAY/INDONESIAN umbrella term for a variety of martial arts forms that have evolved in Malaysia and Indonesia (where it is called *Pencak Silat*). There are in fact more than a hundred known *silat* styles in the region, some involving the use of bladed weapons such as the *khris*. It is a recognized sport in the Southeast Asia Games.

Siliguri Corridor A narrow stretch of land, no wider than 20 km at the most extreme, that (barely) connects India's northeastern states with the rest of India. It was created in 1947 during the partition of the Indian empire into India and Pakistan, and is squeezed by Nepal on one side and Bhutan on the other. It presents New Delhi with serious strategic problems as it could be occupied, thus cutting India from its northeast, by perhaps a single Chinese airborne division.

Silmido Mutiny Shortly after North Korean commandos tried to assassinate President Park Chung-hee at his official residence in January, 1968, the South formed a special commando group called **Unit 684** to assassinate Kim Il-sung. Some 31 men, mostly ruffians and criminals, were recruited and then effectively confined to a bleak, unpopulated island near Incheon called Silmido. In 1971 the unit revolted against the harsh discipline and "invaded" the mainland where they were confronted by regular army units. Of the 31 members, seven were killed in training, 20 in the uprising and four executed for mutiny. The incident was suppressed until 2006 when it was the subject of a highly popular film called *Silmido*.

Soft power A foreign policy term coined by Joseph S. Nye, a Harvard political science professor, to describe how big countries, such as China and the United States, can influence other countries through culture rather than traditional armaments. Soft power can be conveyed through various means, such as popular culture, public diplomacy, business actions and the gravitational pull of the nation's economic strength. Beijing professes to a peaceful rise, but often scares neighbors by sometimes hardline postures on such issues as conflicting claims in the South China Sea. (See **Confucius Institute**)

"splittism" Nothing instills greater fear in China's communist leaders more than splittism. This is the official English translation of *fen lie*, which means to tear up. The notion underscores the deep-seated fear among China's leaders that separatism in one part of China could encourage similar sentiments elsewhere, ultimately threatening the integrity of the entire nation. The authorities have used this word so frequently that it is common parlance. The charge of "splittism" is often directed towards

Tibetans, Uighurs and Taiwanese. The Chinese Communist Party derives much of its legitimacy from its claim to have unified the country following years of disunity caused by Europeans.

Spring Festival The most important holiday for Chinese everywhere. It is something of a misnomer as it takes place during the lunar or Chinese New Year, which is often observed in late January or February. Festivities go on for nearly a week, and are occasioned by innumerable customs. One of them is the exchange of red packet money, known as *lai see* in Hong Kong. The packets are given by married couples to their unmarried juniors or to children. Mountains of the red envelopes are on sale everywhere in the weeks preceding the holiday. People also stand in line at banks to get money to put in them, since it is important that the bills be new and crisp. The giving is usually accompanied by the CANTONESE New Year greeting *Kung Hei Fat Choi*, which means "may you prosper [in the coming year]". (The word *fat* is a homophone of *bat*, which means wealth.) Companies hold Spring Festival banquets in local hotels, featuring the happy clatter of mahjong, a sumptuous dinner and the raffling of dozens of often expensive prizes such as holiday trips.

Snow Country In the winter, cold winds from Siberia pick up moisture over the Sea of Japan and drop it as snow when they strike the mountains of Japan. The Japan Sea side of the mountains is probably, for its latitude (approximately from Cape Hatteras to New York or Morocco to Barcelona), the snowiest region in the world. From December to April the snow in the mountains is often 15 feet deep. Thus the expression "snow country" does not mean anywhere that snow falls, but more specifically that part of Honshu that lies west of the mountain range that is smothered in the stuff. It suggests long, gray winters and life divorced from time through the long winter months, at least before the coming of bullet trains. It is also the title of a famous novel by **Yasunari Kawabata**, who in 1968 won Japan's first Nobel Prize for Literature.

soapland JAPANESE from English as a euphemism for a kind of brothel that gets around Japan's anti-prostitution laws. It was originally called a *toruko buro,* or Turkish bath, until in the 1980s the Turkish embassy waged a campaign against the term as offensive to Turks. The new term, soapland, was chosen in a nationwide contest. It is not known who got to vote.

Songkran THAI The traditional New Year festival in Thailand celebrated in mid-April and now known far and wide for water-throwing antics. In years past, Thai people carried small bowls of scented water from which they sprinkled a few drops on friends as a blessing. Later it became a spree with mostly young people throwing buckets of water around willy-nilly. Anyone venturing out of the house during *Songkran* can expect to be drenched. The festival comes at the end of the dry season when it is mercifully hot. Thailand's other popular and colorful festival, *Loy Krathong,* comes at the end of the rainy season, usually in November. Lighted candles, flowers and joss sticks are floated down rivers or out to sea in coastal communities. *Loy* means to float; *krathong* is the tray or vessel that carries the floating objects. The Burmese observe the same water-throwing festival, called **thingyam**.

songtaew THAI Common form of cheap public transportation in Thailand, similar to the **jeepney** in the Philippines, though less gaudily decorated. It is mainly a small truck with two rows of benches facing each other on the back (literally, *songtaew* means "two rows"). They usually ply a fixed route up and down a town's main street. Riders flag them down and climb on the back. The fee is only about 10 baht (roughly 25 cents). See also **tuk tuk**.

songun KOREAN The word is usually translated as North Korea's "military first" state ideology, which places the armed forces at the forefront in virtually all aspects of the affairs of state. The ideology emerged in the 1990s, is closely associated with the late Kim Jong-il and expanded steadily after he assumed power in 1994. As a state ideology it seems to have supplanted *juche*, or "self-reliance", which was more closely associated with his father Kim Il-sung, although it may be revived under the current leader Kim Jong-un. *Songun* places the North Korean army, one of the world's largest with some one million men under arms, as the vanguard and safekeeper of the revolution – a position that in communist countries is usually assigned to the proletariat or, as in the case of China, to the peasantry. As if to underline the army's new role, North Korea has gradually abolished some civilian positions such as the state presidency (assigned permanently to father Kim).

Southern Weekend A newspaper published weekly in Guangzhou, China. Though it sounds like something a weekend gardener would subscribe to, it is in fact one of the most aggressive investigative publications in China. In 2010 it sent reporters to investigate conditions in a Foxconn factory, a Taiwan enterprise that assembles iPhones and iPods for Apple, and wrote about a spate of suicides over working conditions and pay, investigative reporting by any country's standards.

Spratlys Collective name for hundreds of atolls and tiny islands dotted throughout the South China Sea. They are clustered in two main groups: the northern ones are called the Paracels. These islets are claimed in part or in total by six Asian nations. China asserts its "indisputable sovereignty" over all of the islands, which it claims have been Chinese territory "since ancient times". Indeed, Chinese maps show the national boundary looping in a giant U around the entire South China Sea, almost as far as Indonesian waters. Of the 150 or so atolls in the southern group, 44 are occupied. Taiwan occupies the largest, Itu Aba, which is 1.4 km long and 400 meters wide. The Spratlys have often been described as potentially oil-rich. There are also important issues of navigation. (See **Nine-dash Line** in *Numbers*)

Star Ferry An icon of Hong Kong, the Star Ferry vessels have been making their daily crossings from Kowloon to Hong Kong Island for more than 100 years. Dorabjee Nowrojee, a Parsee from India, started the ferry service in 1898. For reasons now lost to history, he named all of the vessels with the word "Star" as part of the name, and the word has been used on every vessel since. Hence: *Silver Star, Golden Star, Meridian Star*, etc. (but no *Red Star*). The ferries make about 400 crossings a day, or 150,000 a year (give or take a few due to interruptions from typhoons.) A crossing takes about seven minutes. Fares are minimal, but nonetheless have been a sensitive subject. The worst civil discord in Hong Kong's history broke out in 1966 after the Star Ferry raised its rates by the equivalent of a penny. They are still known as the Star Ferry Riots. The Star Ferry Company is a part of the extensive Wharf Holdings, which is content to run the service so long as it doesn't lose too much money. In Hong Kong, that's a big concession.

STDM PORTUGUESE acronym for *Sociedade de Turismo e Diversoes de Macau,* seen everywhere in Macau. This organization, owned by Stanley Ho, held the monopoly on casino gambling in Macau from 1962 until December 31, 2001, when the monopoly expired and was broken into three parts. Two of them were put out to tender, allowing Las Vegas moguls to build and operate elaborate new casinos and other entertainments in the enclave. Now known as *Sociedade do Jogos de Macau* (SJM).

Stein, Aurel (1862-1943) Hungarian-born British explorer known for his discoveries along what used to be the fabled Silk Road in Central Asia. He is most famous for his third expedition in 1907 to Dunhuang, where he discovered (and took home) thousands of priceless ancient Buddhist texts in half a dozen languages, some of them "dead". They included the Diamond Sutra, the oldest surviving printed text in the world. The printing is derived from wood block carvings, not moveable type which would come several centuries later. Most of his finds are in the British Museum, which is a sore point with the Chinese. He died in Kabul and is buried there.

Stolen Generation A term, controversial in itself, meant to describe the practice of taking Aboriginal children away from their parents and placing them under the guardianship of white families or institutions. The stated purpose was to assimilate Aboriginals into the mainstream; another to "breed out" the Aboriginal population through intermarriage. By some estimates, some 100,000 children, living and dead, constitute the "stolen generation". The practice goes back to the 19th century but was only ended in the early 1970s, at about the time Australia also ended its **White Australia** immigration policy. In 2008, the Australian Parliament under a Labor Party government issued a formal apology.

Straits Times The leading English-language newspaper of Singapore, and one of the oldest newspapers in Asia, tracing its history back to 1845. It is published by Singapore Press Holdings. Often criticized as being mainly a mouthpiece for the ruling People's Action Party – but in any case, the tone of the reporting is respectful of the country's leaders. During the Japanese occupation of Singapore from 1942-1945, it was renamed the *Shonan Times*. Not to be confused with the *New Straits Times*, which is the main English-language newspaper published in Kuala Lumpur. Neither publication circulates in the other's territory.

"string of pearls" A geopolitical slang term that is meant to describe China's efforts to project influence, military and diplomatic, along the main sea lanes from the South China Sea across the Indian Ocean to the Persian Gulf. The "pearls" are ports or listening posts to which Beijing wants to achieve access rights or outright bases, such as the port of Gwadar in Pakistan, Hambantota in Sri Lanka, Chittagong in Bangladesh and a listening post on the Cook Islands. (See **Blue Water Navy**)

sufficiency economy A term closely associated with Thailand's King Bhumibol who, in 1997, in the wake of the Asian Financial Crisis, advised the Thai people to change their economic policy and attitudes and adopt a middle way of "self-sufficiency." The idea was meant to insulate Thailand from the shocks of globalization. He never advocated complete autarky with each person growing his own food and making her own clothes, although he did favor devolving more of the economy to the village and town level. Much of the King's considerable good works during his long reign, such as rainmaking, encouraging dairy production and soil conservation, might be considered as helping to promote Thai self-sufficiency. Probably the direct opposite is Thaksinomics, those generally investment-friendly policies of former prime minister **Thaksin Shinawatra**. The country's elite tend to give lip service to the sufficiency economy while working to attract more and more foreign investment that ties the country even more closely to the world rather than the local economy.

"Sukiyaki" Probably the most popular Japanese ballad ever written – in JAPANESE *Ue o Muite Aruko*, or "Look Up While Walking". It is the only Japanese-language song to become number one on the American pop charts (1963). A British music executive reportedly gave the song its "English" title even though the lyrics have nothing to do with *sukiyaki*, a popular hot broth dish. He reckoned that the Japanese title was too much of a mouthful for Westerners, whereas *sukiyaki* is recognizably Japanese while being fairly well known abroad. First released in 1961 and sung by Kyu Sakamoto, a popular singer in the late 1950s and early 1960s.

sukuk ARABIC for Islamic bond. It is an Islamic financial instrument similar to a bond that complies with the Koranic proscription against usury. The issuer sells a certificate to a buyer who "rents" it back at a predetermined price. Malaysia has been promoting Islamic bonds and it became an issue when South Korea attempted in 2011 to ease its tax laws to make Islamic bonds easier to sell and thus help Korean companies raise capital for large Middle East projects. Opposition from the leaders of that country's huge Protestant mega-churches, who feared the spread of Shariah law in the country, helped to kill the legislation.

Suluks of Sabah A term for Filipinos spread over the islands of Tawi-Tawi, Bongao and the mainland of Mindanao in the Philippines which, together with northern Borneo, once formed part of the Sultanate of Sulu. A large number of of Suluks live in the Malaysian state of Sabah which the pretender to the Sultanate claims is his territory. The Suluks of Sabah are citizens and take pains to profess their loyalty to Malaysia and disclaim any allegiance to the Sultanate. In Sabah the community is known as Suluks, while in the Philippines they are known as Tausug. They are part of a wider population of Muslims known as the Moro (see **Bangsamoro**).

Sumo Aside from vistas of Mount Fuji, cherry blossoms and sushi, nothing says Japan as much as *sumo*. Two behemoths enter the ring, stare at each other to psych each other out and then spring at each other, grappling and pushing, until one of them falls outside the ring. This usually lasts only a few seconds. The sport is steeped in tradition and has a strict hierarchy of rank including *ozeki* and the ultimate *yokozuna* or grand champion. It has never caught on globally and isn't even in the Asian Games. But it has become a kind of international sport with the influx of foreign players, led in the 1980s by Kunishiki from Hawaii. Of late, Mongolians dominate (yet *sumo* is not played in Mongolia).

suneung KOREAN Colloquial term for dreaded examinations held once a year for South Korean high school seniors, known officially as the College Scholastic Ability Test. It is one of the most rigorous standardized tests in the world, similar to the American SAT exam but about 50 times more exacting. Source of considerable anxiety for younger high school students and their parents since the results determine a student's future course of life to a great degree, not just which university he can enter. Parents spend a fortune on private, after-school-hours cram schools (*hagwon*) to achieve success in the *suneung*. The test begins in the early morning (latecomers are sometimes rushed to school by police cars), and takes about nine hours.

Sunshine Policy A policy of peace and reconciliation (or appeasement, depending on point of view) with North Korea associated with former South Korean president Kim Dae-jung. Ever since he first ran for president in 1971, Kim had advocated a three-phase program to reunite the two Koreas, starting with contacts, confederation and ultimately reunification. The first stage was the only part of the plan that was implemented, or perhaps could be implemented in the current climate. The most concrete elements were family visits, establishment of the Mount Gumgang tourist site and the Kaesong industrial park. In 2000 Kim flew to Pyongyang for the first and so far only "summit" meeting between the heads of the two Koreas. For this he won the Nobel Prize for Peace in 2000. The glow was later undercut by reports of large bribes paid to the North to stage the meeting. Lee Myung-bak, elected in 2009 as the first conservative president in a decade, was leery of the policy, a skepticism fueled by several northern provocations such as atom bomb tests and the sinking of a South Korean corvette, but he did not dismantle all elements. Tourist visits to Mt Gumgang were stopped after a North Korean soldier fired on and killed a southern visitor, and the industrial park was closed. The main argument against the Sunshine Policy is that it demands too little in return from Pyongyang.

Susanti, Susi (1971-) Chinese-Indonesian badminton player, whose success in the Olympic Games (gold in 1992, bronze in 1996) and numerous other international competitions made her probably the most famous Indonesian athlete in the world. She retired in 1998 to become a full-time mother and partner with her husband, also an Olympic gold medalist, in a sports-equipment business. Born as a kind of English country-house lawn game, badminton has been embraced by Indonesia and Malaysia almost as their national game. It is just about the only world sport in which Indonesians dominate.

Suzuki, Shunichi (1910-2010) Longtime governor of Tokyo and the man who did more to alter the landscape of the world's largest city than anyone since Ieyasu Tokugawa founded the place. While Japanese prime ministers come and go, Suzuki served as governor for 16 years (1979-1995). During his administration the city built the Tokyo International Forum, Tokyo Budokan, the Contemporary Museum of Art and many other public facilities – all designed to make Tokyo a "world-class city" comparable to New York or Paris. He also moved the city government into a towering new 60-story city hall skyscraper in the Shinjuku district. It says something about the stability of Tokyo's government that Suzuki was able to conceive the idea of the towering new city hall, commission its construction and occupy it for a full four-year term.

T

Taeguk-ki KOREAN name for the national flag of South Korea, *taeguk* meaning "universe" and *ki* meaning flag. The design, officially adopted in 1948, is derived from the flag of the short-lived Korean Empire in the late 19th century, just before the country was annexed to Japan in 1910. The symbolism is fairly complex, drawing on ancient Chinese philosophy. The circle in the center represents the *yin-yang* concept of balancing positives and negatives. The symbols at each corner are taken from the *I-ching*, the Chinese *Book of Changes*. Also the name for a Korean film about the Korean War made in 2004, which was one of the most popular Korean films ever produced. (See **Hinomaru**)

taikongnaut Chinese astronaut. Also sometimes *taikongren* or "space man". The word is taken from MANDARIN for space with the suffix -naut at the end (from GREEK for voyager). The term is used by some English newspapers, the English-language version of the *China Daily* and *Xinhua* news releases, although "astronaut" is apparently preferred in official government releases. So far, China has put 14 *taikongnauts* in orbit around the Earth. (See **Shenzhou**)

taishang MANDARIN The term refers either to Taiwan-funded businesses in mainland China or Taiwan businessmen living and working there. The exact numbers range from an estimated several hundred thousand to about a million. That is a politically important voting bloc in Taiwan, a country with only about 23 million people. By and large they strongly support the Kuomintang over the Democratic Progressive Party, as the KMT favors greater economic integration with the mainland while the DPP is skeptical of getting too close. They have to return to Taiwan to vote, something made much easier by the initiative under President Ma Ying-jeou to permit direct flights between China and Taiwan.

tai tai CANTONESE for wife. Among Chinese speakers it has no other connotation, but the word has morphed into something a little different when it is used by expatriates in contemporary Hong Kong. *Tai tai* has come to mean a society wife, a spouse of one of Hong Kong's property magnates, for example, who spends her time organizing charity bazaars or having afternoon tea with other *tai tai* in expensive hotel restaurants.

Taiwanization A political term used in Taiwan to emphasize the importance of a separate Taiwan cultural identity. To advance Taiwanization, history books have been rewritten to put more emphasis on island history, the local dialect emphasized, and the name Taiwan substituted for China in many business names (though significantly not for **China Airlines**). Needless to say, Beijing distrusts this movement which it considers creeping independence. It would rather emphasize everyone's common Chineseness. (See **Chinese Taipei**)

Taklamakan China's largest desert, situated in the Tarim Basin in Xinjiang province. It is also the world's second-largest shifting-sand desert, covering 337,000 square kilometers. Travelers along the storied Silk Road usually skirted the main desert by traversing its northern or southern edges. The name comes from UIGUR, but there is some confusion over its meaning in English. The popular version – he who goes in, never comes out – testifies to its forbidding nature. An alternate translation, the Desert of Death, does too.

Tam, Roman (1950-2002) Hong Kong singer and actor, generally considered the "godfather" of Canto-pop, short for Cantonese pop, Hong Kong's own assembly line of popular music identified mainly by formulaic love ballads. It became a big business in the 1980s and keeps growing. Besides Canto-pop, there is Mando-pop, Mandarin pop music, J-pop, Japanese, and **K-pop**, Korean.

tarento JAPANESE This curious word derived from the English "talent" refers to a kind of celebrity, usually female, who has no discernible talent whatsoever, other than a pretty face and a manager with marketing muscle strong enough to attract a large audience of Japanese girls. Many *tarentos* lead rather bohemian lives, which the fans follow avidly in the gossip magazines but mainly do not emulate. When *tarento* Namie Amuro appeared on television wearing a mini-skirt with fringes and disclosed that she was pregnant and getting married, it set off a fad for wearing mini-skirts with fringes, but not for getting pregnant before marriage. *Tarentos* must be good talkers since they spend a lot of time on television variety shows. Sometimes young women are referred to as *aidoru*, which is the Japanese pronunciation for idol.

Tasaday A small indigenous tribe in Mindanao that was the subject of much attention, claims and counter-claims throughout the 1970s and 1980s. The tribe was supposedly "discovered" in 1971 and billed as the world's only true Stone Age population, cut off from contact with the modern world for a thousand years. This claim was denounced as a hoax, with the tribesmen cynically coerced into pretending to be Stone Age cave dwellers. Then that hoax was later debunked as another hoax. Many outsiders projected onto the Tasaday their own romantic notions of peace-loving, primitive people living a utopian life close to nature. President Ferdinand Marcos declared their home off-limits to visitors with the idea of preserving an idyllic view of the Philippine native culture. The current view takes a more nuanced position, describing the Tasaday as a very poor tribe living close to nature, neither Stone Age nor totally cut off from the world, but manipulated by the media and politicians who imposed their own vision on them for their own purposes.

Tatmadaw BURMESE The word for Myanmar's armed forces. It may be the only Burmese word that most foreigners who follow Asian affairs know. That's because it appears in almost all English-language reports on the country, especially when it was ruled by a military junta. It seems to have a sinister and forbidding tone to foreign ears, much as SLORC

(State Law and Order Restoration Council) used to have. The *Tatmadaw* has been engaged in fighting various ethnic insurgencies for decades, and has been accused of human rights violations such as conscripting civilians into work brigades. It is one of Southeast Asia's largest militaries and has steadily increased in size, thanks to generous support from China.

Temasek Holdings Name of Singapore's sovereign wealth fund, which, as of 2017, managed properties valued at more than $200 billion. Since 2002 it has been headed by Ho Ching, the wife of Prime Minister Lee Hsien Loong. Its most controversial action was to buy shares in Thailand's leading telecommunications company, Shin Corp., from the **Thaksin Shinawatra** family for about $2.2 billion. The sale was seen in Thailand as, in effect, selling one of the country's jewels to a foreign organization. It helped to fuel the anti-Thaksin feelings in the country that led to the September 2006 coup which ousted him from power and sent him into exile. The word Temasek is the name of an older settlement which existed where Singapore now sits and is widely used in other contexts, such as the name of schools, clubs and national honors.

terracotta ITALIAN for a type of clay-based, unglazed earthenware often used for depicting figures. By far the most famous terracotta figures are the Terracotta Warriors that were discovered in 1974 near the Chinese city of Xian. They depict an army of soldiers, with horses and chariots, that form the afterlife bodyguard for Emperor Qin Shi Huang, who died in about 210 BC. So far uncovered are about 8,000 warriors, 520 horses and 130 chariots. After the Great Wall, the Terracotta Warriors are probably China's greatest tourist attraction.

Tet VIETNAMESE for the lunar new year. It is celebrated in Vietnam as in other Chinese-influenced countries with firecrackers, gongs, exchanges of gifts, visits to temples and family gatherings. Officially the holiday lasts three days, although for all practical purposes it lasts about a week. During the Vietnam War, it was usually the reason for a ceasefire and stand-down. But in 1967 the Viet Cong used the holiday as a cover to launch a massive attack on dozens of cities in South Vietnam, known as the Tet

Offensive. The attacks were beaten back, at great cost to the communist side, but they profoundly influenced American public opinion and are credited with turning the public against the war.

Tezuka, Osamu (1928-1989) Generally recognized as the "father of *anime*" and the guru of *manga,* two of the most famous cultural exports of modern Japan. Though trained as a doctor, Tezuka devoted his life to illustration, becoming one of the best-known cultural figures in Japan. Sometimes called the Japanese Walt Disney. He created many of the genres and character types that one sees in *manga* and *anime* today. His most famous creation was Astro Boy. In 1990, a year after his death, the National Museum of Modern Art in Tokyo held a public exhibit of Tezuka's works, the first ever for a "commercial" artist.

Thaksin Shinawatra (1949-) From 2001 until 2006, when he was overthrown in a coup and exiled, the prime minister of Thailand and – for nearly a decade – a lightning rod for royalists, military and other members of the Thai establishment. He was first elected under Thailand's enlightened 1997 Constitution, but once in office he ignored the checks and balances written in the constitution and enriched his family and cronies. For all his shortcomings, Thaksin has an unbreakable hold on Thailand's rural population, especially in the north and the impoverished northeast known as the **Isan**. He introduced a revolving development fund for every village, promoted rural products and services, put a moratorium on farmers' debts and introduced a modest health scheme for the poor in government hospitals. Soon after he was re-elected in 2005 with a massive 401 seats out of 500 in the House of Representatives, he sold his telecoms business to the Singaporean government for about $2 billion. People were disgusted and held massive anti-Thaksin demonstrations in Bangkok (see **yellow shirts**) until the September 2006 coup removed him from power and from the country. The government disqualified his party, the *Thai Rak Thai* (Thais Love Thais) party, but it has reappeared under different names and won two post-coup elections by convincing margins. In August 2011, following the second electoral triumph, his younger sister Yingluck Shinawatra was chosen as prime minister.

Thomas Christians A large Christian group in India with historic roots going back centuries. The Apostle Thomas ("doubting Thomas") is said to have brought Christianity to India in the 1st century. Whether this is true, missionaries in India in the 6th century reported a large indigenous Christian population already there. Thomas is said to be buried near Chennai, and the site is an object of pilgrimages. The Thomas Christians are often said to be Hindu in culture, Christian in faith and Syrian in liturgy. Over the years they have divided into a complicated number of separate sects and churches. The largest is the Malabar Christians, with about 2 million living in the southern state of Kerala. They are also known as *Nazrani*, a word apparently taken from Christ's home town, Nazareth.

Thompson, Jim (1906-1967?) An American who came to Thailand shortly after World War II and almost singlehandedly revived the languishing Thai silk industry. He founded the Thai Silk Company and established a line of upscale garment stores that still bear his name throughout Thailand and some other cities in Southeast Asia. His silk designs were used in the costumes of the Broadway musical *The King and I*. In 1967, while visiting the Genting Highlands in Malaysia, he left friends to take a walk and was never seen again. His disappearance remains one of Southeast Asia's enduring mysteries, along with the death of King Rama VIII and the fate of the Laotian royal family. His traditional Thai-style house in Bangkok is open to the public and a major tourist attraction.

Tiananmen Massacre What most of the world outside of China calls the events of the night of June 4, 1989, in Beijing; when Deng Xiaoping ordered the People's Liberation Army into the capital to clear the massive central square of student protesters. University students had begun gathering in Tiananmen Square, in front of the Forbidden City, in late April following the death of former Communist Party Secretary General Hu Yaobang. They had a number of grievances ranging from corruption, lack of democracy to wretched living conditions in universities. The protests went on for weeks, even after martial law was declared in mid-May. Finally, the government's patience ran out, and Deng ordered the army in. How many people were killed that night may never be known, but there is no question that a paroxysm of killing took place. Yet most Asian publications eschew the word "massacre" for the more euphemistic term "crackdown", partly out of deference to China and partly out of uncertainty over whether anyone was killed on the Square itself, narrowly and literally defined.

Timor Leste Official name for a small republic in the Indonesian archipelago. *Leste* is Portuguese for "east", and the country is also known as East Timor as it occupies the eastern half of Timor island. The name is something of a tautology as the word Timor itself comes from the Malay for "east". In Indonesian it is Timor Timur. The country gained independence from Portugal in 1975 and was almost immediately invaded by Indonesia, which maintained a brutal occupation until on August 30, 1999, Jakarta allowed a referendum on Timor's future. About 78 per cent voted for independence (or more accurately against continued association with Indonesia). Full independence was achieved in 2002. The US officially uses the name Timor Leste; Australia terms the country East Timor. Portuguese and Tetum are the official languages; Indonesian and English are the real ones.

tobashi JAPANESE *Tobashi* literally means "to fly", though it more specifically describes a now-banned practice of hiding bad loans or financial losses in the portfolios of other clients or subsidiaries so that losses don't show up in official corporate financial reports. The practice became a concern in the aftermath of the "Bubble Economy" of the late 1980s. During that time many Japanese companies engaged in the now fading practice of ***zaiteku***, meaning making money through the manipulation of stocks and bonds rather than from core businesses. At its peak, the Toyota Motor Company earned more from financial transactions than it did from selling cars. Supposedly banned in 1992, *tobashi* reared its head again in the 2011 Olympus scandal, in which the company disguised *zaiteku* losses in vastly inflated finder fees for the acquisition of a British medical company and some other transactions. (See ***baburu keizai***)

tofu dregs A Chinese expression that refers to the messy bits left over from making *tofu* and now a metaphor for shoddy construction. The phrase was actually coined by former premier Zhu Rongji to describe a jerry-built dam. It is now applied to all kinds of shoddy construction projects permitted by corrupt local officials. The greatest *tofu dregs* were the several thousand school buildings that collapsed in the **Wenchuan Earthquake** of 2008.

Toki Japanese name for a crested ibis, a magnificent white-plumed crane with a red face and black beak. Once widespread throughout Northeast Asia, it is now virtually extinct. A small colony is maintained at a preservation center on Sado island in the Sea of Japan, the only place where Toki are bred. Some Toki have been spotted in China too. Cranes have figured prominently in Japanese culture and art for at least a thousand years. Children learn how to make paper cranes through the paper folding art of *origami*. Making a thousand such paper cranes signifies peace.

tongzhi MANDARIN for comrade. For many years it was the standard form of address for members of the Chinese Communist Party. It fell out of use as a communist greeting beginning with the opening to the world in the 1980s, at about the time China's leaders shed their Mao jackets and began wearing Western-style business suits and neckties. China's conservative leader Xi Jinping has urged party members to revive the term and be proud of it. One problem. As *tongzhi* fell out of use among cadres, it was embraced by China's gay community, possibly due to its close resemblance to the Chinese word for homosexual, *tongxinglian*.

Tonle Sap CAMBODIAN for "Great Lake", the combined river and inland lake in the center of the country, Southeast Asia's largest body of fresh water. It expands in size from 2,700 sq km to 16,000 sq km depending on the season. The Tonle Sap is to Cambodia what the Nile is to Egypt. Each spring when the Mekong River swells from monsoon rains, its current is so strong that it forces the Tonle Sap River to reverse its course, carrying tons of rich fertile soil and young fish back into the lake. As the lake floods, then recedes, it deposits rich soil on thousands of hectares of land around the lake's periphery. It is one of the world's largest inland water fisheries.

Toyota, **Toyoda** The *Toyota Jidosha Kaishin*, or Toyota Motor Company, vies with General Motors as the world's largest maker of passenger automobiles. It was founded in 1936 by Kiichiro Toyoda and is still largely a family-run enterprise, similar to the Ford Motor Company in the US. In 1937 the Toyoda family changed the name of the automobile company (one of several family businesses; it still makes automated looms and sewing machines) to Toyota, since it was simpler to write in Chinese characters and pronounce. Also the name Toyoda means fertile rice fields, which did not seem an appropriate name for a car company. Chinese still use the Toyoda name, and the characters still mean fertile rice fields. Toyota entered the American market in 1957 with the Toyopet Crown car, but soon dropped the name Toyopet since it implied toys and pets. Many of the earlier Crowns are now collectors' items and much prized by aficionados. The company still maintains its headquarters in Toyota City, about 40 km from Nagoya. In 2009, in the middle of an unprecedented slump in car sales, the board appointed Akio Toyoda as president, the first family member to head the company in 14 years.

Toyota Kijang A minivan assembled and sold in Indonesia by Toyota since 1977. It is reputed to be the most popular vehicle in the country. The same basic car is sold in other Asian countries under different names. The term *Kijang* is INDONESIAN for a breed of deer found in Asia.

transmigrasi INDONESIAN for transmigration. Since independence, and even under the Dutch, it has been state policy to move people from the crowded islands of Java and Madura to the less-populated regions of Sumatra, Kalimantan and Sulawesi, to create a more equal population density across the archipelago and encourage a sense of Indonesian nationality over regional loyalties. It peaked in the late 1970s and early 1980s when about 2.5 million people were transported. It has tapered off due to lack of money and the end of the Suharto regime. The program has resulted in communal conflicts between newcomers and local peoples. The most serious was the Sampit Conflict in 2001 between Dayak people of Kalimantan and Madurese migrants. Some 500 people died. An estimated 20 million people have been relocated under the program.

Trowlan Name of a sprawling archaeological site in East Java; once the capital of the Majapahit Empire, which flourished from the 13th to 16th centuries in Indonesia's pre-Islam period. The import of this site was first realized by **Sir Stamford Raffles** in the early 19th century when he was serving as governor of Java. (He also rediscovered the much more famous Borobudur monument.) The site, now little more than a village, was once a sizeable city, probably larger than central Jakarta today. It boasts numerous temples, gates and public baths. Some of the gates have been reconstructed using red bricks. There is also a museum to help explain it all. The site is an easy day-trip from Surabaya.

Truyen Kieu VIETNAMESE *The Tale of Kieu* is an epic poem that is considered the most significant work of Vietnamese literature. It was written by Nguyen Du (1766-1820) and tells the sad story of a beautiful young woman, Vuong Thuy Kieu, born into a wealthy family but who through a series of misfortunes descends into prostitution. Every educated Vietnamese is familiar with the story and probably can quote passages from memory. It condemns the decadence of the last years of the Li Dynasty with some oblique criticism of Confucianism.

tuk-tuk [took-took] A three-wheeled form of public transportation popular in many forms throughout Southeast Asia but most often associated with Thailand. The name is onomatopoeic, mimicking the sound of the two-cycle motor. Thais have several other forms of cheaper public transportation, such as motorbike taxis and the *songtaew*, so they tend to avoid *tuk-tuks* unless it is raining (the seats are enclosed in plastic) or they are encumbered with packages.

turtle ships Often billed as the world's first ironclads, the turtle ships – or *kobukson* in Korean – were a unique type of warship that were used to defeat the Japanese invasion of Korea in 1592-1598. They are called turtle ships as the head of the dragon at the bow and the slightly curved deck covering made it look sort of like a turtle (or maybe a duck). The term "ironclad" is somewhat misleading, since the sides, with banks of oars, were made of wood. Iron may have been used in the deck covering to protect the rowers from flaming arrows and discourage boarders. Anyway, that is how the several replicas in Korean museums depict the vessel today. Moreover, naval gunfire was not so well developed in the

16th century in Asia to require iron protection against cannonballs. The warships were designed and effectively deployed by Yi Sung-shin (1545-1598), known universally as "Admiral Yi", undoubtedly Korea's greatest military leader (not counting, of course, Kim Il-sung). He won a series of decisive engagements with Japanese ships off the southern coast of Korea, effectively cutting the Japanese invasion army off from reinforcements. Yi won battles as significant to Korea as the defeat of the Persian navy was to the Greeks. The Battle of Myongnyang was the Korean Salamis.

Tycoon, typhoon Two words in English derived from Asian languages, more specifically those denoted by the evocative Chinese character *dai* or *tai* that is formed in the image of a man with his arms and legs outstretched – 大 – which generally means "big" or "great". Tycoon comes from the JAPANESE *taikun*, meaning big man or boss. It was picked up by Commodore Matthew Perry on his mission to Japan in the 1850s. Abraham Lincoln's secretaries called the president the "tycoon" in private, and it later came to mean a wealthy businessman. Typhoon comes from the CANTONESE *dai-fung* or great wind and, of course, has come to mean a tropical cyclone in the western Pacific region. The word crosses cultures, in that "university" in Japanese is *dai gakko* (big school) and in Cantonese *dai-hok* (big school, or literally big learn). Another word with the same character is found in *taipan*, or big boss, a term that once referred to the heads of the British trading companies during colonial times. It is not used in today's Hong Kong, except in historical novels or ironically. There is an American racehorse named Tycoon's Typhoon.

U

Uchinaguchi OKINAWAN A term for the language, or dialect depending on your point of view, native to southern Okinawa but spoken by only a relatively few aging Okinawans. It is unintelligible to most Japanese and perhaps also to many Okinawans. Compared with other Asian nations, such as China and the Philippines, Japan has relatively few linguistic divisions. There is a distinctive Osaka speech called *kansai-ben*. Okinawa has been Japanese for only about a century and a half. It was for several centuries an independent kingdom and a tributary of China, and was annexed in 1879. The small islands south of Okinawa, such as Miyako and Anami, have their own dialects.

The Ugly American A 1958 political novel by Eugene Burdick and William Lederer, which was influential in displaying various American attitudes toward Southeast Asia in the years leading up to the Vietnam War. The action takes place in the mythical Sarkhan, which is generally believed to be Thailand. The term entered the language as a description of boorish, insensitive American attitudes, although the "ugly American" of the title refers specifically to the physical appearance of the main protagonist, who is an aid worker actually sensitive to Asian cultures. Lt. General Edward Landsdale, an influential counter-insurgency expert in that era, makes a cameo appearance in the novel. **Kukrit Pramoj** appeared in the 1963 movie of the novel as the prime minister of Sarkhan. In 1975 he reprised that role in real life, becoming premier of Thailand.

Uigwe KOREAN The name for a collection of documents relating to court ceremony and royal rites during the Joseon Dynasty (1392-1910), many of which were seized first by the French during a brief reprisal for the persecution of several Christian missionaries in 1866, and later by the Japanese during their occupation of Korea from 1910 to 1945. The Koreans look upon these documents in much the same way the Greeks view the Elgin Marbles, taken from the Parthenon and displayed in the British Museum. About 200 of the documents were discovered in 1975 in the National Library of France, mislabeled as Chinese. Seoul formally requested their return, which Paris finally granted in 2011 on liberal lease terms, which presumably means they remain officially French property. Former Japanese premier Naoto Kan also offered to return some 167 royal books and other cultural artifacts that had been removed to Tokyo during the occupation period. Japan had previously returned 1,420 cultural items when the two countries normalized relations in 1965.

Uijongbu Corridor The main northern invasion route leading directly to Seoul. North Korean soldiers and tanks poured down the Uijongbu Corridor in the June 1950 invasion of South Korea. It was the primary attack artery over the next three years as United Nations forces advanced and retreated. For more than 50 years the US Second Infantry Division was deployed to block another advance down the Corridor. As part of a general realignment of forces in South Korea, the 2nd Infantry will be deployed to a new base south of Seoul.

Uiryeong Massacre Before Norway, the modern world's worst case of mass murder by an individual. A disgruntled South Korean policeman named Woo Bum-kon killed 58 people and wounded 35 in Uiryeong county, South Korea, in 1982. Unhappy about being transferred from Seoul, Woo got drunk and went to a police armory where he took a high-powered rifle and a supply of hand grenades, and then went door-to-door in several villages, methodically murdering occupants before he pulled the pin on a grenade to kill himself and a couple of hostages. In South Korea only the military and police are supposed to have guns; unfortunately, Woo was a policeman. The Interior Minister responsible for the police resigned. He was replaced by the hitherto obscure Minister of Sport, one Roh Tae-woo, who went on to become a reforming president of the republic. (See **Port Arthur Massacre**)

Uluru What Australian aborigines call the dull red monolith in central Australia that most of the world calls Ayers Rock. One of Australia's most enduring symbols and tourist attractions, it is located about 200 kilometers from Alice Springs (not on the outskirts – it takes a four-hour bus ride to get there). It was "discovered" in 1872 by an explorer named Ernest Gils and named after an obscure premier of the state of South Australia. A resort town with its own airport has grown around it, making it actually the fourth-largest town in the Northern Territory.

UMNO The acronym for United Malays National Organization, the largest political party in Malaysia's ethnic-based parliament. It is often thought to be the governing party, but the government is actually supported by a coalition called the Barisan Nasional or National Front, of which UMNO is just one partner, albeit the dominant one. The Barisan is also made up of parties that represent the Chinese and Indian minorities and indigenous people from East Malaysia. (See **reformasi**)

unagi JAPANESE A popular cuisine made up of freshwater eels. Rich in protein, it is thought to improve stamina and is a popular energy food in the heat of summer, when people are in need of a pick-me-up. There is even a designated midsummer day for eating eel, based on the zodiac and known as *doyo ushi no hi*.

unequal treaties A general term for treaties that were imposed on China during the height of European imperialism in Asia in the 19th century (or imposed on Korea by Japan in the early 20th century) that generally resulted in payment of large reparations, granting of self-governing treaty ports or outright annexation of land as in the case of Hong Kong. The most famous "unequal treaty" was the 1842 Treaty of Nanjing after the Opium War, in which China ceded Hong Kong Island "in perpetuity." Republican China repudiated the treaties, actions which came to full fruition with the return of Hong Kong in 1997 and Macau in 1999. Of course, all treaties negotiated (or imposed) by the victor on the vanquished are by definition "unequal", but the term usually relates to Asia.

Uniqlo A fast-rising Japanese clothing retailer offering "high quality basics with a little bit of fashion". The company traces its origin to one store opened by founder Tadashi Yanai in 1988 and has been operating under the Uniqlo brand since 2005. It now has more than 800 outlets in Japan and about 500 in Asia, Europe and the US (including one on fashionable Fifth Avenue). In 2012 it was Japan's second most valuable brand according to Interbrand, a brand consultancy. The name Uniqlo is a shortened version of "unique clothing", and it is an example of a fast-growing linguistic trend in Japan to compress English phrases into one short word. Other examples are *combini* for convenience store or *pasacon* for personal computer.

University of Malaya Malaysia's most prominent university is known as the University of Malaya (not Malaysia), or *Universiti Malaya*. It was founded in 1905 in Kuala Lumpur.

Uriminzokkiri (uriminzokkiri.com) is North Korea's official website, which in 2010 added Twitter and Facebook. The only trouble is that nobody in North Korea is allowed Internet access, so the website is aimed purely at international audiences.

Usa A small city on Kyushu famous for a shrine built in 725 but notorious for supposedly using its name to suggest that products made in Japan for export were "Made in USA." True or not, it is definitely a myth that the town changed its name to Usa after the war so that goods made in Japan could be misleadingly labeled. The town has been named Usa for centuries, and in any case has little industry.

Utopia Once the most influential and widely read neo-Marxist website in China, claiming some 500,000 hits a day. It was founded in 2003 as a "patriotic website for the public interest" and as an organ for those nostalgic for life under Mao Zedong. It vigorously opposed privatization of the economy and most of the liberalizing reforms of the current era, not to mention "rightists", i.e. pro-democracy dissidents. Utopia enthusiastically backed Chongqing's communist party boss Bo Xilai and what it called the "Chongqing Model", but it was shut down after Bo was purged from his leadership posts in early 2012. It is also the name for a gay and lesbian website in Bangkok.

V

Valentine, Bobby (1950-) Colorful baseball manager who led the Chiba Lotte Marines to their first Japan Series victory in more than 30 years and the first championship won by a team led by a foreign manager. Japan has had several other *gaijin kantoku* from the US, but none was as influential or beloved by fans as Valentine. He combined shrewd baseball knowledge with a flair for showmanship and a demonstrable love of Japan, which endeared him to Japanese fans but not to the team's higher management (like all Japanese pro ball teams, an organ of a major corporation), who declined to renew his manager contract in 2009. He was happy to sign autographs and pose for pictures with the fans, and he introduced a looser training style. Valentine had a successful career in the US before coming to Japan, having led the New York Mets to World Series victory in 2000. After leaving the Marines, he went on to manage the Boston Red Sox.

Velarde, Mariano (1939-) Known as "Brother Mike", the best-known televangelist in the Philippines. He founded **El Shaddai**, a charismatic movement, in 1984, building it into one of the largest congregations in the world. Often dressed in bow tie and white shoes with a gold chain around his neck, he is a multimedia magnate who dabbles in real estate. He declined to participate in the 1986 People Power revolt against Ferdinand Marcos, or the Catholic-backed uprising against then-president Joseph Estrada.

velotaxi A modern version of the once ubiquitous rickshaw. It is a new version of the cycle rickshaw or pedicab, and is touted as a cheap and environmentally friendly mode of transportation over short distances. They were first seen in Germany but have appeared in Tokyo. Ironically,

Japan is the birthplace of the rickshaw (from *jinrikisha*) but not even the modern pedicab, though common elsewhere in Asia (see **becak**), is seen there now. After their victory in 1949, the Chinese communists eliminated the human-drawn rickshaws as a symbol of oppression.

vending machines Almost every culture has vending machines, but nowhere are they so common, and nowhere do they stock such a variety of goods, than in Japan. By last count there were more than 5 million vending machines in Japan, collectively soaking up the electrical output of about one nuclear power plant. The variety of things that can be purchased from a Japanese vending machine is astonishing. Besides the usual soft drinks, energy drinks and cigarettes, the unmanned emporiums have been known to sell underwear, personalized business cards and alcoholic beverages, not just beer but sometimes whole bottles of whisky. The ministry of health has been working to shut down sales of beer and alcohol from vending machines, and they are less common today than in the past, but not entirely eliminated.

Victory Monument One of Bangkok's most familiar landmarks, located in the middle of a busy traffic circle at the confluence of buses, taxis and elevated trains. Though familiar to everyone in the capital, it is unlikely that one person in a thousand could tell you what victory the monument celebrates. In fact, it commemorates Thailand's "victory" in a two-month war beginning in December 1940 against the French. Japan intervened in the brief struggle and pressured France to cede several provinces in Cambodia and much of Laos. The victory was short-lived as Thailand had to return the lost provinces after the end of World War II. The monument was commissioned by the wartime dictator Phibulsongkram in 1941 and designed by the Italian architect **Corrado Feroci**, who also created the Democracy Monument.

Vietnamese River Cobbler One name for a freshwater white fish – officially called *Pangasius* – that is gaining worldwide popularity as an inexpensive, neutral-tasting, boneless fillet similar to sole. Raised in fish farms, mainly in Vietnam's Mekong River Delta, it is the fastest-growing type of aquaculture in the world and is rapidly climbing the charts of popular seafood (although technically a freshwater fish) in Europe and the US, where it is sold under various names. American catfish farmers temporarily banned imports labeled as "catfish", which merely caused the Vietnamese to change the name. Some environmentalists have urged that it be banned from importation on food safety grounds, claiming that the fish is dangerous to health because it is raised in dirty water and injected with drugs.

"Vietnamization" See **Nixon Doctrine**

Viet Kieu A term for overseas Vietnamese, who number about 3 million, roughly half of them living in the United States. Most of these people fled Vietnam after the fall of Saigon in 1975, but other sectors of the diaspora include Russia, where many northern Vietnamese went to work as laborers. Probably the most famous *Viet Kieu* was Nguyen Cao Ky (1930-2011), former prime minister in the last government of South Vietnam, who moved to Orange County, California, where he opened a liquor store. He returned to Vietnam in 2004, part of a growing number of *Viet Kieu* who now divide their time between Vietnam and America. Hanoi encourages their return and values their investment money, as many refugees have become prosperous in America. According to *USA Today* about half a million *Viet Kieu* now return to Vietnam at least for visits every year. Those born or naturalized in the US are *Viet Kieu Mi*, or Vietnamese-Americans.

Viravaidya, Mechai (1941-) Former politician and advocate of family planning known as "Mr. Condom" in Thailand for his imaginative ways of promoting the use of condoms. These include asking taxi drivers to pass out condoms to passengers and a restaurant chain called Cabbages and Condoms where condoms rather than mints or fortune cookies are given to customers along with the bill. In 2007 his organization, the Population and Community Development Association, received a million-dollar grant from the Bill and Melinda Gates Foundation in recognition of his work in family planning and AIDS prevention.

Visakha Bucha THAI One of the most important days in the Buddhist calendar. It is often called "Buddha's birthday", but it also celebrates the day of his enlightenment and his death, all three of which occurred in the same month: the sixth lunar month of the Buddhist calendar, usually May. It is, of course, observed in many other Asian nations with Buddhist populations under different names: *Waisak* in Indonesia, *Phat Dan* in Vietnam, and elsewhere as Vesak Day.

Vu Quang Ox One of the world's rarest animals, native to Vietnam and Laos, and known to the locals as *sao la*. A British scientist discovered the skeleton of a *sao la* in 1992, and in 1994 two live animals were captured and examined, though they both died in captivity. Informally named the Vu Quang Ox (Vu Quang is Vietnam's largest nature reserve), it resembles a small deer, not an ox. While most attention focuses on species that are becoming extinct, it is noteworthy when a new species is "discovered", that is by scientists – the *sao la* is well known to tribal peoples living in the forests and apparently considered by them to be quite tasty.

W

wai A Thai gesture of greeting in which the person bows slightly and presses his or her hands together. The gesture traces its history back to India and variations can be found in other parts of Southeast Asia, but it has become iconic of Thailand (see *sawasdee*).

Walkman Brand name for a portable audio-cassette player first introduced by Sony in 1979 and still one of the most recognizable Japanese products. Its main revolutionary idea was less technology than marketing. It dispensed with a recording mechanism and was sold only in playback modes, setting the pattern for people to listen to portable music. Sony's legendary chairman, Akio Morita, is said to have pushed for the device because he wanted to listen to opera during long transpacific flights during business trips, but he reportedly hated the name. He was persuaded that it was necessary for marketing, and indeed it has spawned dozens of instruments with the -man suffix, such as the Discman. Sony and competitors have sold hundreds of millions of Walkman products in a couple hundred models, although they are being superseded by newer technologies such as the iPhone.

Washlet Pronounced "woshuretto" by Japanese, a brand name Toto Limited uses to describe a warm-water cleaning toilet seat. It has become a generic term for all such exotic toilet seats, of which Japan offers the greatest number. The *Guinness Book of Records* says that a particular model called the Washlet Zoe holds the world record for the most gimmicks attached to an ordinary toilet seat. It has seven different functions from seat warming to blow-drying.

Weibo Also known as Sina Weibo after its parent company, China's largest – indeed the world's largest – social network. It was launched in 2009 (the domain name weibo.com was registered in 2011) and had 360 million users as of June 2017, compared with approximately 56 million Twitter accounts in the US. It operates similar to Twitter in that users post 140 [Chinese] character messages and gather followers. Firmly embedded in the expanding Chinese middle class, it is becoming a major influence on Chinese society and a marketing tool for international corporations seeking patronage. Several Western celebrities, including the actor Tom Cruise, tennis star Maria Sharapova and Bill Gates have opened Weibo accounts. Chinese authorities tolerate Weibo because the parent company censors politically sensitive messages. (See **Renren**)

Wei Hui (1973-) Full name Zhou Weihui. Chinese novelist famous for pushing the limits of contemporary literature with her landmark novel *Shanghai Baby,* published in 2000 when Wei was 27 years old. The book details the life and loves of a single Chinese woman in contemporary China and her affair with a German expatriate. She was denounced by authorities as a "decadent and debauched slave of foreign culture". Her book was banned and sometimes burned in China, where it nevertheless became an underground best-seller. Above ground the novel has sold about 6 million copies abroad, making it the best-selling Chinese contemporary novel.

wei qi [way-chee] MANDARIN for China's most enduring board game, literally the "game of surrounding pieces." It is played on a heavy wooden table with grid marks on it. Players take turns placing white or black pieces on the board, building up positions of strength while at the same time trying to encircle their opponent's pieces. Outcomes are often ambiguous. The Japanese have the same game, which they call *go.*

Wenchuan Earthquake A severe earthquake that struck western Sichuan province in China on May 12, 2008. The epicenter was located in Wenchuan county, hence the name, although it is also known as the **Sichuan Earthquake**. An estimated 70,000 people were crushed in the quake, making it the deadliest in China since the 1976 Tangshan Earthquake and the 21st deadliest in recorded history. This quake went beyond mere natural disaster because of the large number of schools – some 7,000 – that collapsed during school hours, killing thousands of children and students and awakening great resentment of the shoddy construction methods permitted by corrupt local officials. The aftermath radicalized a number of Chinese, most prominent among them the artist **Ai Weiwei** who was beaten when he visited the county to lend moral support to a local activist on trial for pursing legal actions against shoddy construction work. (See **tofu dregs**)

wet market Fresh food markets still common throughout Southeast Asia and Hong Kong despite the growing popularity of supermarkets. The term comes from the extensive use of water to wash down the floors and to keep vegetables, fish and meat looking fresh. In Hong Kong wet markets compete easily with local supermarket chains Wellcome (spelled with two 'l's) and ParknShop. *Pasar Pagi*, MALAY for morning markets, are found throughout Malaysia and Indonesia. Sometimes live animals, such as chickens, are kept in bamboo cages, which can cause hygiene problems. **Bird flu** has been traced to wet markets.

White Australia Policy A restrictive policy that limited immigration only to people from Europe and North America and excluded Asians despite a need to fill a nearly empty continent. The restrictions were some of the first pieces of legislation approved by the new federal parliament when the Commonwealth of Australia was united in 1901. The restrictive provisions were only repealed in the 1970s, and yet immigration, especially concerning refugees from places like nearby Papua or Indonesia, is still a very volatile political topic in the country. The history of the White Australia Policy, not to mention the cultural makeup of the country, have hampered Canberra's occasional efforts to claim that Australia is a part of Asia. It should be remembered that the US maintained similarly racial immigration policies, such as the 1925 Japanese Exclusion Act, until after World War II. (See **Stolen Generation**)

"white coolies" An ironic term that was current in the final few years before Britain turned Hong Kong over to China. Large numbers of British citizens were attracted to Hong Kong in the few remaining years because jobs were plentiful, and they could enter and work in what was still British territory without taking the trouble of obtaining a work permit like other foreign devils. As there were many big construction projects underway at the time, such as the new airport, many of them were doing what was once called "coolie work" on these projects (albeit highly paid "coolie work"). The term alone, referring to unskilled labor, is seldom heard in modern Asia.

White day March 14 in Japan, exactly one month after Valentine's day, when men are supposed to reciprocate the attention they received from women on February 14 with gifts of chocolate. Called "white day" as the confectionery companies that promoted the day of giving back in 1978 suggested buying white chocolate. Today any kind of chocolate is welcome, as well as other non-candy gifts such as jewelry or lingerie. Two phrases are associated with white day: *honmei-choco*, or chocolates out of love, and *giri-choco*, or gifts out of a feeling of social obligation.

Winton The quintessential Australian outback town, located in the middle of Queensland. The population is slightly less than 1,000, yet it has an outsized place in Australia's cultural history. The country's flag airline **Qantas** was born in Winton as Queensland and Northern Territory Air Service. It is also connected to *Waltzing Matilda*, which was composed at a sheep ranch (station) north of the town and first performed at the North Gregory Hotel in Winton. The nearby Combo Waterhole (**billabong**) is thought to be the setting for the lyrics. A Waltzing Matilda Centre opened in Winton in 1998.

Woyla Name for an aircraft formally known as Garuda Flight 206, a DC-9 that was hijacked on March 28, 1981, while flying from Palembang to Medan, by an Islamist splinter movement in West Java called *Komando Jihad*. They were Muslim radicals responsible for various acts of sabotage in Indonesia from 1977-1981. The hijackers ordered the plane to fly to

Colombo, but due to lack of fuel it landed in Penang, Malaysia and later flew to Bangkok instead. The Indonesian army's **Kopassus** special forces were flown to Thailand and, forming three teams, invaded the grounded aircraft and quickly overwhelmed the terrorists. All five hijackers were killed, as was the pilot and one commando. But the rest of the crew and passengers survived. News of this successful raid may have been overshadowed by the attempted assassination of US President Ronald Reagan, which occurred at the same time.

Wukang Road Shanghai's best-known street is probably Nanjing Road, a major shopping avenue lined with stores filled with brand-name products. But Wukang Road is like a living museum of architecture, bearing witness to the city's atmospheric past. This road was paved in 1907 and originally named after the American missionary John Calvin Ferguson. It was the home of numerous celebrities including the actress Zhou Yuan, the writer Ba Jin, and Soong Ching Ling, the wife of Sun Yat-sen and a former vice president of the PRC. Wukang Road ends at the Normandie Apartments, built in 1924 and designed by Hungarian architect Ladislav Hudec. It is shaped like a ship and was named after a famous liner.

Wuliangye Name of one luxury brand of Chinese spirits that go under the generic name of *baijiu*, made in the western city of Yibin. The potent brew is made by the Wuliangye Group, which dominates the economy of this city of 4.5 million at the head of the Yangzi River in Sichuan province. The company, which employs about 20,000 people, contributes some 70 per cent of the city revenues and about 60 per cent of the town's gross domestic product. It even plans to name its new airport after the spirit that made the city famous. Another luxury spirit is Maotai (sometimes spelled Moutai). Although often associated with the communist regime, it is not named after Mao Zedong but after the town of Maotai in Guizhou province where it is made.

wushu MANDARIN *Wushu* literally means martial arts. It is now considered a competitive sport, on par with other sports originating from martial arts such as judo or taekwondo, and it is said to be China's most popular sport. The rules were codified in the early years of the People's Republic as basically a judged sport where the players are graded on various moves, kicks and throws. The International Wushu Federation organizes the World Wushu Championship tournament every two years. Efforts to make *wushu* an official Olympic sport have not been successful so far, but it is a medal sport in the Asian Games.

X

Xiali Name of Beijing's once-ubiquitous taxicabs, fondly remembered by the city's expat community for their low, 1.2 yuan (roughly 15 cents) flagfall. At one time about 40 per cent of the capital's some 30,000 taxis were Xiali, basically a Daihatsu Charade. The Xiali had replaced Beijing's fleet of *mianbaoche* – literally bread loaf minivans – as taxis and have now been all but eliminated themselves, mainly in the name of reducing emissions, by more modern and expensive Hyundais, Volkswagens and Citroens. The city's then three-tiered taxi fare system was also unified at the highest level, although it is still cheap by the standards of other Asian cities.

Xianggang What people in Beijing call Hong Kong. Both the Mandarin and Cantonese version of the name mean the same thing – "fragrant harbor." The more generally recognized name is a slight corruption of the CANTONESE Heung Gong.

xiangqi Better known in the West as Chinese chess (literally "elephant game" in MANDARIN; the animal is featured on some of the pieces). It is a two-person strategic board game, popular throughout the Chinese world and Vietnam. It is played with round discs and the object is to capture the king. The Asian Xiangqi Federation bestows the title of grandmaster. It is one of three board games played in the Asian Games – the Olympics not having board-game contests – the other two are chess and ***weiqi.*** A World Mind Sports Games championship, a kind of cerebral Olympics, was begun in 2008. To the three games listed above, it adds bridge and draughts (checkers).

xiao huangdi MANDARIN for "Little Emperors", a term given to only children raised under China's **One Child Policy**. Depending on who is doing the study, the Little Emperors are spoiled brats basking in the full attention of parents, or strivers, constantly pushed to succeed and make money by parents who, growing up in an earlier impoverished China, want their child to have more than they had. By some accounts, about 20 per cent of China's people under 25 years of age are only children, or about 100 million.

xiaokang MANDARIN A Confucian term that roughly translates as the goal of everybody being moderately well off, a state of affairs that is only now coming even close to reality in modern, post-Mao China. Deng Xiaoping picked up on the term, saying that his reforms had as their eventual goal the "*xiaokang* society," which is sometimes translated as a "middle class", or what the communists used to disdain as the bourgeoisie. The Communist leadership in Beijing now refers to this idea from classical Chinese, as opposed to the former Marxist ideal of class struggle.

Xin Cae [Zhen Kay] HOKKIEN for newcomer: the Chinese who migrated from Fujian province to Malaysia, southern Thailand and elsewhere in Southeast Asia (*Nanyang*) in the early 20th century to work the tin mines.

Xinhai Revolution The name given to the events leading up to the overthrow of the Qing Dynasty and the formation of the Chinese Republic. The rebellion took place in 1911 and the "last emperor" **Puyi** abdicated in 1912. The name comes from the year name – *Xinhai* – in the Chinese 60-year cycle calendar. The rebellion did not lead to democracy, which would eventually be established for the first time in China's 4,000-year history 80 years later on Taiwan. A period of warlord rule, disunity and civil war preceded the ultimate victory of the communists and the proclaiming of the People's Republic in 1949. China's leaders tolerate the 1911 celebrations but prefer to honor their own holidays, such as the founding date of the Chinese Communist Party. On the 100th anniversary

in 2011 the Chinese released a historical film called *Xinhai Revolution* starring Hong Kong superstar Jackie Chan. (See **Double Ten**)

Xizang MANDARIN What the Chinese call Tibet, or more accurately the Tibetan Autonomous Region. The word Tibet is English and dates back to the 18th century. Tibetans call their country Bod in their own language.

Xuan MANDARIN China invented the process for making paper, so it is appropriate that *xuan* paper has become a favorite of collectors and calligraphers. It is made from the bark of blue sandalwood trees from Jingxian county in Anhui province. In Tang-dynasty times this area was administered as part of Xuanzhou prefecture, which gives the paper its name. Production was largely a family affair from as far back as the late Song dynasty, although it is now produced in other factories. Increasing demand has pushed production to 1,000 tons a year.

Y

Yadana gas field An offshore natural gas field located in the Andaman Sea about 60 km from Myanmar and containing approximately 150 billion cubic meters of gas. The gas is carried by pipelines across Myanmar to serve Thailand. They were completed in1998 and can carry 500 million cubic meters of gas a day. The building of the pipeline was controversial because of the regime's alleged use of forced, unpaid labor and other human rights abuses.

yakuza See **8-9-3** in *Numbers*

Yamanote Line The most heavily used commuter line in downtown Tokyo, instantly recognizable by the green stripes painted on the side of the cars. It traces its beginnings to the late 19th century and became a full loop in 1925 with the construction of the elevated line between Ueno and Kanda. Hardly anyone moving around town can avoid a ride on this line, which touches on all the main centers: Shinjuku, Shibuya, Ikebukuro and, of course, Tokyo station, to name a few. It takes about one hour to complete the 34.5 km circle, and it is probable that the true Tokyoite can recite the names of all 29 stations along the way. In many ways, the Yamanote line defines the parameters of Tokyo better than any political boundary. Anything inside this great circle is by common agreement the inner city; anything outside, the beginning of the suburbs or the fading old city. It is named after that hilly part of Tokyo (see **Edo**) where feudal lords had their mansions, as opposed to the more plebeian *shitamachi*, or low-lying city, around the Sumida River.

Yang di-Pertuan Agong MALAY The ruler of the state or, for short, King of Malaysia. Not many people realize that Malaysia is a constitutional monarchy. The office passes every five years to one of the nine hereditary sultans who are the ceremonial heads of nine Malaysian states. Other monarchies in Asia include Japan, Thailand, Cambodia and Brunei. Nepal abolished its monarchy and became a republic in 2008.

Yanjing For most foreigners, the only Chinese beer they recognize by name is **Tsingtao Beer**, perhaps because the brewery was founded by Germans. But the most popular beer in China by a long shot is Yanjing, brewed in Beijing and preserving one of the city's former names from when it was the capital of the northern Yan state during the Warring States period. The Beijing Yanjing Brewery is the largest in Asia. Tsingtao Beer, brewed in present-day Qingdao, preserves the older Wade-Giles spelling of the city's name.

Yashukan War Museum The war museum attached to the Yasukuni Shrine in downtown Tokyo is dedicated to "the truth of modern Japanese history". It includes many static displays, such as a "Zero" fighter plane and some personal effects of departed soldiers, that one would expect to find in any war museum, but it basically proclaims the most extreme nationalist interpretation of recent history, especially World War II, and the years leading up to it. In the museum's view, by seizing Taiwan or Korea, Japan was simply doing what the European colonial powers had done in the years previous. The museum takes as its starting point Commodore Perry's mission to open Japan in the 1850s. The Yasukuni Shrine is dedicated to preserving the souls or *kami* of approximately 2.5 million soldiers and sailors who have died in Japan's wars since the Meiji era. The admission in 1978 of 1,068 "Martyrs of Showa", that is, people convicted in war crime tribunals including 14 classified as "**Class A**", is one reason why no emperor has visited the shrine since 1975.

Yazhou Zhoukan The world's only Chinese-language international newsweekly magazine, published for more than 20 years. The title is roughly "Asia week" in MANDARIN, reflecting the fact that it was founded in 1991 by the English-language newsweekly *Asiaweek*. It was acquired from Time Inc (*Asiaweek's* owner) by the Hong Kong newspaper *Ming Pao* and is currently published by Media Chinese International in Malaysia. The English-language parent ceased publication in 2001.

Year Zero A political term connected with the short but bloody Khmer Rouge reign in Cambodia (1975-79). It conveys the fundamental idea that the country needed to be stripped of all culture and traditions so that a new social system could be constructed essentially from scratch. The phrase may have been inspired by the Year One of the French Revolution, although the Khmer Rouge atrocities vastly exceeded anything done by the French. Solath Sar (better known by his *nom de guerre* as Pol Pot), studied in Paris before returning to Cambodia. (See **S-21**)

yellow cab The term "yellow cab" is a nasty nickname given to promiscuous young Japanese women who go overseas in search of sex with foreign men. The "yellow" probably refers to the Asianness of the women, but could also refer to real Yellow Cabs, since New York is supposedly the prime destination for the fun seekers. The phrase was popularized by a 1992 book *Yellow Cab* by Shoko Ieda, who made some extravagant claims about Japanese women's behavior abroad, claims that were later debunked. Nevertheless, it is a theme often pushed by the more sensational elements of the Japanese press. A similar phrase, Sarong Party Girl (SPG), was current in Singapore and Malaysia to describe women who act and dress in a provocative manner.

yellow dust A term the Japanese use for dust that originates in China's denuded Inner Mongolia province and other parts of Central Asia and is blown east by prevailing winds, settling over Tokyo and other cities. Cities are bathed in a kind of yellow haze similar to smog, and the particles get into everything. Television news channels plot the approaching dust and recommend that people refrain from hanging clothes out of doors. In extreme cases the dust can cut visibility to the point where airports close temporarily. The heaviest concentrations seem to come in the spring at the height of the hay fever season, which only aggravates respiratory problems. (See **haze**)

Yellow River Elegy *Heshang* in MANDARIN. An influential and highly controversial six-part Chinese television documentary that aired in 1988. In it, the muddy Yellow River was depicted as a metaphor for China's backwardness and isolation. While the British, Dutch and Portuguese sailed the pristine blue waters of the high seas discovering the riches of the world, China just paddled along the silted Yellow River, hardly ever venturing out of sight of land. It underscored "the debate whether traditional Chinese culture should be glorified or scorned, whether the nation's poverty is best diagnosed as the result of foreign imperialism or a rotting indigenous civilization," wrote Nicholas Kristof of the *New York Times*. The documentary was initially tolerated as it did not directly attack the ruling Communist Party, but following the Tiananmen crackdown a year later, the government came down hard on some of the documentary's producers.

yellow shirts In Thailand, yellow is the color of respect for the King. Days are given their own colors, and yellow is the color of Monday. As King Bhumibol was born on a Monday, it is the *de facto* royal color. Go into the post office, the bank or a restaurant and chances are everyone is wearing a yellow T-shirt or batik. But during the disturbances that followed the ouster of former prime minister **Thaksin Shinawatra**, it came to be the color of opposition to his controversial rule. Thaksin supporters decided they needed a color of their own and adopted red, hence the term "red shirts". Yellow is often the color of reform or change in Asia. It was the color of the People Power revolt in the Philippines in 1986 and often worn by President Corazon Aquino. It is also the symbol of reform movements in Malaysia (see ***Bersih***).

Yeosu [yuh-sue] A relatively small city of about 300,000 people on the southern coast of South Korea, which in 2012 became the smallest city to host a recognized World's Fair since Spokane in the US hosted one in 1974. It helped catapult this once out-of-the-way city into the front ranks of Korean tourist attractions.

Yeouido This is Seoul's main business, financial and political district, also known as Yoido, similar to Wall Street and Capitol Hill in America combined. Located on a large island in the Han River, it is the location of the National Assembly Building, the stock exchange and the Yoido Full Gospel Church, the largest protestant church in the world.

yinsi MANDARIN The Chinese word for privacy, which is still a fairly modern idea for them. It connotes secrecy, conspiracy and illicit behavior, in contrast with the Western concept which is linked to individual rights and personal liberties. Younger Chinese increasingly object to intrusion into their private lives such as intercepting and reading emails (which doesn't seem to deter state censors, who keep an eagle eye on the Internet for evidence of subversive ideas.)

Yodogo (strictly speaking, Japan Airlines Flight 351) Name of a flight from Tokyo to Fukuoka that was hijacked in 1970 by the Red Army Faction, a precursor to the Japanese Red Army, and flown to Pyongyang, where the hijackers were given political asylum and where some of them still live. Before the rise of the Aum Shinrikyu and its sarin gas attack on Tokyo's commuter lines, the Japanese Red Army was the most feared indigenous Japanese terrorist group. The communist army was dedicated to the overthrow of the Japanese government and world revolution. Despite its name and the fact that most members were Japanese, the army actually perpetrated few actions in Japan. Their most famous terror attack took place on May 30, 1972, at the international airport in Tel Aviv, Israel, when 26 people were murdered and 80 injured. Other actions took place in Holland, Indonesia, Singapore, Kuala Lumpur, the skies over the Indian Ocean, anywhere but Japan. The exception was the 1974 bombing of the Mitsubishi headquarters in Tokyo. Now considered defunct, although former members appear in the newspapers from time to time seeking, usually unsuccessfully, to have their prison sentences reduced or to return to Japan.

yoga SANSKRIT meaning union. Yoga is a form of exercise and meditation with deep philosophic roots in India. In the West yoga is usually practiced as an innocent form of exercise, something associated with the gymnasium, not the temple. But it is more controversial in countries with large Muslim populations. Muslims frown on the practice as it traces its roots to Hinduism, uses non-Muslim holy words such as *namaste* and usually involves women wearing skimpy clothing. Singapore banned yoga in 1980, and in 2006 Muslim clerics in Malaysia issued a *fatwa* against yoga, claiming it was *haram* (forbidden). Hindu nationalists

in India regularly push to make yoga compulsory in public schools, riling the Muslim minority.

Yokota, Megumi (1964-1994?) The most famous of more than a dozen Japanese who were kidnapped and brought to North Korea in the 1970s and 1980s, supposedly to train North Korean spies in the Japanese language and customs. She was only 13 when she was snatched on a quiet Niigata street while walking home from school on the evening of November 15, 1977. Megumi was among the dozen people that North Korea's supreme leader Kim Jong-il admitted in 2002 were kidnapped. His government maintains that she committed suicide in North Korea in 1994, when she would have been around 30. Her remains were returned in 2004 but Japanese technicians, using DNA techniques, say the remains belonged to others. The Japanese government officially maintains that she may be alive. A satisfactory accounting for 17 officially identified abductees, their return if alive and the extradition of the kidnappers are Tokyo's terms for any normalization of relations between the two countries. Her parents appear frequently on television to keep their cause alive. In 2009 they were received at the White House by President George W. Bush.

Yonaguni Monument A mysterious underwater rock formation located off the coast of Yonaguni, the southern-most island in Japan's Ryukyu chain. Since their discovery in the 1980s no consensus has emerged as to whether they are man-made or natural formations or natural formations reshaped by man, a kind of Japanese Atlantis. Published underwater photos seem to support the man-made idea with what appear to be stepped terraces with sharp edges and right angles. Signs of prehistoric habitation have been found on Yonaguni, but the population would seem to have been too small to mobilize the effort needed to build such formations (either submerged or above water). About 1,500 people live on the island and earn their livelihood partly by catering to scuba divers.

Yongbyon North Korea's main nuclear weapons development site, located about 90 km north of Pyongyang. The main facilities include a 5 MW magnox nuclear reactor, which is believed to be the source of plutonium for the country's atomic bomb program but now disabled, a fuel fabrication plant, a fuel reprocessing plant and associated technical training schools. More recently Western visitors have observed construction at Yongbyon of a new 30-50 MW light water reactor and a surprisingly sophisticated uranium enrichment plant to supply fuel for the new reactor and possibly weapons-grade uranium for bombs. The facility dates back to the 1960s with help from the Soviet Union, but work really started in the 1980s, eventually leading to major confrontations with neighbors and the US. Washington considered destroying these facilities with air strikes, but settled on the 1994 Agreed Framework which froze nuclear activities until 2002, when the new administration in Washington, charging that Pyongyang was secretly seeking to enrich uranium, suspended its part of the agreement. North Korea then "unfroze" its nuclear program. In 2006 and 2009 North Korea exploded low-yield atomic bombs in two underground tests. (See **Six-Party Talks**)

Yonsama JAPANESE nickname for the Korean actor and heart-throb Bae Yong-joon. He won the hearts of middle-aged Japanese women in the 2002 soap opera *Winter Sonata* and later the hit show *April Snow*. He seemed to be more popular in Japan than in his homeland, where he is basically famous for being famous in Japan. He is emblematic of the success of Korean soaps and other cultural exports (see *hanryu*). In 2006 Bae was picked for a leading role in what was then the most expensive drama series in South Korean television. He played a king who expanded the **Kogaryo** empire throughout the Korean peninsula and into present-day Manchuria. The production coincided with a row between South Korea and China over the meaning of the Kogaryo empire for today.

yuefenpai MANDARIN A distinctive Chinese poster art style, which grew out of calendar girl art in the late 19th century and blossomed as an advertising medium in the 1920s and 1930s. Kwong Sang Hong, one of the first cosmetic companies in China, set the pattern with its poster showing two elegant Chinese women in flower-patterned *qipao* looking sweet and demure. The Kwong Sang Hong Company still exists, and it still uses the "two girls" advertisement. Rather than try to blend the models into a vague, semi-European look, the women pictured are unmistakably Chinese. The women depicted in later posters were more vampish, with rosy cheeks, arch eyebrows, painted lips, slender waists and full hips and a come-hither look on their faces. They are very evocative of the Shanghai of the 1930s. Posters and postcards featuring the *yuefenpai* illustrations are now collectors' items.

Yunus, Muhammad (1940-) Bangladeshi economist generally considered the father of micro-financing, that is, giving small loans without collateral to encourage small-scale businesses often owned by women. These borrowers previously had to turn to loan sharks or do without. He founded the Grameen Bank as the principal vehicle for making these loans. His first loan was the equivalent of about $27 from his own pocket, which he distributed among 42 women. For his efforts he was awarded the Nobel Prize for Peace in 2006. In recent years, as Yunus toyed with forming a political party, he ran into trouble with Prime Minister Sheikh Hasina Wajed and in 2011 was forced to surrender his position as head of Grameen Bank because of age and allegations of misusing funds.

yurt TURKIC name for a portable, round, wood-framed dwelling that is common throughout Central Asia. Not to be confused with a *ger*, which is the MONGOLIAN version of the hut, slightly different in that it uses poles to support a heavier roof.

Yushin KOREAN word for the October, 1972 internal coup in which President Park Chung-hee assumed near-dictatorial powers. The period from 1972 until Park's assassination in 1979 is known as the Yushin Regime. At the heart of the regime was a new constitution – the Fourth – in which an electoral college was created to choose the president (who had no term limits) and a third of the National Assembly. Park chose the word himself as it was similar to the Japanese word *ishin* as in *Meiji Ishin* or the Meiji Restoration in Japan. It was this modernization and industrialization that Park wished to emulate in his country, and which he did emulate with considerable success in the economic field.

Z

zainuchi JAPANESE for "staying in Japan". It refers to ethnic Koreans living in Japan, who mostly trace their ancestry to the time when Japan ruled Korea as a colony (i.e. not recent immigrants, businessmen or students, and so on). At the end of World War II an estimated 2 million Koreans were in Japan; many returned after the surrender. About 500,000 *zainuchi* remain in Japan, making them the country's largest minority. As Japan does not recognize birthright citizenship, many Koreans are considered aliens, even if they are second- or third-generation and have Japanese names. Considerable prejudice against Koreans persists, though it is abating. In arranged marriages, the parents of the bride may hire investigators to determine whether the prospective groom is really a Korean. Two groups purport to represent Koreans in Japan. *Chongryon* is closely affiliated with North Korea and runs its own schools that parrot Pyongyang propaganda. The South Korean opposite is *Mindan*. Membership in the *Chongryon* is declining as the cash-strapped North has cut subsidies and as younger Koreans seem more interested in integrating into Japanese society than singing the praises of Kim Il-sung and his offspring.

zaiteku JAPANESE During the bubble economy years of the late 1980s many Japanese companies earned more money from investing in financial instruments, such as stocks and bonds, then they did in making things. That spawned the vogue word *zaiteku*, literally "financial technology" (*zai* means economy; *teku* is short for technology). One of the biggest practitioners was Toyota, which for a time earned the sobriquet the "Bank of Toyota". After the bubble burst in late 1989, Japanese companies mostly went back to making things and *zaiteku* as a word dropped out of the vocabulary.

Zaitokukai JAPANESE meaning literally "citizens against special privileges for the ***zainuchi***". An anti-Korean group known for organizing street rallies that verbally attack local Korean residents, especially in areas where they concentrate, such as the Shin-Okubo district in Tokyo and Tsuruhashi in Osaka. Choice phrases include "Koreans you die!" or "You stink of kimchi!" Such phrases have led to calls for Japan to enact laws against hate speech. The organization says it wants to abolish "special privileges" accorded to ethnic Koreans in Japan, especially the 1991 law that accorded them permanent residency.

zakka [zak-kah] JAPANESE Literally meaning "many things," a kind of fashion or design phenomenon which has spread throughout Asia in the century's first decade. They are often ordinary, even mundane objects that have a subtext. A plastic ashtray would not be *zakka,* but a plastic ashtray bought at a Paris flea market might. Or it could be a colorful cloth strap on a cell phone. "We Love Zakka" is a *zakka* website run from Singapore.

Zarganar (1961-) Popular Burmese entertainer and probably the most famous political prisoner in Myanmar after Aung San Suu Kyi. Generally considered the country's leading comedian and film director, his acid tongue has got him in and out of prison as far back as the demonstrations that began on August 8, 1988 (See **8888 Uprising**). In 2006 his work was banned, and in 2008 he was imprisoned for 35 years on vague public disorder charges stemming from his criticism of the junta's reaction to **Cyclone Nargis** that devastated the Irrawaddy River Delta in 2008. He was freed during a general amnesty in 2011.

Zhang Yimou (1951-) Noted Chinese film director famous for such sumptuous films as *Red Sorghum* (1987), *Ju Dou* (1990), *Raise the Red Lantern* (1991) and *Hero* (2002) that exposed post-liberation Chinese films to the world's consciousness. *Ju Dou* was the first Chinese film to be nominated for an Academy Award; *Raise the Red Lantern* was the second. He brought actress (and sometime paramour) Gong Li to prominence in a dozen films in which she was the star. He was also chief designer of the spectacular opening ceremony for the 2008 Beijing Olympics.

Zhenbao Island Incident Chinese name for an island in the Ussuri River where Siberia abuts the Chinese frontier, better known by its Russian name Damansky. It was the site of a serious border clash in March, 1969, which some at the time thought might be the prelude to a Russian attack on China's nuclear facilities, or even outright war. This and other border incidents helped to create a climate favorable to détente with the United States, which began in earnest in mid-1971 with Henry Kissinger's first exploratory visit to Beijing and culminated in President Richard Nixon's trip to China in early 1972. Most border disputes were resolved in a 2004 agreement in which Moscow conceded that Zhenbao belonged to China. (See **Ping-pong diplomacy** and **Polo**)

Zhonghua minzu MANDARIN for "Chinese nation". A term that partly replaced **One China** as a means of describing the tricky relationship between Taiwan and mainland China. Taiwan's former president Ma Ying-jeou used the term in his inaugural speech, although it was translated more like "Chinese of common heritage". There is no consensus on the use of this term in Taiwan. (See **1992 Consensus**)

Zhongnanhai The main seat of power in China, located in Beijing immediately west of the Forbidden City. The irony is that the "Forbidden" City is open to the public and overrun with tourists, while Zhongnanhai is closed to the people and closely guarded. The compound is named after the central and southern lakes, two artificial bodies of water fully enclosed by vermilion-colored walls. In Imperial times, it was a kind of park next to the palace where the emperor lived. Since Republican times, it has been the seat of government. China's leaders have villas and offices inside the compound, plus halls for receiving foreign dignitaries and holding special conferences. Mao Zedong lived there in a small villa (although former premier Zhu Rongji chose to live outside the compound and used it only as an office). The name Zhongnanhai can also be used as shorthand for the Chinese government, in the same way as **Nagata-cho** in Japan or the White House in the US. A large silent demonstration outside the walls by a Buddhist sect called the **Falungong** in April 1999 led to the sect's harsh suppression.

Zhongshan jacket A form of Chinese men's apparel better known in the West as the "Mao jacket". It was introduced by Sun Yat-sen shortly after the **Xinhai Revolution** of 1911 as a new form of national dress, discarding the older gowns worn by Qing-dynasty mandarins. It is a tunic with a single row of buttons and four outside pockets, usually in black or gray. It became widely and popularly associated with the first generation of communist leaders. Mao Zedong wore the Zhongshan jacket when he proclaimed the People's Republic in 1949 and later when he met with President Richard Nixon in 1972. In recent years it has fallen out of fashion among China's elite who prefer to present themselves to the world wearing ordinary Western-style business suits with neckties. However, they occasionally don the jacket during state occasions, especially those associated with the communist party. Then-president Hu Jintao wore one on the reviewing stand for the 60th anniversary extravaganza of the founding of the People's Republic in 2009.

Numbers

One Child Policy China's policy of limiting families to only one child was introduced by Deng Xiaoping in 1979 to limit the country's population growth. The law is enforced through fines, societal pressure and, it is alleged though denied by Beijing, by forced abortions. Supposedly a "temporary" measure, it has been enforced for more than 30 years. The policy applies to urban residents, not rural, and to Han Chinese, not minorities. One of the unintended consequences has been a growing gender imbalance, as parents abort girls in order that their one legally permitted child may be a male. Another consequence, some say, is the growing presence of spoiled only children, known in China as **Little Emperors**. By some accounts, China would have about 300 million more people than it does today save for the One Child Policy. Indeed, as in other Asian countries, Chinese are now beginning to fret over their aging society.

One China Policy The proposition that there is only one China and Taiwan is a part of China. It is a useful fiction that has governed how the world deals with the legacy of the Chinese Civil War that left Taiwan in the hands of the defeated Nationalists and the mainland to the Communists. Up until the early 1970s both Beijing and Taipei claimed to be the legitimate government of all of China. Taipei no longer portrays itself that way. The two sides have agreed to disagree on the definition of what "China" really is. All governments, including the United States, that wish to do business with China or maintain normal relations pledge allegiance to this proposition. It is also professed by the Kuomintang government on Taiwan but not so fervently by the opposition Democratic Progressive Party. (See **Shanghai Communiqué** and **1992 Consensus**)

One country, two systems A pithy way of describing the arrangement by which Hong Kong reverted to Chinese sovereignty in 1997. Under provisions of the Joint Declaration between London and Beijing, Hong Kong would enjoy its capitalist system and other liberties for 50 years. For its part Beijing amended the Chinese constitution to create Special Administrative Regions (SARs) which enjoy considerable autonomy for Hong Kong and Macau. In this regard Hong Kong keeps its own money, issues special passports, maintains its own immigration system, and many more. Beijing is responsible for foreign relations and defense. (See ***gangren zhigang***)

One *Lakh* Car Informal name for what has been billed as the world's cheapest car, known more formally as the Nano. It is a two-cylinder, four-door road vehicle, built in India by the Tata Motor Company and aimed at India's expanding middle class. A *lakh* represents 100,000 in India's unique and often confusing numbering system. That was the approximate local price for the car, equivalent to about $2,000, when the car was first introduced to the market in 2009. The cost of the tiny car was kept down by dispensing with non-essentials, such as power steering (not needed due to the car's light weight), such safety devices as air bags and by judicious use of steel. Despite its billing, the cost has been rising due to increasing material costs. As of 2010, a Nano went for the equivalent of about $2,900.

1Q84 Enigmatic title for an enigmatic novel by **Haruki Murakami** (1949-), Japan's most important contemporary writer. The novel was published in three parts in Japan but collected into a single blockbuster of a book when issued in English in the fall of 2011. Murakami published his first novel, *Hear the Wind Sing,* in 1979. His big break came with *Norwegian Wood,* published in 1987, which sold an estimated 4 million copies in Japan. His new books are now instant cultural events on six continents. However, many readers find the novels difficult to follow. The debut of *1Q84* elicited a scathing review in *The New York Times*: "*1Q84* has even his most ardent fans doing back flips as they try to justify this book's glaring troubles. Is it consistently interesting? No, but Mr. Murakami is too skillful a trickster to rely on conventional notions of storytelling."

QE2 The nickname for the cruise ship *Queen Elizabeth 2* of the Cunard Line that used to sail the waters of Asia until it was retired in 2008. The ship is not named, as often thought, after the reigning Queen Elizabeth. It is named after the late Queen Mother, widow of King George VI, and is the second ship named after her. Thus it is correct to use the Arabic numeral 2 rather than the Roman numeral II after the name. The original *Queen Elizabeth* was sold to a Hong Kong businessman named Tung Chao Yung, who wanted to turn it into a floating university, but in 1972 it caught fire and sank in Victoria Harbour.

Second Artillery Force The unit of China's People's Liberation Army that controls China's stock of ground-based nuclear weapons and conventional tactical missiles, under the direct command of the Central Military Committee. It is comparable to the US Strategic Command (formerly Strategic Air Command) and the Soviet/Russian Strategic Rocket Force. China exploded its first nuclear weapon in 1964, and the Second Artillery Force was established in 1966. China is thought to have about 400 nuclear weapons and about 20 ICBMs with MIRVed warheads. Officially, its mission is to deter a nuclear attack on the homeland. Both US Admiral Mike Mullen, former chief of staff, and former defense secretary Robert Gates have visited the Second Artillery Force headquarters as guests of the PLA. (See **596**)

Second stove A Chinese expression indicating a parting of the ways, as in "we don't like what you're cooking up, so we'll build a second stove and cook our own dish". In the Hong Kong context, it meant China's plans to nullify Chris Patten's political reforms (see **Fat Pang**) by forming a parallel legislature. Then Foreign Minister Qian Qichen added another twist when he dismissed further debate with another curt Chinese culinary expression, *"This rice is cooked!"*

Taepodong-2 Name given to a North Korean ballistic missile that Pyongyang periodically threatened to launch whenever it felt that the world wasn't giving it enough attention. In 1998 North Korea fired a Taepodong-1 missile from its east coast missile test site provocatively over Japan. The North Koreans claimed that it successfully launched its first orbiting satellite, which beamed back messages in praise of Dear Leader Kim Jong-il, but independent sources never confirmed this. Most analysts in the West believe that the third stage failed to ignite, and that the missile crashed somewhere in the north Pacific Ocean.

PAC-3 What Japan has to defend itself against North Korean missiles. The term is short for Patriot Advance Capable-3 surface-to-air missile. The American-made anti-missile missile has been deployed in friendly Asian countries including Japan, Taiwan and South Korea. In September, 2008, the Japanese recorded their first successful interception, but it has never been really tested even though Tokyo has, with great fanfare, deployed the missile at vulnerable points whenever North Korea has tested a long-range missile. Not to be confused with the P-3 Orion, a maritime search and anti-submarine aircraft.

3K words JAPANESE for undesirable jobs that are either *kitsui* (demanding), *kitanai* (dirty) or *kiken* (dangerous) – or all three. At one time many of these jobs were done by *eta,* a kind of lower caste.

Three Nos Japan's official policy on nuclear weapons, first articulated in 1967 by Prime Minister Eisako Sato (1964-70). The Three Nos are: 1. Never to possess a nuclear weapon, 2. Never to produce a nuclear weapon, and 3. Never to allow the introduction of nuclear weapons to its territory. While faithful to the first two, Japan for many years turned a blind eye to port calls by American naval vessels carrying these weapons, even though that appeared to run counter to the third No. That became moot in 1991 when President George H.W. Bush ordered the navy to remove these weapons on vessels, save for ballistic missile-carrying submarines (which do not call on foreign ports). The policy helped Sato win the Nobel Peace Prize in 1974.

Three Represents A vague Chinese political theory associated with former president and communist party boss Jiang Zemin and probably understood by only a few dedicated **China watchers**. It was first enunciated by Jiang during an inspection tour of Guangdong province in 2005. "Being the vanguard of the Chinese working class, the Chinese Communist Party always "represents" the fundamental interests of the Chinese people in terms of development trends for advanced productive forces, advanced culture and the "fundamental interests" of the overwhelming majority of the people of China."

Three Self Movement An organization to which all Protestant Christian churches in China are supposed to belong, there being no independent or mainline denominations such as Presbyterians, Baptists or Methodists. The three "selfs" are self-governing, self-financing (meaning no foreign funding) and self-propagating (meaning no foreign missionaries). These values represent a reaction to both Western imperialism and to the communist victory in 1949. The TSM was suspended during the Cultural Revolution (1966-76) when all expression of religion was banned. It was revived following a relaxation of religious persecution after Mao Zedong's death in 1976, the opening to the world under Deng Xiaoping and a realization in Beijing that the repression had simply driven Christianity underground. This wariness persists in the number of house churches that decline to register with the government or join the TSM. The Roman Catholic counterpart in China is the **Chinese Patriotic Catholic Association**.

May Fourth Movement This important event in 20th-century China took place on May 4, 1919, when hundreds of university students from Peking University and other institutions held a mass demonstration aimed ostensibly at Japan but more at the Chinese government. The spark was China's acceptance of the decision at the Versailles peace treaty conference to give Japan the former German concessions in China as a reward for its declaring war on Germany during World War I. It grew into a larger movement and boycott of Japanese goods.

Fifth Modernization In 1978 Chinese dissident Wei Jingsheng posted a large-character poster on Beijing's "Democracy Wall" calling on the government to add democracy to the Four Modernizations propounded by Deng Xiaoping. The four modernizations – agriculture, industry, national defense, and technology – had been advanced by communist party leaders even before Mao Zedong's death in 1976, to make China a great power in the 21st century, but they were pushed aggressively by Deng to help jump-start reforms. Democracy was never part of his agenda, and Wei was arrested and sentenced to 15 years in prison. (See **Democracy Wall**)

Six-Party Talks On-again, off-again negotiations tasked with persuading, bribing or threatening North Korea to end its nuclear weapons program. The six parties are North and South Korea, China, Russia, Japan and the United States. China, which maintains relations with both Koreas, usually officiates. This negotiating platform was created in 2002 following the collapse of the Agreed Framework plan under which the North "froze" its existing nuclear program in exchange for heavy fuel and prospects of additional aid and recognition. All parties have been accused from time to time of failing to meet their obligations, and the talks were suspended in late 2008. Since negotiations began under this format, North Korea has exploded two nuclear weapons.

KAL 007 Korean Airlines Flight 007 from New York to Seoul was shot down by a Soviet interceptor on September 1, 1983, killing all 269 passengers and crew. Somewhere between Alaska and Hokkaido the Boeing 747 strayed off course and flew over prohibited Soviet airspace on the Kamchatka peninsula; it crashed off the northern tip of Hokkaido. The grim report from the Russian pilot – "the target is destroyed" – entered the lexicon. The incident came at a tense time in US-Soviet relations, as Washington was proposing to introduce short-range Pershing missiles into Europe and build an anti-ballistic missile defense system nicknamed "Star Wars."

Charter 8 A manifesto signed by some 300 Chinese intellectuals in December, 2008, calling for greater freedom of expression, multi-party elections and an independent judiciary. It was inspired by a similar document signed by dissidents in Czechoslovakia in 1977 called Charter 77. Charter 8 was drawn up by writer and later Nobel peace laureate Liu Xiaobo and was signed by more than 300 others. Liu is detained by the Chinese government and many other Charter 8 signers have been questioned or harassed. Without freedom of expression, association, to assemble and protest, "China will always remain far from civilized ideals", it reads. A similar movement in communist Vietnam goes by the title Bloc 8406, from the date – April 8, 2006 – when it was formulated.

Article 9 The famous clause in Japan's American-written constitution that renounces war as a sovereign right and prohibits establishment of armed forces. It reads in total: "Aspiring sincerely to an international peace based on justice and order, the Japanese people forever renounce the use of force as a means of settling international disputes. In order to accomplish the aim of the preceding paragraph land, sea and air forces, as well as other war potential will never be maintained. The right of belligerency of the state shall not be recognized." Encouraged by Washington, and the outbreak of the Korean War, Japan began to undermine the letter of this clause with the establishment of a national police force that evolved into the Self-Defense Forces, or *jieitai* in JAPANESE. The country gets around the prohibition by pretending that the army, air force and navy are a kind of super police force, albeit one with F-15s, submarines and Aegis missile-equipped destroyers. Conservatives have been agitating for years to drop the Article or revise it in order to make Japan once again a "**normal nation**."

Document No. 9 refers to a memorandum issued by the General Office of the Chinese Communist Party Central Committee to warn cadres of what it termed "subversive currents" that could undermine the party's rule. It was supposedly issued in April, 2013, and first leaked outside China by a Hong Kong publication in August of that year. It has the hallmarks of president Xi Jinping and is meant to be read and discussed at lower party levels. The seven "subversive" Western values include such things as advocating constitutional democracy, multi-party elections and an independent judiciary. Such ideas are to be avoided "to preserve the party's grip on power."

Nine-Dash Line Heavy dashes, nine of them, that loop from China's Hainan Island at the South China Sea's northern end down south nearly 1,200 nautical miles close to Indonesia and back. The lines were first published in 1947, predating the communist era, and have been repeated on subsequent editions of official Chinese maps. It makes it appear that Beijing is claiming the entire sea, not just disputed islands and atolls, as part of its national territory, although it has never made such a claim officially. By some estimates, the nine dashes incorporate about 80 per cent of the South China Sea. Needless to say, any such assertion is fiercely opposed by the countries along the littoral, as well as other maritime nations including the United States. (See **Spratlys**)

Double Ten The tenth day of the tenth month, aka October 10. On this day in 1911 a rebellion against the Qing Dynasty broke out in Wuchang, a city on the Yangzi River, which was a precursor to the **Xinhai Revolution** that overthrew the monarchy and established the Chinese republic. It is widely celebrated in the Republic of China, aka Taiwan, where it has become something of a national day holiday. Mainland China prefers to celebrate October 1, the day in 1949 when the People's Republic was proclaimed. Before the 1997 handover, ROC supporters in Hong Kong decorated the territory with nationalist flags. The Double Ten is still observed quietly in Hong Kong, but police usually confiscate the flags.

13th Month's Salary A bonus equal to one month's salary paid usually at the beginning of the new year. It is common, but not legally mandatory, in Hong Kong, Singapore and Malaysia. It is required in Indonesia and paid usually as part of the end of Ramadan celebrations.

S-21 Security Prison 21, also known as Tuol Sleng, was housed in a former high school on the outskirts of Phnom Penh. It opened shortly after the Khmer Rouge seized power in Cambodia in 1975 and operated until overrun by the Vietnamese in 1979. It was used as a secret prison for torturing "traitors" who were later sent to nearby execution grounds. The head of the prison, one Khang Khek Leu – better known as Comrade Duch – was a former mathematics teacher. He was tried at a special war crimes tribunal and convicted of crimes against humanity in 2010 and sentenced to 30 years in prison (later expanded to life in prison). He was the only senior Khmer Rouge official to admit responsibility for his crimes. The prison was converted into the Tuol Sleng Genocide Museum. The fact that the Khmer Rouge meticulously documented their crimes with photographs makes the museum an especially poignant, or ghoulish, place.

Article 23 A time-bomb lurking in Hong Kong and Macau's post-handover constitutions, called in both territories the Basic Law, which requires that each Special Administrative Region government "enact laws on its own to prohibit any act of treason, secession, subversion against the Central People's Government or theft of state secrets, to prohibit foreign political organizations or bodies from conducting political activities in the region and to prohibit political organizations or bodies of the Region from establishing ties with foreign organizations or bodies." The Hong Kong government's first crack at passing such a law in 2003 led to the largest popular anti-government demonstration in the territory since the **Tiananmen Massacre**. The government backed down and has not, as of 2017, tried to pass it again. But Macau quietly enacted its enabling legislation in February, 2009, nearly 10 years after its return to Chinese sovereignty.

Article 24 Long before its own aborted effort, the Americans wrote an equal rights amendment (actually an article) into Japan's post-World War II constitution. It reads: "Marriage shall be based on the mutual consent of both sexes and shall be maintained through mutual cooperation with equal rights of husband and wife as a basis. ... laws shall be enacted from the standpoint of individual dignity and the essential equality of the sexes." It was written at the personal insistence of a young American woman, **Beate Sirota Gordon**, the only woman among the 24 other Americans who drafted Japan's post-war constitution. She is a hero to the Japanese women's movement. After **Article 9**, this provision is one that conservatives in Japan would most like to alter, arguing that it puts too much emphasis on the rights of the individual. They would like to raise family and community over individual rights.

28 degrees centigrade The extraordinary high setting for summer air-conditioning in Japan in light of the power shortages stemming from the Fukushima nuclear power plant disaster. Some companies encourage workers to come to work in shorts and tennis shirts to keep cool. Such a high setting would be considered torture in air-conditioning-obsessed Hong Kong. (See **cool biz**)

31 Planes of Existence In classical Buddhism this number represents the planes of existence into which a person can be reincarnated. Humans occupy the fifth level, above common animals but below *devas*, or godlike figures. The new parliament complex of Myanmar in Naypyidaw has 31 buildings, representing the planes of existence.

Bureau 39 Sometimes known as "Office 39." It refers to a shadowy agency that manages the North Korean leadership's slush fund gained mainly from illicit business dealings such as selling drugs, pirated cigarettes and high-quality counterfeit US$100 notes known as "super dollars". Reputedly operating since 1974 and housed in a well-guarded, nondescript concrete building in Pyongyang, it reports directly to the North Korean leader, now Kim Jong-un. He dispenses the money to the elite to win their loyalty. Washington clamped down on their operations in August 2010, with an executive order freezing assets of five North Korean agencies or state companies.

55 The number of women still living, in early 2014, who were registered with the South Korean government as being former sex slaves to the Imperial Japanese Army. Their average age was 88. Some historians estimate that as many as 200,000 women, mostly Korean but also Chinese and other nationalities, were conscripted into the army's brothel system. (see *ianfu*)

60 A propitious age for Asians in countries influenced by China. The body is deemed to have passed through the five 12-year zodiacal cycles that constitute the proper lifespan. Once one has completed the 60-year cycle then all time beyond is considered a bonus. You take your ease and let your children make you as comfortable as possible. The parties to celebrate this auspicious event are known in Korean as the *hwan-gap*, and are a big business.

Detachment 88 Crack Indonesian anti-terrorism group (in INDONESIAN *Detasemen Khusus 88*). It was formed after the deadly Bali bombing of 2002, and is heavily subsidized and supported by the FBI and other American counter-terrorism groups and also the Australian Federal Intelligence Service. It has had considerable success in tracking down and arresting or killing Islamic terrorists, especially those linked to the Islamist movement *Jemaah Islamiyah*. The special force is comprised of about 400 people including investigators, explosive experts and a unit of snipers. The unit supposedly got its name after a senior Indonesian policeman misheard the letters A-T-A (Anti-Terrorism Assistance) as being the number 88. Also the number eight is auspicious throughout Asian cultures.

Type 094 The NATO designation for the Chinese navy's newest nuclear-powered ballistic missile submarine, also known as the *Jin* class. The first submarine of this class was reportedly launched in 2004 and a second in 2007. They replace an earlier, cruder type of missile-carrying sub called the *Xia* class. The submarine can carry up to 12 missiles with 8,000 km range, each capable of deploying three nuclear warheads. It is believed that these submarines are to be based at a naval base constructed on Hainan Island.

100 yen shops In JAPANESE *hyaku-en shoppe*. Common Japanese retail stores where everything is priced at 100 yen (actually 108 yen with the 8 per cent sales tax included). Thousands of 100-yen shops are dotted throughout Japan's major cities, ranging in size from multi-story department stores to small shops in shopping malls. They offer an amazing range of products such as kitchenware, tools for small repairs, stationery such as pens and notepads. Similar shops can be found in other parts of Asia, such as the 10-dollar shops in Hong Kong. (See *sari sari* **store**)

Shibuya 109 This iconic department store just outside Shibuya station is Tokyo's Mecca for the young, with-it generation. Many of the stores have numbers instead of names, giving the neighborhood a kind of spacey look. The 109 name is taken from the Japanese words *to* (meaning 10) and *kyu* (meaning 9), hence Tokyu, after the department store chain of that name. The gray, cylindrical ten-story building at the main Shibuya crossroads opened in 1979 and was designed by Minuro Takeyama. The store was once the meeting place and fashion supply depot for the *gyaru* subculture, typified by girls with dark fake tans and bleached hair. Fashion styles have moved on but 109 lives on.

113 The number to call in South Korea if you happen to spot a North Korean spy.

333 Beer Vietnam's national brew, which traces its origins to a French brewery in Danang in 1893, nationalized after the communist victory in 1975 and well known to American troops during the Vietnam War. Originally called "33" or *ba moui ba* [bam-me-bah] in VIETNAMESE, the name was changed to 333 – *ba ba ba* – apparently to play down colonial origins. Some outside brewers still brew "33" beer, which can cause confusion. The origin of the name "33" seems to be lost in history.

596 Code name for China's first atomic bomb test on October 16, 1964, at the **Lop Nur** test site. The number refers to June, 1959, when Beijing initiated its own nuclear weapons development after the Soviet Union stopped helping them. It was an implosion device using U235 core and yielding 22 kilotons. Since then China has conducted 45 tests including a thermonuclear bomb in 1967 and a neutron bomb.

609 The number of Chinese dollar billionaires, according to the Hurun Richest Chinese report as of March, 2017. The richest man in China was Wang Jianlin, who made his fortune in real estate. *Forbes Magazine* also listed Wang as the richest Chinese but valued his net worth lower. The Hurun Report, a research firm founded in 1999, vies with *Forbes* for reporting the richest Chinese.

Unit 684 See **Silmido Mutiny**

689 The number of votes that Hong Kong's third Chief Executive, Leung Chun-ying, received from the 1,200-person election committee in the 2012 election. It was turned into a label of derision in the heavy "Umbrella Movement" demonstrations that broke out in Hong Kong in 2014 protesting Beijing's plan to allow city-wide voting in 2017 – so long as it and its Hong Kong allies controlled who were the candidates.

Unit 731 A covert unit of Japan's wartime Kwantung Army that carried out bacteriological, chemical and "medical" experiments on mostly Chinese prisoners of war and Koreans, located near Harbin in northeast China. It was in fact the headquarters for a widespread network of laboratories, including at least one in Shinjuku in downtown Tokyo. It was given the cover name of Epidemic Prevention Unit, ironic as its main mission was to develop the means of creating epidemics. Over about a decade and a half the Japanese conducted experiments on several thousand victims. However, it is not clear how much of this was actually used in battle or how many died from it (Chinese sources, not always reliable, put the figure at 300,000). The unit's commander Shiro Iishi was granted immunity from prosecution by American occupation authorities, and no evidence of what happened at Unit 731 was ever presented at the Tokyo Trials after the war. (However, the Soviet Union did put some Unit 731 participants on trial in the 1949 **Khabarovsk War Trials**).

798 District This part of Beijing was in the early 1950s the site of large armament factories built with help from the Soviet Union (the number seven before a factory number denoted military use). After the break with Moscow and the economic reforms of Deng Xiaoping, these factories went into decline, replaced by more modern facilities elsewhere. However, that coincided with the rebirth of Chinese contemporary art, and the artists needing display space began to occupy the old factories, turning the district into an art center, sort of like SoHo in New York. Lately many artists and gallery owners have been migrating to another art district in the village of Caochangdi northeast of Beijing, near the Fifth Ring Road. Contemporary artist **Ai Weiwei** was instrumental in creating this new art center.

8-9-3 The hand that will lead to a score of "no points" in a traditional Japanese *hanafuda* card game. Roughly translates as *yattsu ku san* from which is derived the word *yakuza*, the traditional term for Japanese mobsters. It referred to "useless people" or gamblers in feudal Japan. At the request of the police, who find the traditional term too romantic-sounding to impressionable youth, the media now calls mobsters *boryokudan,* meaning violent groups, or use other euphemisms such as "anti-social groups".

969 Movement A rapidly expanding mass movement in Myanmar led by extremists determined to purge the country of Muslims. The number 969 has special meaning for Buddhists, who make up the vast majority of the people of Myanmar, and is increasingly seen on decals attached to entrances of shops and on motorbikes denoting that the bearer is a proper Buddhist. Numerology has a strong appeal for many people in the country. Much of the violent Buddhist-Muslim tension has been directed at the **Rohingyas,** a stateless people residing in the far northwestern state of Arakan. Things took a more ominous turn in March, 2013, with vicious attacks on Muslims and Muslim businesses in the central town of Meikhtila near Mandalay, allegedly backed by Buddhist monks. It showed that animosity was not just racial but directed against ethnic Burmese who practice Islam. The movement leaders have been likened to "neo-Nazis" as the more extreme among them make no secret that their goal is to remove all Muslims from Myanmar.

AP1000 The first "third-generation" nuclear power reactor design to be licensed by the US Nuclear Regulatory Commission will likely be built mostly in China. The advanced Pressurized Water Reactor design was developed by Westinghouse, now owned by the Toshiba Corp. Its simplified design is aimed at reducing costs, and its passive core cooling system to help prevent core meltdown in the event that outside electric power is lost. As of 2016, four AP1000 reactor-plants were under construction in China.

1955 System In 1955 various Japanese political parties congealed into the dominant Liberal Democratic Party, *Jiminto*, named from a merger of the Liberal and Democratic Parties, and the perpetual opposition, the Japan Socialist Party. During the boom years that began in the 1960s Japanese voters repeatedly returned the LDP to power. Only in the early 1990s did the "system" begin to break down as more and more voters turned against the LDP's dominance, and the opposition went through various permutations before coalescing into the Democratic Party of Japan, *Minshuto*, which finally ousted the LDP in the 2009 general election.

1992 Consensus A tacit understanding between China and Taiwan that both agree there is only one China, but that each side is free to interpret what that one China is. The consensus was supposedly negotiated between the two organizations responsible for cross-strait relations in Hong Kong in 1992. It is considered the foundation of China-Taiwan relations, at least by Beijing and the Kuomintang party on Taiwan. The Democratic Progressive Party, which in theory supports independence for Taiwan, denies the existence of the 1992 consensus. (See **One China Policy**)

1993 Kono Statement A statement by the then Chief Cabinet Secretary Yohei Kono admitting and apologizing for at least indirect Japanese government involvement in the forced recruitment of Asian women to work in army brothels. It is a deeply emotional issue, especially in South Korea, and a source of tension even today between Japan and the South Korean government, which claims Tokyo has never truly owned up to it. Hardline nationalists in Japan want to repudiate the statement. (See *ianfu*)

2002 The year of one of the worst outbreaks of communal sectarian violence in post-independence India. Since then, the number "2002" in India immediately brings to mind the massacre in the same way "9/11" does for Americans. It began when 59 Hindus were burned to death on February 27, 2002, on a train in the town of Godhra, Gujarat, which is mainly populated by Muslims. The new Chief Minister Narendra Modi declared a day of mourning, which many Hindus took as an open invitation to rape and kill Muslims in the state's largest city of Ahmedabad. Ever since, Modi has stood accused of being at best indifferent to the attacks that killed an estimated 1,080 or at worst encouraging them. (See **Modi, Narendra**)

7,000 The number of people working to decommission the destroyed Fukushima Daiichi nuclear power station on any average day. The task is expected to take decades. See *ichifu*.

Unit 8341 Common designation for the guard unit responsible for protecting China's leaders and their families. It was once the number for a strategic warehouse in Beijing but was reassigned to the guard unit, which had several previous number designations. The official title was discontinued in 1971 but is still in common use. The unit, made up of several thousand soldiers and policemen, has guarded every Chinese leader from Mao Zedong to Xi Jinping as well as important venues such as the Great Hall of the People. It played an important role in Chinese history when its then commander, Wang Dongxing, threw his weight behind the "coup" against the **Gang of Four**.

8888 Uprising Nationwide popular uprising against a longtime dictatorship that had turned Burma (Myanmar) into one of the poorest nations on earth. It began on August 8, 1988 – hence the name – with student demonstrations joined by Buddhist monks in Yangon. It quickly spread to the rest of the country. It ended in September after a bloody coup put into power a new junta that went by the name "State Law and Order Restoration Council" or SLORC. The generals countenanced a general election in 1990, but refused to recognize the results when the pro-democracy party won an overwhelming majority. Aung San Suu Kyi, daughter of Burma's independence hero Aung San, rose to prominence and eventually won a Nobel Prize for Peace around this time. The generals put her under house arrest, which ended only in 2010. In the 2015 elections, her party won a landslide victory, and she took the newly created role of State Counsellor.

Executive Order 9066 Of the thousands of orders signed by American presidents, Executive Order 9066 may be the most notorious. President Franklin D. Roosevelt signed the order on February 19, 1942, about 10 weeks after the attack on Pearl Harbor. Technically it authorized the Secretary of War to designate certain areas of the country as military zones, giving the commanding generals wide authority to deal with possible sabotage or espionage. It paved the way for the internment of about 120,000 Japanese-Americans (roughly 60 per cent of them native-born Americans) for two years in bleak internment camps. The word "Japanese" was never specifically mentioned in the order. It was not officially rescinded until 1976 by President Gerald Ford. In 1988 President Ronald Reagan signed a law granting an official apology and $20,000 in restitution to the surviving internees. (See **Koramatsu, Fred** and *issei*)

man JAPANESE for the numeral ten thousand (10,000). Japanese count in multiples of ten thousand rather than one thousand, which can be a source of confusion if one is not careful when calculating large numbers. Japanese count in the common fashion up to 9,999. Then they switch to one *man,* two *man,* etc. One million would be expressed as *hyaku man,* or one hundred ten thousands. It is advisable to write things down on paper when discussing high numbers with Japanese. Koreans use the same word and also count in multiples of ten thousand.

61398 Military designation for the People's Liberation Army's Unit 61398, which US security officials believe is the main army unit engaging in cyber warfare against American and other nations' corporations. The unit supposedly operates out of a nondescript, 11-story building in Shanghai. It cannot be ascertained conclusively that this unit is actually attacking foreign targets, since it is difficult to know for certain where attacks originate. The accuser, an American computer security firm called Mandiant, had an impressive amount of detail in making its allegations.

100,000 Defined as one *lakh* in the cumbersome numbering system common in India and throughout South Asia. A *crore* equals ten million, or 100 *lakh.*

$1,740,000 The annual state salary in US dollars for Singapore's prime minister, making that post the highest (legally) paid government position in the world. By contrast, the president of the United States earns $400,000. This figure actually represents a 35 per cent cut in salary after Singapore's overly generous compensation became an issue in the 2011 general election in which the opposition gained six seats in parliament. The salary for an entry-level cabinet member is the equivalent of $1,100,000 a year, compared with $147,000 in the US. Singapore justifies the huge salaries as needed to attract capable people to government and keep them honest.

1,000,000,000,000,000 The size in yen (one quadrillion) of Japan's national debt as of mid-2013.

10,000,000,000,000,000 The number, standing for ten quadrillion, of computations that Japan's K (or *Kei*) supercomputer can make in a second, making it the most powerful such instrument in the world – for a time, at least. The computer was built by Fujitsu and is located in the

Riken Advanced Institute for Computerability in Kobe. It was ranked as number one in 2011 and was fully operational in 2012. As of June 2017, however, K ranks only as the world's eighth-fastest computer. *Kei* is the Japanese word for ten quadrillion.

Appendix: Colonial-Era Names

In Asia, Europeans left behind a plethora of place names such as Victoria and George Town during their two centuries of dominance, names which are gradually being replaced with ones more familiar to the local languages and nationalities. As a rule, journalists use the names that the locals either use themselves or which they want to be known by others.

When I first went to work for *Asiaweek* in the late 1980s, we still referred to China's major cities by their colonial-era names: Peking, Canton, Amoy and so on. Only later did we join most other journals in using the names that the Chinese preferred: Beijing, Guangzhou and Xiamen. We bid the old names farewell with some sadness, as the words were softer to our ears, the new ones full of harsh-sounding Xs and Zs. While most of the world calls China's capital Beijing, its leading university is still known as Peking University. The old name for Beijing survives in other uses such as Pekingese (a breed of dog) and Peking duck (though probably morphing into Beijing duck). The French, of course, continue to refer to China's capital as "Pekin".

The Asian names for the principal cities of China, Japan and South Korea may sound exotic to the Western ear, but they are especially prosaic in their own tongue. Beijing simply means "Northern Capital" (Nanjing is the former Southern Capital). Tokyo is the Eastern Capital and Seoul simply means "the Capital."

We should be thankful at least that the Chinese have never objected to the universal "China" in international usage (taken from the name of the first emperor Qin, pronounced "chin"). What the Chinese call their own country is a little complicated. In MANDARIN it is *Zhongguo*, but there are different words for different occasions, as well as different words in different dialects.

The Japanese have no objection to our using the word "Japan" (derived from the Chinese word *Cipan*) instead of *Nihon*, even as they tolerate reproducing their names in Western word order instead of placing the family name first like the Chinese. The word "Japan" appears at all international functions, and the three-letter shorthand "JPN" or simply "Japan" appears at the Olympic Games and other international sporting events. Japan's cities, such as Tokyo, Osaka and Kyoto, never had colonial-era names so there is no need to learn new ones.

Southeast Asia has more or less purged its colonial-era names. Thus Batavia is now Jakarta, Tourane is now Danang, Brunei Town is Bandar Seri Begawan. Not many realize that Bangkok is actually a colonial-era name. It is, of course, Thai, but refers to a small part of the city that later grew into what the Thais themselves call Krungthep. However, the ever-accommodating Thais don't mind our using Bangkok. Even the road signs in Roman letters point the way to "Bangkok".

Of course, the word "Thailand" is a hybrid, since "land" is English. Since 1948 Thais have called their country Muang Thai, rather than Siam (see entry for the reason).

Some colonial-era names persist, such as George Town in Malaysia. Maps and postal addresses still show the center of Hong Kong (in MANDARIN Xianggang) as "Victoria", even though that name has long fallen out of usage, replaced simply by "Central" (though there remain even after the 1997 handover to China a Victoria Harbour, Victoria Park and Victoria Peak, not to mention innumerable streets still named after colonial governors.)

Another major pair of name changes is Yangon for Rangoon and Myanmar for Burma, but here things get a little sticky. Both Burma and Myanmar approximate how the locals call their country, and so the word itself is not very controversial, only the way it was named. In 1989 the military junta that ruled Burma, then known as the State Law and Order Restoration Council (SLORC), let it be known that Burma was a colonial-era name and they wanted the country to be called Myanmar henceforth. As the SLORC was a dictatorship, many have questioned what authority it had to change any name. Most international bodies, such as the UN, Japan, and all neighboring countries and most news organs use Myanmar; but the US state department and dissident publications still use Burma. Many international news organizations use Myanmar, but add "also known as Burma". It raises the question of what to call a citizen of the country. "Myanmese" seems awkward but may be catching on.

India's largest city and financial center, formerly known as Bombay, has been officially Mumbai since 1995 when the right-wing Hindu nationalist party Shiv Sena won control of the state of Maharashtra of which Mumbai is the capital. Following the election, the new government announced that Bombay had been renamed Mumbai after the Hindu goddess Mumbadevi. Government agencies were ordered to adopt the new name. Initially there was resistance, both at home and abroad, in part because the Shiv Sena Party was unsavory. However, the name has now gained universal acceptance. By some accounts, "Bombay" was a corruption of "Mumbai", which is how speakers of the local dialect MARATHI have always called the city. Other accounts say the colonial name is an anglicized version of the PORTUGUESE "Bombaim", which is believed to have derived from Bom Bahia, or Good Bay. In HINDI, Mumbai is still called Bambai. However the Shiv Sena was not so successful in changing the term for Mumbai's film industry to "Mollywood." It is still "Bollywood".

Other major Indian cities have followed the trend in order to promote local culture and languages. Madras is now Chennai, Pondicherry is Puducherry and Bangalore, capital of Karnataka state and a major international outsourcing center, seems destined to become Bengaluru from the native KANNADA dialect. In 2001 Calcutta's name was officially changed to Kolkata, reflecting more closely the native BENGALI pronunciation. The capital Delhi remains Delhi for now rather than Inraprasth favored by some nationalists.

Even "India" is not immune to revision. After all, the word comes from the River Indus, which is in Pakistan. Some push for Hindustan, while the more extreme nationalists favor Akhand Bharat. The latter is reflected in the name of the main nationalist Hindu political group, the Bharatiya Janata Party.

Also by Todd Crowell and available from Blacksmith Books:

Explore Macau
A walking guide and history

ISBN 978-988-19002-2-7   HK$98 / US$11.95

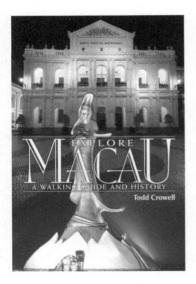

Walking is the best way to get to know any city, and Macau — the former Portuguese colony returned to China in 1999 — is made for walking. Only seven miles square, one can easily walk from the Border Gate to the A-Ma Temple at the tip of Macau in a day.

This guidebook describes eight routes around the urban peninsula and its outlying islands, sufficient to explore and understand this fascinating old city and its unique blend of European and Asian architecture, cuisine and cultures.

"An invaluable pocket guide that is perfect for the first-time visitor as well as old hands."
— *South China Morning Post*

Tales from Victoria Park
Short stories of Indonesian women in Hong Kong

ISBN 978-988-16139-3-6   HK$108 / US$13.95

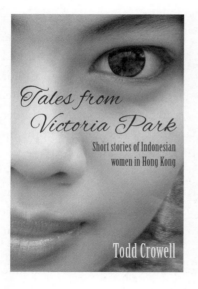

Victoria Park, the largest expanse of open space in Hong Kong, is the crossroads and away home for thousands of Muslim women who come from Indonesia to find their fortunes, or at least support their families, in the teeming Chinese city. Most come initially as maids, but some lose their employers and descend into the netherworld of overstayers, illegal street hawkers and disco "PR" girls. Whoever they are, they all know Dina: a woman who sells phonecards, changes money, dispenses advice and listens to their tales of exile.

From the comic to the bizarre to the heart-breaking, these cross-cultural tales build on a sensual evocation of place and character.

EXPLORE ASIA WITH BLACKSMITH BOOKS

From retailers around the world or from *www.blacksmithbooks.com*